WOLFE
and NORTH AMERICA

MAJOR-GENERAL JAMES WOLFE AT ANSE DU FOULON (WOLFE'S COVE) ON THE MORNING OF 13TH SEPTEMBER, 1759. From an engraving made from a water-colour painted by Wolfe's aide-de-camp, Captain Hervey Smith, during the campaign.

Frontispiece.

WOLFE
AND NORTH AMERICA

by

Lieut.-Col.

F. E. WHITTON

C.M.G., p.s.c.

Late The Prince of Wales's Leinster Regiment
(Royal Canadians)

Frederick Ernest Whitton

E
199
W62
1971

629152

KENNIKAT PRESS
Port Washington, N. Y./London

WOLFE AND NORTH AMERICA

First published in 1929
Reissued in 1971 by Kennikat Press
Library of Congress Catalog Card No: 76-118509
ISBN 0-8046-1257-9

Manufactured by Taylor Publishing Company   Dallas, Texas

CONTENTS

CHAPTER		PAGE
I.	—FRANCE AND ENGLAND IN NORTH AMERICA UP TO THE TIME OF WOLFE'S BIRTH	9
II.	—THE EARLY MILITARY CAREER OF JAMES WOLFE	64
III.	—THE SITUATION IN NORTH AMERICA AFTER THE TREATY OF UTRECHT. THE FALL OF LOUISBURG IN 1745 AND THE FRENCH EFFORTS TO RECAPTURE IT	120
IV.	—WOLFE'S EARLY MANHOOD. THE BEGINNING OF THE FINAL STRUGGLE FOR NORTH AMERICA IN 1755	174
V.	—THE SEVEN YEARS' WAR. FRENCH SUCCESSES IN NORTH AMERICA. THE TURN OF THE TIDE. SIEGE AND CAPTURE OF LOUISBURG IN 1758	234
VI.	—THE CAPTURE OF QUEBEC AND THE DEATH OF WOLFE	298
VII.	—THE SURRENDER OF CANADA TO THE BRITISH CROWN	382

ILLUSTRATIONS

	FACING PAGE
MAJOR-GENERAL JAMES WOLFE AT ANSE DU FOULON (WOLFE'S COVE) ON THE MORNING OF 13TH SEPTEMBER, 1759	*Frontispiece*
ROOM IN WESTERHAM VICARAGE WHERE WOLFE WAS BORN, JANUARY 2, 1727	66
MONUMENT TO WOLFE IN WESTMINSTER ABBEY, WITH CANADIAN REGIMENTAL COLOURS DURING THE GREAT WAR	200
QUEBEC HOUSE, WESTERHAM, KENT	386

MAPS

	FACING PAGE
MAP TO ILLUSTRATE THE SIEGES OF LOUISBURG, 1745 & 1758	296
MAP TO ILLUSTRATE THE QUEBEC CAMPAIGNS, 1759 & 1760	380
MAP TO ILLUSTRATE MILITARY OPERATIONS BETWEEN FRENCH AND ENGLISH IN NORTH AMERICA	*At end of book*

" The incalculable Yankee Nations, shall they be in effect *Yangkee* (' English' with a difference) or *Frangcee* (' French ' with a difference) ? "

  Carlyle, *Frederick the Great, Book XVI, Chapter XIV.*

" This will, some time hence, be a vast empire, the seat of power and learning. Nature has refused them nothing, and there will grow a people out of our little spot, England, that will fill this vast space."

  From a letter written by James Wolfe *to his mother, dated Louisburg,* 11th *August,* 1758.

WOLFE AND NORTH AMERICA

CHAPTER ONE

FRANCE AND ENGLAND IN NORTH AMERICA UP TO THE TIME OF WOLFE'S BIRTH.

ALTHOUGH the contest between France and England for empire in America is one of the outstanding events of history, even the main details of it are not always fully understood. Every schoolboy knows that in the year 1759 Wolfe won a great battle under the walls of Quebec, but from that pinnacle of fact the descent into inaccurate conclusions is abrupt yet easy. It is the common belief, not only amongst schoolboys, but amongst those old enough to know better, that, with the capture of Quebec, French resistance collapsed and that in a moment British supremacy over North America was once and for ever assured. Actually this was far from being the case. Although, with the capture of Quebec, a position of outstanding strategical importance fell into the hands of the British, the French covering army, so far from being forced to capitulate, passed round the British left and made its way towards Montreal. Early in the following year an attempt was made to retake Quebec, and the scene of Wolfe's dramatic triumph of 1759 now witnessed a stinging British defeat. The French prepared to take the place by storm. The attackers were elated with victory and burning for revenge; the defenders were reduced in numbers, shaken by their defeat, decimated by sickness and weakened by bad and scanty food. The river was free from ice; either French or British ships might appear at any moment. It was well understood that upon the nationality of the first comer the fate of the city hung. On May 9th, 1760, a ship of war was discerned standing up the St. Lawrence. Her colours were British, and then, but not till then, the French grip upon the river fortress was relaxed.

The popular delusion as to the completeness of Wolfe's dramatic success does injustice, not only to many others, but to Wolfe himself. It is unjust to Wolfe, for it implies that the French dominion of the New World was a structure with foundations so insecure that the superstructure could be brought down by a few volleys of musketry. It is unjust to others, for not only does it not take into account the brilliant operation by which, later, three widely-separated British columns converged successfully upon Montreal—at which place, and not at Quebec, the French capitulated—but it entirely overlooks the share of the British navy in the conquest of Canada. In the story of the particular operations which culminated on the Heights of Abraham on September 13th, 1759, it is inevitable, if unfortunate, that the solid assistance of the fleet should be overshadowed by the more vivid occurrences of the actual battle on land. But there is no excuse for overlooking Hawke's splendid victory at Quiberon Bay, in European waters, on November 20th of the same year. Wolfe's capture of Quebec was not permanent. It was quickly challenged, and the fate of the fortress depended upon which side could secure the sea communication between Quebec and Europe. It is no exaggeration to say that the destiny of Canada was decided amid the shoals of Quiberon no less than upon the Heights of Abraham.

The struggle for empire between France and England which Wolfe did much to bring to a close had been of long duration. For exactly a century and a half friction had existed, and time after time actual collision had occurred in North America between the representatives of the two nations. In 1759 Quebec was no virgin fortress. Nearly a hundred years before Wolfe was born the fleur-de-lys had been lowered, and for three years the English flag had waved above its battlements. Twice since then attempts had been made, but without success, upon the fortress. These things are little known. So completely has France, as a European Power, been ousted from North America, that among the English-speaking race her one-time empire is little realized. How many are there aware that, five years before the Pilgrim Fathers gave thanks for their safe arrival at New Plymouth, a French priest, five hundred miles inland, had celebrated Mass and had raised the Host before the eyes of astonished Indians by the shores of Lake Huron? How many realize that, nearly half a century after the death of Wolfe, France still owned almost a third of what is now the United States of America? Yet these things were so. To trace the story of this rivalry between France and England; to tell why one nation succeeded and the other failed; to survey the long struggle chiefly from a military standpoint; to sketch the part which was played by Wolfe; to describe what he achieved, and what he left perforce to be accomplished by others—these are the objects with which this volume is written—*nostri farrago libelli.*

To go back to the earliest days, the award, in 1493, of Pope Alexander VI, by which the bulk of the New World was assigned to Spain and Portugal, granted practically the whole of North and South America to the former Power. But in the great upheaval brought about by the Renaissance and the Reformation such an arbitrary decision was certain to be defied. Two Powers so fitted by geographical situation for expansion westward—as were France and England—were not likely to pay undue deference to a ruling by which they were barred from half the world, particularly as the Pope was ignorant of the globular shape of this planet. In those countries various causes contributed to extension overseas—hostility to Spain; religion, either the desire to disseminate the Catholic faith or the desire to escape from religious persecution ; the craving for gold, and especially gold got without labour, and the discovery of a route to India and China quicker and more certain than that by the Cape of Good Hope. There was, too, a vague longing for exploration for itself, and a still vaguer urge towards an imperialism overseas. Last in this list, though not least in importance, was the supply of fish, a requirement bound up, especially in France, with the question of religion.

Long before the arrival of the Pilgrim Fathers, long before the foundation of Quebec, France and England had come into contact, if not into actual collision, in American waters. In England there still exists a hazy belief that the *Mayflower* was almost " the first that ever burst into a silent sea." Nothing can be further from the truth. In January and February, 1545, about two vessels a day sailed from French ports for Newfoundland, and twenty years later there were complaints that the French " ruled despotically " in those parts. There is some reason indeed to believe that this fishery existed before the voyage of Cabot in 1497 ; at any rate, it is certain that it began as early as the year 1504, and by 1517 it was well established. Ten years later eleven French and two Portuguese fishing-vessels were to be found in the Bay of St. John. In 1578 there were 150 French vessels in Newfoundland waters, besides 200 of other nations, Spanish, Portuguese and English. Added to these there were twenty to thirty Biscayan whalers. Thirteen years before the arrival of the Pilgrim Fathers there was living in what is now Nova Scotia an old French fisherman who had crossed the Atlantic more than eighty times.

Although to England is due the credit of the discovery of the North American continent, it was France who took up the first task of exploration. Sebastian Cabot in 1498 had reached the North American continent and proceeded along the shores of the United States to the southern boundary of Maryland; but the names connected with exploration in these waters during the years immediately following are those of voyagers in the service of France. The fishermen of Brittany and Normandy thronged to the coast of Newfoundland. The island of Cap Breton acquired its name from their remembrance of home. A map of the Gulf of St. Lawrence was drawn by a citizen of Honfleur in 1506. During 1523 and 1524 Verrazano—a Florentine in the employ of the King of France—reached the American coast in the latitude of Wilmington. Turning northward, he landed in what is now North Carolina, visited New York harbour, spent fifteen days in the haven of Newport, and, leaving the waters of Rhode Island, sailed along the whole coast of New England to Nova Scotia, thus giving to France some claim to an extensive territory based on the rights of discovery.

Such claims were strengthened and the direction of French efforts was determined by the voyages of Jacques Cartier, a seaman of St. Malo ; and these fixed the attention of France upon the great waterway of the St. Lawrence. On July 12th, 1534, upon a point of land at Gaspé, a lofty cross was raised bearing a shield on which were displayed the lilies of France. Leaving the Bay of Gaspé, Cartier discovered the great river of Canada, and, in a second voyage in the following year, explored it to that hill to which he gave the name Mont Real. As early as 1541 an attempt—but an unsuccessful one—was made to inaugurate a new France, but, although the project collapsed, a step further was taken on the path of exploration. Cartier ascended the rapids beyond Montreal. In the annals of discovery the name of Cartier is now replaced by that of Champlain. In 1605 there was founded Port Royal, in Acadia, the first French settlement in the New World. In the same year Champlain entered Massachusetts Bay and, on July 18th, took shelter in that harbour of Plymouth where, fifteen years later, the Pilgrims made their memorable landing. In 1610, at Port Royal, Poutrincourt took the first step in that great task of Christianizing the New World which marked the first years of France's imperial policy. A priest baptized the old Indian chief Membertou. His squaws, his children, his grandchildren, and his entire clan were next won over. Membertou was named Henri, after the King, and his principal squaw Marie, from the Queen of France. One of his sons received the name of the Pope, another that of the Dauphin. His daughter was called Marguerite, after the divorced Marguerite of Valois, while amongst the remainder of the tribe were distributed names of French princes, nobles and ladies of rank.

In the first decade of the seventeenth century France and England had become so definitely committed to colonization in North America that a struggle for definite supremacy was merely a matter of time. Quebec was founded in 1608, and the establishment of this settlement was anticipated, twelve months earlier, by the English settlement at James Town, in Virginia. But although a slight chronological priority in favour of England is here suggested, James Town came into existence two years after the foundation of the French settlement of Port Royal already referred to. The name of England is so pre-eminently connected with sea-power and maritime enterprise, and the age of Elizabeth fills such a place in the naval annals of the world, that it is difficult at first to comprehend how in the initial exploitation of the New World England not only failed to keep step with France, but definitely lagged behind.

Much of the difficulty will disappear if it is remembered that up to the middle of the sixteenth century the English people were not particularly distinguished either for seamanship, commerce, or love of adventure overseas. The impulse of the crusaders had died away long before the voyages of Columbus, and overseas expeditions were alien to English life. In the middle of the sixteenth century the English were an easy-going, stay-at-home people, loving hard fighting and good living, but so indifferent to trade and money-making that they were still content that the larger share of the external trade of their island should remain in the hands of foreigners. The discovery of the New World could not fail, however, to exert an influence. The indifference to trade and money-making which had characterized the English gave way before the new conditions, and signs of a new spirit of activity are dimly discernible in early Tudor times. Curiously enough, Henry VII, who had won the crown by his sword, displayed, during his reign, a commercial rather than a martial instinct. He was avaricious, a shrewd man of business, and gained for himself the title of the "Huckstering King." He definitely gave up all designs for military glory to be won on the Continent, and particularly in France, and decided that England should look for new possibilities for expansion beyond the western horizon.

The desire to avoid complications with Spain fixed the zone of English exploration in the Northern Atlantic, but the discoveries of the Cabots led to no immediate results which could challenge the importance of the discoveries already made. There is nothing in the English story of the time comparable with the expeditions of Verrazano, Cartier and Champlain. Henry VII died within a few years of the discoveries made by the Cabots, and when upon his death the crown passed to Henry VIII, much of the guidance of the destinies of England passed into the hands of Wolsey. That statesman undid much of the work of Henry VII. His eyes looked ever eastwards towards Europe rather than towards the New World. He failed to realize that a new era had dawned, and he strictly forbade all transatlantic voyages. As for Henry VIII himself, his attention during his reign was almost entirely fixed upon two subjects in which he was intimately and personally concerned. The long-drawn-out process to free himself from Catherine of Aragon had scarcely reached a conclusion when the Reformation began, and the abolition of Papal Supremacy in England, with the reversion of it to the English sovereign, became the great and absorbing question of English contemporary history. Both these questions deeply involved England in Continental affairs. As a result, the long period of nearly forty years covered by the reign of Henry VIII, famous as it was for improvements in the navy and the construction of new ships, was almost barren of mercantile expansion, maritime discovery, or any other form of enterprise overseas.

The reigns of Mary and Elizabeth tell indeed a different tale, but here again causes were in operation which afforded immunity to France in the great task she had set her hand to in the New World. Chief of these causes was the tendency in England to regard the New World not as a possession particularly valuable *per se*, but as a means of approach or a gateway to the known, as well as suspected, riches of the Far East. To this paradise the Portuguese had found their way by the Cape of Good Hope, while Magellan, in the service of Spain, had forced a way to the Moluccas by the strait which still bears his name. Both these routes, though one was easterly and the other by the west, had this in common—that they involved rounding the land masses of the world in the south. Sebastian Cabot pondered deeply upon the matter, and to his logical mind it seemed that there were probably similar passages in the Northern Hemisphere, one passing north of Europe and the other north of the newly discovered continent of America, and he wished England to possess them both.

The attention of England was, therefore, diverted from the exploration and penetration of a continent to the attempt to circumvent it. The North-East Passage was, however, attempted first in the opening year of Queen Mary's reign. Although it proved a complete failure so far as a route to India and China was concerned, a landing was made at Archangel, and Chancellor travelled in sledges as far as Moscow, where he laid the foundations of a remunerative Muscovy trade. The spirit of adventure and enterprise was thus stimulated, and a Russian Company was started to develop this new opening for commerce. Soon it was clear that the North-East Passage opened out little possibility for a route to the Indies, and under Queen Elizabeth the patronage of the Crown was transferred to the

North-West Passage. Here again failure had to be acknowledged, but it was long before the struggle was abandoned, and for years the prosecution of the attempt involved the neglect of the American continent.

The search for a route to the Far East was prompted by no such considerations as, in more modern times, has induced governments or men to undertake expenditure and risk in exploration. There was very little scientific impetus. As a corollary, there was a certain impatience over failure. A new school of thought came into being of which the chief apostle was Hawkins. To him it seemed foolish to pursue the quest for an all-English route to India when more profitable opportunities lay neglected. New markets could obviously be found in the growing overseas empires of Portugal and Spain. The Spanish, however, kept their American colonies under strict control and proclaimed the absolute monopoly of trade with them. On the other hand, such monopoly raised the cost of living to the Spanish colonists, who were prepared to welcome any foreign merchants willing to disregard the navigation laws and sell them goods of which they were in urgent need. Smuggling goods into Spanish colonies had, therefore, financial possibilities far exceeding those held out by the floes and bergs of Novaya Zemlya and Baffin's Bay, or by colonization in territories already discovered in America.

The special want of the Spaniards in America

was labour for their plantations and mines. The climate militated against the performance of this work by the colonists themselves, and the natives died off like flies when forced to toil for their new masters. Hawkins discovered that an easy way to amass wealth was to kidnap strong and hardy negroes in Africa, to transport them across the Atlantic, and to sell them to the Spanish in America and the West Indies. The voyages of Hawkins were amazingly successful. He had powerful backing, for Queen Elizabeth " stood in " with her kidnapping subject and looked to share his profits. Not unnaturally the Spanish authorities at home were incensed at this illicit trade, but though on his third voyage Hawkins was overborne by the Spaniards and lost most of his ships and profits, he returned safely to England and showed to other adventurers where " easy money " lay.

From mere smuggling to plunder was but a short step, and to the era of Hawkins immediately succeeded that of Drake. Whether Drake was actually a pirate—as some historians bluntly assert —or merely an " unlicensed privateer "—as other historians suggest with regard to his first voyage— is a question which need not concern us now. The main facts are that, with the widening of the breach in the relations between England and Spain, his position was legitimized, and that the booty he secured was prodigious. Naturally, when the minds of Englishmen were full of the fortunes to be made by looting the commerce of a rich and hostile State, the exploitation of the sterile regions of North America fell somewhat into the background. The last years of Elizabeth's reign did, however, witness attempts to establish English colonies across the Atlantic. As early as 1583 Sir Humphrey Gilbert had striven to plant an English settlement on the dreary coast of Newfoundland, but failed utterly and perished at sea on his way back to England. His half-brother Raleigh took up Gilbert's ideas, and between 1585 and 1590 made three attempts to set up an English colony in a part of North America which he called Virginia in honour of the virgin queen. But Raleigh was too busy pushing his fortunes at court to go himself to Virginia, and the effort came to nothing. Thus it resulted that when Elizabeth died, after a reign marked by some of the most splendid maritime efforts of English history, there was not yet a single English settlement in the continent of America.

More than a century had now elapsed since the discovery of the North American continent, but neither England nor France had made much headway in extending their dominion in the New World. There was, however, a balance, which, though slight, was well marked, in favour of France, owing to the fact that the River St. Lawrence formed a highway into the interior, and promised an access to regions unknown denied to English colonists. Even as late as 1612, one hundred and fifteen years after the first voyage of Cabot, the picture of North America as painted by the historian Parkman is a curiously depressing one. " On the banks of James River was a nest of woebegone Englishmen, a handful of Dutch fur traders at the mouth of the Hudson, and a few shivering Frenchmen among the snowdrifts of Acadia; while deep within the wild monotony of desolation, on the icy verge of the great northern river, the hand of Champlain upheld the fleur-de-lys on the rocks of Quebec." But, poor though the record of each country had been in the long period which had been available, France could show the greater achievements in exploration. It is true that from James Town the Englishman Captain John Smith made some short ventures towards the interior, and the story of Pocahontas preserves the memory of his exploits. Between 1614 and 1616 he traversed also the coast as far east as the mouth of the Penobscot and as far south as Cape Cod, writing an attractive description of the country, preparing a map of it, and suggesting for it the present name of New England. It is true, too, that in 1609 Hudson sailed up the river named after him as far as Albany, heading, all unconsciously, towards Champlain, then moving down from the north, although it is untrue to say —although the statement is frequently made—that Hudson's vessel was the first to float on the waters of the river, for Verrazano, in 1524, had pushed up some distance in a boat, and for many years following French vessels occasionally ascended the Hudson to trade with the Indians. The efforts of the English were eclipsed by those of the French. In exploration France led. In 1611 Champlain had founded a trading post at what is now Montreal, and by his entry two years earlier upon the waters of the lake which still bears his name he had unconsciously inaugurated that policy of trying to encircle the English settlements which was to be the chief cause of the eventual struggle between the two nations for the mastery of North America.

In those early years of rival effort France was impelled, either as a nation or as represented by her pioneers, by two driving forces which did not affect the English settlers in Virginia. The first was the hope of discovering a route to the Indies *through* the North American continent. Although the discovery of a route to the Far East was absorbing much English attention, the way sought *via* the New World was an ocean one across the northern limits of America, while to the French the vastness of the St. Lawrence seemed to promise a waterway, the headwaters of which might be situated near the further shore of the continent or the source of which even lie within Chinese territory. The second driving force in the case of France was that of religion. Although the motives of Champlain have been questioned, it is certain that he was largely influenced by a desire to bring the heathen tribes into the embrace of the Church. With Champlain considerations of material and territorial advantage, though clearly recognized, were often subordinated to the spiritual. He would fain rescue from perdition a people living, as he said, "like brute beasts, without faith, without law, without religion, without God." This impulse, which tended to exploration and to relations with the Indians, was peculiar to the original French settlement when contrasted with that of England. Small though the population of Europeans in North America was at the time, and remote though the nearest French settlement was from the tiny English colony at Jamestown—at least 800 miles lay between them—collision occurred as early as 1613, and in that year the first shot was fired in a struggle which was to last for a century and a half. In 1606 James I had granted privileges to two English companies to settle on the new continent between the 34th and 45th degrees of latitude. Two years earlier, however, the King of France had empowered the Sieur de Monts to explore and take possession of all lands in North America between the 40th and 46th parallels. Reduced to language more easily understood to-day, the English claimed the coast-line from about Cape Fear, in North Carolina, to the middle of Nova Scotia, while the French nobleman asserted his rights from the latitude of Philadelphia almost to Cap Breton. A reference to the map will show that the French settlement of Port Royal in Acadia, as well as St. Sauveur—on the coast of what is now Maine—were in debatable territory claimed by either nation.

At this time Sir Thomas Dale was the Governor of Virginia, and "understanding there was a plantation of Frenchmen in the north part of

Virginia about the degree of 45," he decided to destroy them. Suitable means were at hand, for Samuel Argall, the master of an illicit trading vessel and a man of daring and ruthless character, was in Virginian waters with a ship of 130 tons and carrying 14 guns. He made two voyages in pursuance of Dale's orders. In 1613 St. Sauveur was wiped out, and later in the same year Port Royal was reduced to ashes. The expeditions were of very questionable legality, for the London Company, to which Virginia had been assigned, had no jurisdiction over Acadia, which fell within the geographical boundaries of the Company of Plymouth, and, further, France and England were not at war. The conduct of Dale in constituting himself the champion of English rights led to complaints from the French ambassador in London, but, owing to the disturbed state of France, the matter dropped. In spite of their reverses the French, however, maintained their hold on Acadia. Though now long forgotten, these episodes form an important feature of North American history. They show how even at that early stage the English were vigorously asserting what they believed to be their territorial rights, and in the vindication of those rights in an obscure stroke of lawless violence began that strife between France and England, Protestantism and Rome, which for a century and a half shook the struggling communities of North America.

A period of half a generation now ensues, marked by a continuance of official peace between France and England, but closing with actual hostilities on the continent of Europe which reacted sharply on the New World. These sixteen years between 1613 and 1629 were distinguished by events of outstanding importance for the future of America, and a synoptical view of the progress of the work carried out by England and France across the Atlantic will reveal much of historical interest. Paper concessions, lavishly bestowed by both Governments, were bound to force the question of ultimate ownership to a decision. In 1621 James I of England granted to Sir William Alexander territory which included the French Acadia and changed its name to Nova Scotia. Six years later Richelieu created the Company of New France, granting it entire possession of American soil from Florida to the Arctic Circle. But this visionary domain had been invaded by a force whose weight was eventually to turn the scale not only against France but against the Old World. A new charter from James I in 1620 had conveyed to the New England Council—the successor of the Plymouth Company—the territory of North America known as New England. In the same year another and famous settlement was made. A small body of religious dissentients—101 men, women and children, including some who had fled to Holland to escape the discipline of the Church of England— sailed in the *Mayflower* and landed near Cape Cod, where they founded the settlement of Plymouth.

But although an English settlement, which was

to prove one of the foundation-stones of a mighty nation, had been established in North America, the French were making steady strides along the arduous path of exploration. The space of sixteen years now under review was marked by great achievements. In 1613 the intrepid Champlain had passed far up the Ottawa, and two years later he and his companions gazed upon the waters of *La Mère Douce*, the freshwater sea of the Huron, the first white men to do so except the French friar Le Caron. Working south-east, the Frenchmen struck the eastern end of Lake Ontario, put out boldly on its waters, and landed within the borders of what is now New York State. Champlain's interpreter, Étienne Brulé, with a small party of Indians, reached the headwaters of the Susquehanna and, with an enterprise worthy of his commander, spent the winter of 1616-17 in further exploration. Descending the Susquehanna, he followed the course of the river through what is now Pennsylvania and into Maryland to the outlet in Chesapeake Bay, returning by the same route and rejoining his leader at Montreal after an absence of three years and astounding adventures.

This period of the history of North America may appear too early to afford any useful comparison between the political system of the English and French settlements respectively. Nevertheless, the contest between the two nations can be perfectly understood only if the early stages of colonization are passed closely under review. The arrival of the Pilgrim Fathers is—in England at least—almost universally believed to be coincident with the birth of the United States, and their name is so interwoven with conceptions of democratic government and religious freedom that there is a danger lest it may be believed that such conditions attended the earliest English colonization in America. Actually the first written charter of a permanent American colony—Virginia—reserved to the King of England absolute legislative authority and denied to the emigrants any right whatever of self-government. Religion was to be established according to the doctrines and rites of the Church of England, and dissent was prohibited. Succeeding charters within a few years diminished the absolute authority of the sovereign. Nevertheless in 1611 a code akin to martial law was in force; in religion, though conformity was not strictly enforced, yet indifference could be punished with stripes and infidelity with death. This condition of affairs should be borne in mind by those who are wont to believe that the ultimate British triumph was largely due to freedom of conscience enjoyed from the earliest days, and that the downfall of New France, on the other hand, was due to an ultramontane and reactionary priesthood.

Civil liberty was won by Virginia, only to suffer a sharp setback in 1623, when James extinguished the Company. The constitution, however, assumed the form in which, although the governor and one chamber were nominated by the Crown, one chamber was popularly elected, and the death of James I prevented him from carrying out his projected task of drawing up a legal code. It is within the sixteen-year period of which we are now treating that two features of American economic history came into being in Virginia, and mark off the English sector of the continent from New France. The first of these was the cultivation of tobacco, which became not only the staple industry, but for a time the very currency of Virginia. As early as 1615 the fields, the gardens, the public squares and even the streets of Jamestown were planted with it. The second feature is one of those cynical paradoxes in which history often takes delight. At the very time when the first colony was striving to become an asylum of human liberty, it became a gaol of hereditary bondsmen. Slavery was introduced into Virginia in 1619.

While Virginia developed into what may be described as a Crown colony, Plymouth quickly assumed the status of a corporate colony deriving its chief authority from the whole body of its freemen. This contrast may perhaps appear to be without much significance, seeing that after six years' existence the new settlement numbered but three hundred souls and was ultimately absorbed into the colony of Massachusetts. Nevertheless, the difference is worth more than passing note, since it shows the germ of that system by which the English colonies became, and continued to exist as, separate entities, whereas the note of French transatlantic expansion was unity and solidarity. It is true that Acadia and the two adjacent islands of Cap Breton and St. John were distinct from Canada, and received different treatment from the French Government, but this was owing to geographical conditions and difficulties of communication rather than to any deliberate diversion from French colonial policy. Where France—or with greater truth a French statesman—showed a wider vision of the future and of the possibilities of America than can be noticed in English records was in the creation of the Company of New France in 1627. Champlain and Richelieu perceived that it was not by monopolies to commercial organizations, whose efforts were limited to the maintenance of mere trading posts, that the cause of France could best be served. Exploration and conversion were the motives which urged on Champlain; more practical, if more worldly, were the views of Richelieu. His desire to secure sea-power made him perceive the wisdom of enlarging the limits not only of French trade but also of French settlement. Commercial and political principles combined to point to the necessity of a navy strong enough to protect the colonial trade. For this end matters moved in a favourable circle, and the line of argument which guided Richelieu may be thus briefly summarized: colonies produced saleable commodities; to protect this trade a strong navy was required; but the actual carrying trade would automatically develop a mercantile marine; and from this mercantile marine the fighting navy could be recruited. From the trade itself would, therefore, grow the protection which that trade required. From this ingenious policy there ultimately developed the project of making Canada of assistance to the mother-country in shipbuilding ; a royal dockyard was established at Quebec and a constructor-in-chief was there stationed. These views, although broad and statesmanlike in comparison with the rather haphazard system in which the English colonies grew up, were, however, actually limited in scope. Nothing had yet occurred to France to suggest hopes of a great racial expansion overseas, and indeed the possibility of depopulating the mother-country was felt to be a serious danger.

Two important features distinguished this Company of New France. It was under royal auspices, and for the first time French government support was offered to supply the want of adequate voluntary contributions. Secondly, the ecclesiastical element was strong : all emigrants were to be not only French but Catholic, and for each *habitation* three ecclesiastics were to be provided for the Company. Then definitely began, for better or worse, that feature of the French colonizing régime over which argument will continue until empires are ended and nations are no more. France, like Spain before her, aimed at keeping the New World free from all taint of heresy. This policy implied the exclusion of the Huguenots and drove them to the English plantations. History has abundantly proved, be the explanation what it may, that colonizing instinct, adaptability to altered circumstances, and capacity for success were possessed to a marked degree by these refugees. But if France undoubtedly suffered by their exclusion, it must be admitted that she was loyally served by her Catholic priests. The Jesuits sent their first member to North America in 1611, and his arrival was followed in 1625 by a definite mission to Canada. A new feature was now introduced into French colonization, for it is important to remember that the Society of Jesus was a society not French, but Spanish in origin and policy. Its members differed considerably from those liberal Catholics of France who, side by side with the Huguenots, had made head against the League and its Spanish allies, and had placed Henry IV upon the throne. Indeed, the earliest settlers in Acadia feared the arrival of Jesuits who, with their fierce ultramontane principles, represented something at the time definitely un-French.

The story of the world-wide missionary enterprise of the Jesuits is a history in itself. It was just a year after they had reached the sources of the Ganges and Tibet, and nearly half a century since they had evangelized Paraguay, that priests of the Order reached the banks of the St. Lawrence. The strength of the French missions lay thenceforth in the enormous range that they covered. The Jesuits were, if not primarily at least inevitably, geographical explorers. Their intellectual superiority over the later English missionaries was marked. Their aim was to bend, not to break—and certainly not to exterminate the savage red man. Many of them lived wholly with the Indians, slept and fed in their tents and, what was more important from the imperial point of view, made themselves masters of the dialects of various tribes. It should not be inferred that the English were blind to the question of the propagation of religion. Raleigh, King James I, and later Laud interested themselves in varying degrees in the matter. But the Jesuits had got the start; they were, in the technical sense at least, more "devoted," and they were subject to an organization more autocratic and complete than any which guided the efforts of the missionaries from England. A survey of the general condition of affairs in the northern part of the American continent towards the year 1630 will justify the following conclusion. On the one hand there is New France being fitted with a machinery ecclesiastical, administrative and military; endowed with the solidarity that comes from a broad statesmanlike outlook of those at home; and supplied with explorers who viewed death in the service of exploration as a title to paradise. On the other hand are a couple of separate English colonies, lacking that power of territorial penetration afforded to their rivals by the Jesuits and other Catholic orders.

In 1625 Charles I, King of England, married Henrietta Maria, the sister of the King of France, a union which promised a rise of friendly relations in the partition of the New World, particularly in Acadia, where jarring pretensions existed as a result of conflicting concessions. The promise was, however, not to be fulfilled. War broke out between England and France over the question of the Huguenot revolt in the latter country. The attempts of Sir William Alexander to colonize Acadia had turned the attention of England towards the New World, and on the breaking out of the war an expedition was set on foot to capture the French possessions in North America. The enterprise was a private one undertaken by London merchants but furnished with letters of marque from the King. Many Huguenots were among the crews, and amongst the leaders was an Englishman, Gervase Kirke, who had long lived at Dieppe and there married a Frenchwoman. A summons to Quebec to surrender was rejected, and the assailants withdrew. Soon, however, owing to the non-arrival of supplies, the garrison was reduced to extreme suffering, and when Kirke reappeared in the following year Quebec capitulated. On July 20th, 1629, the cross of St. George was hoisted over the settlement. For nearly three years Quebec remained an English possession, but by the treaty which concluded the war not only Canada but Cap Breton and the undefined Acadia were restored to France.

The restoration of Quebec by England is an action at first sight difficult to understand, for the advisability of retaining the key of the St. Lawrence must have been obvious even in those days when the importance of overseas expansion was but dimly grasped. The solution of the mystery is to be found in the internal state of England. Charles I was at issue with his Parliament; he was in desperate need of money; half of the promised dowry of his queen was still unpaid. In these circumstances he traded Quebec and Port Royal—which had also been captured—for the 400,000 crowns due to him on his marriage with Henrietta Maria. A letter to the English ambassador in Paris is extant, directing him, under the King's authority, to make good the territorial transfer on, but not before, the payment of the money. It is doubtful, however, whether Charles made a bargain so poor as to justify the indignation of the American historian Parkman. The King of England would have found it exceedingly difficult to maintain his hold upon Quebec. He had no money. He had no standing army. As for a navy or a mercantile marine, his father had allowed these services to drift into a condition of inefficiency in startling contrast with the glorious era of Elizabeth. Callender, the English naval historian, paints a gloomy picture of England as a naval power in the years when the fate of Quebec was in the balance. He frankly describes them as the saddest in the maritime history of England. Not an English river nor an English harbour was safe from insult. Pirates infested the lower reaches of the Thames and

Severn. Portsmouth was entered by foreign ships which levied blackmail. The citizens of Plymouth were seized by alien privateers and carried off to serve before the mast. The west of England and the south of Ireland were raided by Barbary corsairs in search of galley slaves. London could count no more than ten ships over 200 tons. Foreign fishermen landed in Lincolnshire to mend their nets, and drove off with musketry the outraged owners of the soil. In five years Algerian pirates carried off 266 ships from English harbours, and in every case of capture sold the ship's company into lifelong servitude. The honour of England suffered a special indignity in 1631, when the royal fleet fled before a squadron of foreign privateers. England was powerless at sea ; in France, Richelieu had built up a navy. To imagine that in these circumstances Charles I could have permanently retained New France is to imagine a vain thing.

Little over half a century takes us to the year 1688, and during that period both French and English made such strides in the colonization of North America that, looking back, the student of history will clearly discern the shadow of the approaching struggle. It was a period in which North America had to a great extent to work out her own destiny, for both France and England were seriously occupied with European affairs. From the Thirty Years War France emerged into the Fronde. In England there was a civil war, the downfall of a monarchy, the restoration, and a great naval war with the Dutch. It was a period marked by the rise of two great statesmen, Cromwell and Colbert ; and in sea affairs by the resurrection of England as a maritime Power and, under the influence and guidance of Colbert, of an intensive growth of the French marine. The era closes with the Revolution in England and the beginning of that trilogy of wars with France, those of the Spanish and Austrian Successions, and the Seven Years' War, in which the imperial dreams of France and her colonial empire, like an insubstantial pageant, faded and left not a wrack behind.

Confining our attention to North America, and looking at the period as a whole, we shall see that the bureaucratic, over-centralized, and ecclesiastical system of France failed to achieve the vigour which distinguished the more independent and haphazard method of English settlement. Obviously in a contest to decide the question of supremacy in a New World the factor of population becomes one of immense importance. Here France was at a marked disadvantage. In the year 1663 the number of French inhabitants throughout the whole of Canada was a mere 2,500, at a time when Boston alone had 14,000 citizens, and the population of Virginia was over 80,000. It is true that under the fostering care of Colbert the population of Canada was quickly trebled, and by 1679 had almost reached five figures, but against this must be set a continued influx to the English colonies and the natural increase of the population already

FRANCE AND ENGLAND 39

settled. In the middle of the seventeenth century there was no real motive for emigration to New France. No persecution expelled the colonist from his home, for none but good Catholics were tolerated in Canada. The fur trade was an opening for the solitary adventurer rather than for a collection of families. The rigour of the climate was an added deterrent, and the government and regulations of Company and Church were hardly of a nature to entice a settler overseas. As regards the latter, should the immigrant neglect to go to Mass he was liable to be made fast to a post with collar and chain like a dog. This failure on the part of France to compete numerically with the Anglo-Saxon stock almost entirely counteracted the benefits of that homogeneity which distinguished Canada as compared with the settlements of England. In these latter, except for a New England confederation, which embraced Massachusetts, Connecticut, Newhaven and Plymouth, the tendency was for autonomy, as far as possible, along lines of administration common to every settlement. Differing from the case of Canada there was, here and there on the English seaboard, a kind of fierce attempt to found and maintain independent " settlements " of microscopic size, sometimes mere townships. These, be it noted, were not mere trading posts, but Lilliputian republics with political organizations to correspond. Inevitably these were absorbed by some larger entity, but their foundation implies an individualism and independence which may supply the solution, in part, of the success which attended the English as the colonizers of North America rather than the French. The end of the period, which closes with the year 1688, found the English strip of North America occupied by a dozen colonies differing much in origin, religion and industrial conditions, while politically they included chartered, proprietary and crown colonies.

Between the years 1632 and 1688 there stand out certain incidents, features and developments in North America peculiar to France or England, or directly affecting the colonists and settlements of both countries. In the first category are the continued penetration westwards of Jesuit priests—assisted by the penetration, even if with a quite different object, of the hardy *coureurs de bois*, who united in themselves the virtues and faults of explorers, pioneers, bushrangers and illicit traders; the formation in 1664 of Colbert's great Company of the West; and the discovery of the Mississippi and the navigation of that river to its mouth, with the claim of the whole Mississippi valley for France under the name of Louisiana. As for the English portion of America, apart from the growth of new colonies, there stand out the introduction of Quakers and the capture of New Netherlands from the Dutch. Directly and immediately affecting both French and English was the triumph of the Iroquois—or Five Nation—Indians over the Hurons, among whom most of the French evangelization was carried out, and the fact that during this period several Indian tribes—the Iroquois in particular—had received firearms through the Dutch.

If dauntless heroism, self-sacrifice and endurance, and an iron fortitude, under tortures too horrible to describe, were all that was required to extend an empire, then New France would have grown into strength as the result of the efforts of her Jesuit missionaries. It was not commercial enterprise nor royal ambition which brought the name of France into the heart of America. The motive was religion. Nevertheless, the missionaries were explorers by force of circumstances. The history of their labours is connected with the origin of every celebrated town in the annals of French America— "not a cape was turned, nor a river entered, but a Jesuit led the way." Their kindness, their patience and charity, their indomitable coolness in the hour of danger, and the utter absence of any self-seeking conduct on their part, did not fail to impress the Hurons and Alonquins, if not at first, yet eventually, in favour of France. By September, 1646, a mere fourteen years after the restoration of Quebec, the Jesuits had religious settlements on the shores of Lake Huron, with outposts on the Kennebec. As early as 1634 there was raised to the north-west of Lake Ontario the first humble house of the Society of Jesus among the Hurons. In 1641 Montreal was founded. In the same year the religious zeal of the French bore the cross to Sault Ste Marie and the confines of Lake Superior, five years before Eliot, of New England, had addressed the tribe of Indians that dwelt within six miles of Boston harbour. A map, prepared by the Order of the Jesuits at Paris in 1660, proves that they had already traced the highway of waters from Lake Erie to Lake Superior, and had gained a glimpse at least of Lake Michigan. Men with the culture and intelligence such as the Jesuits possessed could not but grasp the strategic importance of certain positions. In 1640 the lion-hearted Brebeuf, who had been sent to the villages of the neutral Indians along the Niagara, realized the necessity of a position south of Lake Ontario to guarantee the navigation of the St. Lawrence long before any Englishman had even reached the basin of that river.

But although France gained by having in her service such courageous pioneers who, in the intervals of religious work, could prepare rough maps, report upon a territory, and even construct a passable fort, these missions lacked the military backing which was essential. Not that protection was wholly absent. By 1644 soldiers were being sent from Quebec, from time to time, to escort the Fathers on their way and to defend them on arrival. Further, some of the inhabitants of Canada were allowed to settle with the missions, and, in return for helping in their defence, to trade with the Indians and to sell the furs to the Company at a fixed price. Even artillery was not altogether wanting, for in 1648 a small cannon was sent to

Sainte Marie, on Lake Huron, by Huron canoes. But these handfuls of men were unable to supply the resisting power required against the formidable Iroquois. What famine and pestilence had spared of the Hurons the Iroquois tomahawk and the Iroquois bullet almost exterminated. As a tribe the Hurons practically ceased to be. Of the survivors some dispersed among friendly Indians, some went over to the Iroquois, and the remainder accompanied those of the Jesuits who still remained to Quebec. In 1650 the Huron mission was abandoned.

In addition to their distant labours amongst the Hurons the Jesuits had worked upon the northern outskirts of what is now Maine. This brought them into touch with an Indian tribe near the colonies of New England, and, in addition, into touch with the outposts of the English settlements, where their emissary was well received. In the autumn of 1650 the Jesuits reappeared upon a diplomatic and political mission. Massachusetts had made representations to Quebec with a view to reciprocity of trade, and the French governor of the latter place hoped, by granting the privileges asked for, to secure military aid against the Iroquois, who were harrying the Abenakis. Druilletes, a Jesuit priest, made two journeys to New England, visiting Boston, Salem and Newhaven, and making his representations to the governor of Massachusetts. He was well received, but his errand proved bootless, for the commissioners of the Four Colonies declined either to declare war or even to permit volunteers to be raised in New England against the Iroquois. Even the bait of free trade with Canada failed to tempt the Puritan. The circumstances of this mission are, however, of interest as showing how, even as far back as 1650, there was a kind of dawn of commercial relations between the French and English colonies. From the strictly military point of view the policy of the Puritans was probably sound. The Iroquois were the best fighting savages in North America, and while there was little to be looked for by provoking them, a good deal was to be gained by allowing them to harry the French and to exhaust themselves and the French in continued hostilities.

In Canada, in spite of the failure of the Huron enterprise, the Jesuits were still a power, and a great one. The Canadian mission was under most exalted patronage in France. The Superior of the Jesuits at Quebec occupied an important position in the temporal administration of New France. But although the charge of sacerdotalism and religious tyranny may be levelled against the Canada of that day, it would be a delusion to imagine that spiritual freedom was indigenous in New England. In 1656 two Quaker women landed at Boston. They were subjected to the grossest indignities, imprisoned and transported to Barbados. In 1658 Mary Clark came to Boston to warn the persecutors to leave off their cruelties, but, in addition to imprisonment, she was flogged with a three-corded whip upon her naked back. Each cord was knotted and as thick as a man's little finger, and the handle of the whip was so long that the hangman made use of both his arms to wield it. An Act imposing the penalty of death in cases of extreme obstinacy was carried—though by a very small majority—and, under its provisions, four Quakers were hanged. Nor was it only against Quakers that intolerance was directed. In 1635 Roger Williams had been banished from Massachusetts for heterodoxy, and a few years later a similar fate overtook the clergyman John Wheelwright and his sister, Mrs. Hutchinson, owing to a persistent but trifling divergence from the accepted creed of the colony. As for Roman Catholicism, in 1647 Massachusetts enacted that Jesuits entering the colony should be expelled and, if they returned, should be hanged.

A few pages back, in summarizing the outstanding features of this period of from 1632 to 1688, there were mentioned the foundation of the Company of the West in 1664, on the part of France; and on the part of England the gaining of what is now New York. These two important episodes should be reviewed together. The Company of the West was due to the genius of Colbert, whose imperial vision and whose persistent efforts for the maintenance and increase of the French navy and mercantile marine mark him as a statesman of a high order. So far as New France was concerned, the foundation of the new organization implied that the real power was concentrated not in a company but in the Crown. An important result was the reinforcing of the Canadian militia by " King's " troops. Colbert clearly appreciated the necessity of sending out disciplined and well-officered regulars to break the Iroquois. The Carignan Regiment, and details, some 1,200 strong, was despatched to Canada. This was a hard-bitten unit, raised in Savoy, with a record of good service against the Turks. The regiment operated against the Iroquois with success, though without decisive success. In one of the expeditions a French force reached Schenectady, and French and English gazed upon each other with astonishment. Courtesy, however, prevailed, provisions were supplied to the French on payment, and quarters were offered, but declined. The French campaign was attended by important results. Roads were made and forts established along the line of the River Richelieu and Lake Champlain, which pointed at New York. The importance of this line, with its continuation by the Hudson, was to be most marked not only in the struggle between France and England, but in the American War of Independence, and the strategic value of it will be referred to later at greater length. As for New York, the English had seen, in the year that Colbert founded his new Company, the necessity of removing the feeble Dutch power, which by the possession of New Netherlands—to which they had added the adjacent New Sweden in 1655—was the one obstacle to continuous

English settlement. In exchange for Surinam the Dutch New Netherlands became the English New York, while from what was New Sweden sprang New Jersey and Delaware.

In consequence of this readjustment of territory, portion of the English sector of North America now marched with the hunting ground of the Iroquois, and this new state of affairs tended to place that tribe in the position of holding the balance between the colonies of England and France. From henceforth this Iroquois problem, and the possession by the French of the waterway to Lake Champlain, must always expose the English settlements—or, at least, New England and New York—to attack from the rear. Further, when the Carignan regiment was disbanded in Canada every effort was made to form military settlements of officers and men to protect the line of the Richelieu River. The *heroum filii* who might result from such colonization, and who would be brought up in a military tradition, would be a distinct asset in case of hostility with the English settlements. These latter had a great preponderance in population ; but Colbert, and Talon the Canadian *intendant*, by encouragement of immigration, bonuses on marriage, fines for celibacy, the despatch of shiploads of young women, and the forcible prevention of return, strove hard to adjust the inequality. The experiments, however, were not a success, and France thus forfeited much of the advantage which she might otherwise have enjoyed.

France, however, was by no means backward in the question of the vast possibilities of trade with the western Indians, for which her claim to, and part occupation of, the immense area bordering on the Great Lakes placed her in a favourable position. The Huron shores had been the scene of much of the Jesuit labour. In 1669 two Sulpicians erected a cross and took possession in the name of the King of France of the territory extending from Lake Erie to the north. Two years later a " congress of nations " was held at Sault Ste Marie, where Indian chiefs, assembled from the head-waters of the St. Lawrence, the Mississippi and the Red River, were informed by French officials that henceforth they were under the protection of the French king. A cross was erected, and by its side was planted a column which bore the lilies of the Bourbons. Another two years elapsed and Frontenac, the governor-general of New France, took another step in the commercial struggle which was now becoming clearly marked. The question at issue was whether the great fur trade of the west should find an outlet to the sea by Albany and the Hudson, or by the River St. Lawrence. It was a question difficult to solve, and two centuries later the problem whether the commerce of the Upper Lakes could be more profitably passed to the seaboard at New York or by Montreal had not been decided. In Frontenac's time the Iroquois traded with the western Indians of the Mississippi Valley, bartering what they themselves received from Europeans for the furs which the western Indians possessed in abundance. It seemed to Frontenac that by the construction of a fort at the eastern end of Lake Ontario most of the traffic would be placed under French control, the Iroquois crossing the Lake Ontario to meet the western Indians at this *entrepôt*. At the same time the fort would be a definite and material witness of French military power. The fort was built in 1673, and was called Fort Cataraqui. Later the name was changed to Fort Frontenac, and on its site stands the Kingston of to-day.

This was but the beginning of much greater things. The indefatigable French missionaries had already borne the cross through eastern Wisconsin and the north of Illinois. The long-expected discovery of the upper waters of the Mississippi was at hand, and, in the same year as that in which Frontenac built his fort at Kingston, the cross and the emblem of France stood in the valley of the Mississippi. Marquette and Joliet were the first white men ever to tread the soil of Iowa. Descending the Father of Waters, the two travellers proceeded past the entrance of the Arkansas. Apart from actual exploration two incidents are noteworthy. In the vicinity of the mouth of the Ohio, Indians were met carrying guns and wearing cloth ; at the Arkansas the travellers learnt that it was dangerous to proceed owing to the presence lower down the river of Indians with firearms, and that the informants themselves never descended the river for that reason. The news induced the explorers to return. It is not without significance in connection with the contest between France and England in the New World that, as early as 1673, red men from the St. Lawrence to the Gulf of Orleans were in possession of muskets.

Marquette and Joliet had not reached the mouth of the Mississippi, but it was clear that the river which they had descended must be the same great waterway, the lower reaches of which had been traversed by Spanish explorers. At this time there dwelt at the outlet of Lake Ontario René Robert Cavelier, Sieur de La Salle, a young Frenchman of good family with a passion for exploration. In his wanderings he had discovered the Ohio River, and had passed through Lakes Huron, Erie and Michigan, and some distance down the Illinois River. When Joliet, on his return, passed Fort Frontenac, he spread the news of his discoveries, and the young and enthusiastic La Salle immediately framed vast plans of colonization and of commerce between Europe and the Mississippi. Twice he repaired to France and interested Colbert, and Colbert's son, Seignelay, in his scheme. On his return to Canada disappointment and delay were encountered, but, passing down the Illinois, La Salle entered the Mississippi in February, 1682, and, floating down the river, reached the mouth on April 9th. There cross and column were erected in due form, and La Salle claimed the territory through which he had passed for France and gave to it the name of Louisiana.

Returning to Quebec, La Salle sailed for France once again. Colbert was no more, but Seignelay, now minister for maritime affairs, listened confidingly to La Salle's ambitions. The explorer aimed at nothing less than to make France mistress of North America. He pointed out that the Mexican mines of Spain could be attacked; that all the articles of commerce which had enriched Virginia and New England—timber, salted meat, tallow, corn, sugar, tobacco, and so on—could now be obtained; and he emphasized the fact that if foreigners should anticipate the French in settling the Mississippi Valley, New France would be completely hemmed in. The King of France was won over, and in the summer of 1684 four ships were despatched with 280 colonists of both sexes and including 100 soldiers. The expedition, however, was not a success. The mouth of the Mississippi was passed, an error which made Texas part of Louisiana. After searching in vain for the great river, the indomitable La Salle attempted to return to Canada overland, but left several of his followers near the Trinity River in the present Texas. Starvation, sickness, and the guns and tomahawks of the Indians effected the destruction of the infant colony left behind.

Meanwhile, in the English strip of North America, events had taken place of importance as regards the growth of the Anglo-Saxon element in the continent. In 1673 England and Holland were again at war, and the Dutch recovered New York and

New Jersey. No measures had been taken for the protection of these new colonies, and, in face of a Dutch fleet of twenty-three vessels, with sixteen hundred men on board, resistance was manifestly useless. Fortunately for the English race the whole of the reconquered territory was restored to England by the treaty which concluded the war, and the continuity of seaboard, so essential for expansion, was thus ensured. New York soon began to divert some of the lucrative fur trade from French channels. Traders were sent from Albany to carry English goods to the Upper Lakes. They traded successfully and won golden opinions from the Indians, who begged them to return. Rum was conveyed by the adventurers, and the fact is the subject of tart comment in a correspondence between Denonville, the governor-general of Canada, and Dongan, the Catholic governor of New York. To an indignant query from the former appealing to their common religion, Dongan replied that English rum did no more hurt than French brandy, and, " in the opinion of Christians, is much more wholesome." Another important event was the founding of the colony of Pennsylvania in 1682, when a tract of territory unoccupied, although included in the original patent of Maryland, was transferred to Penn. The new colony neither was, nor was designed to be, composed exclusively of Quakers. The Quaker element, however, undoubtedly preponderated, and the qualities of industry, frugality and sobriety were offset by that abhorrence of war peculiar to the sect. This tenet was to prove a serious hindrance on a future occasion when it became needful that the colonists should be united against French and Indian enemies.

The French were now not only in possession of New France and Acadia, Newfoundland, and practically all of Hudson's Bay, but claimed also a moiety of Maine, of Vermont, more than a moiety of New York, the whole valley of the Mississippi, and Texas, even as far as the Rio Bravo del Norte. In view of this strong position held by France, the period, beginning with the English Revolution and closing with the Treaty of Utrecht —containing as it does two great wars in which France and England were opposed—deserves more than a passing mention. These two wars reacted upon North America, and although there was no Beachy Head nor Blenheim fought in the New World, blood and treasure were expended in the struggle between the rival settlements. It was not likely that in those days of slow and infrequent communications the denizens of North America should interest themselves particularly in the question of the personal rivalry between William and Louis, or should care one way or another whether a Bourbon sat on the Spanish throne. The strife between the colonies was frankly on more parochial issues—for the fisheries and for territory north and west. Each side on occasion took the offensive, and some of the expeditions are of peculiar interest in that they foreshadow the events of the two further great Anglo-French contests in America, and reveal the importance of certain strategic points which was to be stressed in the lifetime of Wolfe.

If the issue had depended on the population of the colonies it could hardly have appeared doubtful. The French census for the North American continent in 1688 showed 11,249 persons—scarcely a tenth part of the English population on its frontiers, and about a twentieth of that of English North America. As against this, Canada was under a unified military control, while the English colonies were distinct and without co-ordination. The question of solidarity or disunion was, however, secondary to that of the attitude of the Indians. The savages still held the keys of the great west, and, to a really definite extent, held the balance of power between French and English. When Frontenac, once more governor-general of Canada, on the outbreak of war in 1689, planned the conquest of New York, his hand was stayed by the capture of Montreal by the Iroquois. In the moment of consternation Fort Frontenac was evacuated and razed, and from Three Rivers, on the St. Lawrence, to Mackinaw, at the outlet of Lake Michigan, there remained not one French town and scarcely one French fort.

The effect was important and twofold. To prevent the French "losing face" with the Indians, Frontenac resolved to make a triple descent—from Montreal, Three Rivers and Quebec—upon the

English settlements, aided by Christianized Iroquois. Schenectady was destroyed and the settlement at Salmon Falls met a similar fate. Both engagements were bloody; many were massacred and many were taken prisoners. In the expedition from Quebec the fort and settlement at Casco, near the present Portland in Maine, were captured. These incidents, however, taught the English colonies the necessity of some kind of union. On May 1st, 1690, New York beheld the momentous example of an American "Congress." Invitations were extended to all the colonies—as far, at least, as Maryland. The tomahawks of Christian Indians, led by French commanders, brought into being the idea of unification, which was to lead to the formation of the United States of America.

The plan adopted by the Congress was first suggested by the Iroquois. It was bold and, strategically speaking, sound enough. An "amphibious" operation was to be undertaken, the objective being not mere isolated raids and massacres, but the full conquest of Canada. By land an army was to move by the Lake Champlain route against Montreal, while Massachusetts, with a fleet, was to attack Quebec. The scheme, however, was beyond the resources of the colonies, and, to be frank, beyond the capacity of the leaders employed on it. The projected attack by land broke down through lack of supplies and through differences between Connecticut and New York, and petered out into a mere raid. And although the fleet of thirty-four sail reached Quebec, it could effect nothing in view of the failure of the expedition against Montreal. A landing was made and the fortress was hotly bombarded by the fleet, but the rude courage of the fishermen and farmers of the Massachusetts force could not prevail against the discipline and training of the garrison of French regulars at Quebec. Repulsed from Canada, the English colonies could then do little more than attempt the defence of their own frontiers. The French continued their raids, and by the late summer of 1696 French dominion was extended into the heart of Maine. Acadia was once more under the French flag. The Treaty of Ryswick of 1697 left France secure in her American possessions. She retained all Hudson's Bay and all the places of which she was in possession at the opening of the war. The fighting for Hudson's Bay is of interest, but, being subsidiary to the main issue in America, needs no detailed description beyond the record that a French vessel of thirty-four guns—isolated from her consorts—defeated three English ships carrying 120 guns between them off Fort Nelson in 1697.

To utilize the discovery of the whole course of the Mississippi was the object of France when peace had been brought about by the Treaty of Ryswick. D'Iberville obtained a commission for establishing direct maritime intercourse between the Mississippi and France. In March, 1699, the river was, for the first time, entered from the sea. The progress of France in this quarter had now begun to excite uneasiness not only in the English colonies, but at home, where William III and his counsellors were perturbed by the progress which France had made. The English king declared his intention of planting settlements on the Mississippi at any cost, but various reasons prevented the design from being put into execution. France was left in control of Louisiana, but, as in Canada, the bigotry and intolerance of the French Government checked the growth of the colony. French Protestants had petitioned to be allowed, under French sovereignty and in the enjoyment of freedom of conscience, to plant the banks of the Mississippi. "The King," was the reply, "has not driven Protestants from France to make a republic for them in America."

After a few years of peace there followed in Europe the War of the Spanish Succession, in which France and Spain were allied—a condition which gave the English colonists in America two enemies to fight. There, however, the struggle was localized. The central colonies were practically unaffected. New York was protected by the neutrality of the Iroquois, now at peace with France and England. In the south, South Carolina, bordering on Spanish Florida, was engaged, and in the north, New England again witnessed rapine and bloodshed. Dearfield was destroyed early in 1704 by a party of about 200 French and 140 Indians, who, by the aid of snow-shoes, had made their way on foot from Canada. In the following year the Indians stealthily approached towns in the heart of Massachusetts, as well as along the coast. In 1708 Haverhill, near the Merrimac, was the scene of another massacre by a Franco-Indian expedition.

The great victories of Marlborough on the continent of Europe shattered the prevailing belief in the invincibility of French troops, and restored to the English army that prestige which it had lost since Agincourt. Freed from anxiety in Europe, the minds of Englishmen turned to colonial acquisitions. In one season Acadia, Newfoundland and Canada were to be added to the British Crown. Acadia was seized in 1710 by a force which included six English vessels joined by thirty of New England, and four New England regiments. Flushed with victory, Nicholson returned to England to urge the conquest of Canada, and five chieftains from the Iroquois were brought to London and given audience by Queen Anne. Protests from America, pointing out that the French, by their hold on the Mississippi, could take the English colonies in reverse, stimulated the English Government to despatch in 1711 a naval and military expedition under the command of Sir Hovenden Walker. There were fifteen ships of war, with forty transports, carrying seven veteran regiments from Marlborough's army and a battalion of marines. The force reached Boston on June 25th. The campaign was to be carried out from three points. The English expedition was to proceed by sea to

Quebec; from Albany a colonial army, reinforced by 600 Iroquois, was to move on Montreal, while from Wisconsin the Fox Indians were to harry the French in Michigan. The incompetence, however, of Walker ruined the chances of success at Quebec. Montreal was unmolested, and in the west the French managed to hold Detroit against the Indians.

The war was brought to a conclusion by the Treaty of Utrecht in 1713. The principal object for which England had entered the war—the exclusion of the Bourbons from the throne of Spain—had not been secured, but, in America, England obtained from France large concessions of territory, namely, Hudson's Bay, Newfoundland, and Nova Scotia, or Acadia "according to its ancient boundaries"—a vague expression pregnant with dispute. Further, it was admitted that the Iroquois were in the sphere of influence of Great Britain, and France pledged herself not to molest them. Nothing, however, was done to counteract French influence and possession in the basin of the Mississippi. New York, Pennsylvania, and Virginia had more than once directed the attention of the English Government to the progress of the French in the west, and Penn had urged that the valley of the Mississippi should be secured for England. The English prime minister himself was frankly uneasy about "the future undertakings of the French in North America." The colonization by Great Britain had been proposed to Queen Anne. Nothing, however, was done, and

France was left free to exploit the boundless spaces of the Mississippi valley.

The territorial concessions made by France had been of great extent, but the loss of Hudson's Bay, Newfoundland and Acadia, enabled her to concentrate upon the continental issue, and the question whether to France or England would fall the dominion of the West. The surrender of Acadia, it is true, gave England an admirable harbour, which was later to be Halifax, but the French discounted this future advantage by the construction of the fortress of Louisburg on Cap Breton Island. The plans were from the great Vauban himself, and thirty million *livres* were spent upon the place. At the other extremity of New France, New Orleans came into existence, and a vast, though unsuccessful, scheme for the development of Louisiana was begun.

This sketch of the relations between France and England in North America has now been brought up to the years immediately preceding the birth of Wolfe. It may be further summarized by a brief comparison of the colonial systems, and of the attitude of the two countries towards the momentous question whether France or England was to be mistress of the West. It has been well said that the French colonies were apt to be treated too much as household plants, when a hardier culture might have suited them better; whereas the English colonies, like thistles planted by the hand of Nature, seemed to grow apace out of sheer wilfulness. The

English colonies were separate, jealous of the Crown and of one another, and incapable as yet of acting in concert. Instead of concerting for defence they were "crumbled into little Governments." When Queen Anne nominated a commander-in-chief of the militias of the various colonies, the proposal was resisted, and only a grudging compliance made to supply quotas required. In trade, too, the colonies became rivals of England, and the mother country, urged on by selfish commercial interests, enacted legislation against them. In Canada, on the other hand, colonial produce never competed with home manufactures sufficiently to cause professional alarm. New France was treated as a child, and a favoured one; the English colonies remind us rather of the young exiles of Dotheboys Hall. The neglect in which the English court left them was wholesome in some respects, but it left them unfit for aggressive action. Without troops, without commanders, without political union, with neither military organization nor military habits, they were at a disadvantage in comparison with the highly centralized and military regime of Canada. At the same time it should be pointed out that the union and solidarity of New France were merely comparative. Actually within Canada there were frequent internal bickering and dissension. The era of Frontenac particularly is distinguished by a triangular duel between himself as viceroy and the civil *intendant* and the Jesuit Superior. The ships which started for France each year, when the ice on the St. Lawrence had disappeared, were crammed with dispatches and letters of mutual recrimination. There was, too, a long-standing jealousy between Montreal and Quebec, and some friction between the Jesuits and other religious orders, while the *coureurs de bois*, with their illicit trade and the occasional corrupt alliance between them and high officials, from the viceroy downwards, were an added problem. Where, however, Canada was in a position superior to the English colonies was in this : for any dispute from the mouth of the St. Lawrence to the Great Lakes there was one supreme and autocratic referee—the King of France.

In their views upon territorial expansion the colonies of the two nations present a striking difference. Canada lived by the fur trade, and for this required free range and indefinite space. In the English colonies agriculture played an important part. This could be carried out in limited areas, and there was, therefore, no present need to cross the forest-covered Alleghanies. The tendency of the English was, therefore, to take firm root before they spread, while the French shot offshoots far out and quickly into the wilderness. The French colonists were the more military by training and tradition ; they were quicker in recognizing strategic points. These they seized and held by armed force, forming no agricultural basis, but " attracting the Indians by trade and holding them by conversion." But the advantages which France enjoyed—and they were not a few—were blasted by her religious intolerance. The French people were divided into two parts—one eager to emigrate and the other reluctant to do so. The one consisted of persecuted Huguenots, the other of favoured Catholics. France chose to endeavour to people the New World not with those who wished to go, but with those who preferred to stay at home. England adopted practically the opposite policy, and at the time of the Treaty of Utrecht, while the population of Canada was but 20,000, that of the English colonies was ten times that amount, and there were 158,000 inhabitants in New England alone. The downfall of the French empire in America was due in part to the genius of Wolfe, but perhaps more to the united skill of other capable soldiers. Still more was it due to the remorseless action of sea power. But none of these might have prevailed had not the flow of a stream of hardy French settlers been ruthlessly dammed at the source. Had it not been for bigotry and intolerance New France might well have survived. The story of the fall of Quebec might never have been written. *Troiaque nunc staret, Priamique arx alta maneres.*

CHAPTER TWO

THE EARLY MILITARY CAREER OF JAMES WOLFE.

THE Treaty of Utrecht left England in a condition in some ways analogous to the state of affairs existing after the Great War of the twentieth century. A long struggle had been brought to a victorious conclusion, but in each case there was an aftermath of lesser contests before peace was really secured. The rebellion in Scotland two years after Utrecht may be compared, in a loose way, with the post-1918 war in Ireland, while the fighting, or the probability of fighting, in Russia and Turkey, after the Treaty of Versailles had been signed, bears some resemblance to the hostility and the actual fighting between England and Spain after the formal conclusion of the War of the Spanish Succession. Common to both periods was the reduction of the fighting services, and the retirement or quasi-retirement into civil life of many veterans of the longer struggle.

Amongst those who fought with Marlborough, and who soon found themselves quickly engaged in the little war in Scotland in 1715, was an officer, Edward Wolfe by name, who, at the time of the Old Pretender's landing, was thirty-one years of

EARLY CAREER OF WOLFE 65

age. He came of Anglo-Irish stock—a stock from which many of the great soldiers of England have been recruited. The family of Wolfes, or Woulfes, appears to have emigrated to Ireland in the fifteenth century and became connected by marriage with another famous Anglo-Irish family, the Goldsmiths, whose name appears for the first time in official Irish records about 1500. This Edward Wolfe was born at York in 1685, both his father and grandfather having been soldiers before him. At the age of sixteen, in the first year of the reign of Queen Anne, Edward was appointed second lieutenant of Marines, and three years later was promoted captain in Temple's regiment of Foot. This regiment was raised during the war by Sir Richard Temple, afterwards the first Viscount Cobham, and was disbanded on the conclusion of peace. In 1708 a detachment distinguished itself by a stubborn defence of the citadel of Ghent, when the town was treacherously surrendered to Vendôme by French partisans. In 1708, the year of Oudenarde, Edward Wolfe was serving with Marlborough in Flanders as a brigade-major, and continued in the field until the Peace of Utrecht. Two years later he took part in the suppression of the rebellion in Scotland under General Wade. On the conclusion of the campaign he received a lieutenant-colonelcy, and in the inevitable and drastic reduction which always follows England's wars Edward Wolfe settled down into a state of quasi-retirement. In 1723 this Wolfe married Henrietta, daughter of

Edward Thompson of Marsden, in Yorkshire—a lady some eighteen years junior to himself. The couple appear to have resided at York for several years, and then, in 1726, a migration was made to the little town of Westerham, in Kent, some twenty-two miles from London, where Colonel Wolfe and his wife occupied a gabled Tudor house named " Spiers." During the winter of 1726 Colonel Wolfe was temporarily away from home, and his wife, during his absence, passed much of her time at the vicarage. Here, during the evening of what was then Christmas Eve, but, according to the reformed calendar, we now call January 2nd, 1727, Henrietta Wolfe gave birth to a son—James Wolfe, the future victor of Quebec.

Both James Wolfe and his younger brother, Edward—born a year later—were delicate children and of indifferent health, aggravated probably by the ministrations of their mother, in whose cookery book appears, written in her own hand, the following :—

" Good water for consumption :

" Take a peck of green garden snails, wash them in Bear (beer), put them in an oven, and let them stay till they've done crying ; then with a knife and fork pick the green from them, and beat the snail shells and all in a stone mortar. Then take a quart of green earth-worms, slice them through the middle, and strow them with salt ; then wash them and beat them, the pot being first put into the still with two handfuls of angelica, a quart of rosemary flowers, then the snails and worms, the

ROOM IN WESTERHAM VICARAGE WHERE WOLFE WAS BORN,
JANUARY 2, 1727.
(*By permission of A. E. Wolfe-Aylward.*)

egrimony, bears' feet, red dock roots, barbery brake, bilbony, wormwood, of each two handfuls ; one handful of rue tumerick and one ounce of saffron, well dried and beaten. Then powder in three gallons of milk. Wait till morning, then put in three ounces of cloves (well beaten), hartshorn, grated. Keep the still covered all night. This done, stir it not. Distil with a moderate fire. The patient must take two spoonfuls at a time."

Wolfe carried ill-health with him to his death, and one can only wonder how he cheated the grave so long, nurtured as he may have been on such a pharmacopœia as that. Save for this reference to the strange paregoric with which the young James may or may not have been dosed, there are few details extant as to his childhood. It is known that the nurse of both the lads in their infancy was a young woman, Betty Hooper by name, whose two sons in due time enlisted in the regiment in which James Wolfe was then lieutenant-colonel. When the latter was some five years old, Squerryes Court at Westerham was taken by a Mr. John Warde, a widower, whose wife had been the sister of two countesses. Between the second son, George, and the elder Wolfe boy there sprang up a warm friendship, in which the military ambitions and fighting tastes of both lads seem to have been foreshadowed. James Wolfe and his brother were sent to a school in Westerham kept by a Mr. Lawrence, and it was here that James formed his boyish friendship with young Warde. Of traditions of the schooldays of Wolfe none endures, and, leaving him for the moment imbibing history and geography under Lawrence's ferule, we may turn to note some conditions of international affairs by which his life was to be closely affected.

The Peace of Utrecht had been soon followed by the death of Queen Anne. She died too suddenly for the Tories to engineer the restoration of the Stuarts; and the Elector of Hanover, under the terms of the Act of Settlement of 1701, came to England as George I—a circumstance which provided for Wolfe two of his earlier lessons in war, for he fought in Europe for the defence of Hanover, and in Scotland in defence of the Hanoverian dynasty. Nevertheless, for over a quarter of a century after Utrecht, England enjoyed a period of almost unbroken repose. Louis XIV died in 1715, and, for a great part of the twenty-four years which followed, both France and England were guided by peace-loving ministers—Fleury in the one country and Walpole in the other. Hence, not only were there no hostilities in Europe, but even at times an alliance or informal co-operation between the two Powers—a very unusual state of affairs in the eighteenth century and one which will be considered shortly as regards its effect upon the contest in America.

In the New World the questions at issue with France were attended with great difficulty. By the Treaty of Utrecht she had surrendered Acadia and Nova Scotia " with its ancient boundaries." About these boundaries disputes arose, and there was actual fighting in connection with the eastern frontier of Massachusetts, in what is now Maine. The French and English would probably have come to an amicable settlement, but there was a third party, often unconsidered in these questions—the Indians. The Abenakis, alarmed by the arrival of claimants from New England, appealed earnestly to the French. Assistance was not forthcoming, and the Abenakis were badly worsted in an attempt to withstand the English settlers, who now definitely established the eastern boundary of New England. In 1724 Massachusetts established Fort Dummer on the site of Brattleborough, and a settlement was made in the present Vermont. A still greater difficulty attended the delimitation of Canada. In those days of discovery, when merely the chief physical features could be taken as the basis of a claim, it was customary in the case of a river to claim the whole basin. The entrances of tributaries could be marked upon a rough map and, by a kind of convention, all the land drained by such tributaries came to be included. Canada, by its original charter, comprised the whole basin of the St. Lawrence, and the logical interpretation of this clause would prevent the northern extension of New York. A still further complication was brought about by the question of the Iroquois. By the Treaty of Utrecht these were explicitly made subjects of England, and every effort was made by the English in America to exaggerate the rights and claims of the Five Nations. Accordingly, in

1726, the year before the birth of Wolfe, a treaty was made by the governor of New York, at Albany, with the Iroquois, by which much of the territory adjoining the Great Lakes, which had always been regarded as French, came nominally under the King of England. Considerable confusion and probably actual conflict were bound to ensue from these vague claims and counter-claims.

The people on the spot realized that, whatever might be the value of such expressions as " river basin," or whatever worth might be attached to treaties endorsed with the red man's symbol, it was actual possession which would count. The English started by converting a trading-post at Oswego, on the south shore of Lake Ontario, into a fort, but, before the transformation had been made, the French fort at Niagara, at the western end of the lake, had been renewed, and the flag of France floated from it before Oswego had assumed any real military value. A few years later the French entered Lake Champlain and constructed a fort at Crown Point. The batteries, by defending the approach to Canada by the Hudson-Lake Champlain-Richelieu route, gave security to Montreal. But the French authorities in Canada were soldiers enough not to be contented with mere defence. The works at Crown Point would clearly facilitate a French invasion, and were a pistol aimed at the heart of New York. The net result was that, except for Oswego and the territory controlled by the fort there, the entire country watered by the St. Lawrence and its tributaries was still in the possession of the French. And the exploitation also of Louisiana gave France a further grip upon an enormous part of what is now the United States. By claiming the " valley of the Mississippi " La Salle had unconsciously extended the dominion of the King of France by an area bounded on one side by the Rocky Mountains and on the other by the Alleghanies. The western limits may be disregarded, although it is of interest to note that within them would have been included portions of Montana, Wyoming, Colorado and Texas. It is on the east that the real significance of the claim will be observed. Not a fountain bubbled west of the Alleghanies but was claimed as being within the French Empire. All the Ohio country was thus French. The fort which the French erected where Pittsburgh now stands, at the junction of the Alleghany and the Monongahela, was built as a result of a claim to Louisiana, not of Canada. Its riverine father was not the St. Lawrence, but the Mississippi.

France and England were, however, not the only two European Powers involved in the destiny of the New World. Spain had been first in the field, and during the long interval of peace between the two former countries it was England and Spain who fell out, and the quarrel gave young James Wolfe his first glimpse of soldiering. By the Treaty of Utrecht the monopoly of the supply of slaves to the Spanish-American colonies was transferred from a French company to British subjects, who were authorized to introduce 144,000 slaves in thirty years. Further, once a year a British vessel was authorized to proceed with manufactured goods to the fairs of Porto Bello and Vera Cruz. The privilege was transferred to the South Sea Company, and was grossly abused. Under pretence of renewing her provisions, the trading vessel was followed by tenders from which she filled up again with merchandise. A vast and lucrative contraband trade was thus established, and, to meet it, the Spanish Government established a fleet of revenue cutters which insisted on searching all English vessels approaching the Spanish colonies. Considerable friction was thus caused, and when James Wolfe was a child in his fifth year it may be that he sometimes heard his father discussing with some old military cronies a curious story of the dastardliness of the Spaniards, and of an Englishman who was moving about the country exhibiting an ear as a proof of outrages he had undergone. It was in the year 1731 that a certain English skipper, master of the *Rebecca*, Jenkins by name, was met at sea and overhauled by a Spanish *guarda costa*. As he had nothing contraband on board which could be seized, the master himself was laid hold upon by the spiteful visitors. They nearly hanged him, frightened him to death, and at last, so it was alleged, tore off one of his ears. " Carry that to your king and tell him of it," cried the revenue officers, casting the ear at Jenkins. Bleeding and furious, the poor man set sail for England and, " with his owners," hurried to Hampton Court to lay the facts before the Duke of Newcastle. But Walpole was at the height of his pacific reign, and the ministry had no desire to be made acquainted with facts which might disturb the peace of the nation. Poor Jenkins wrapped his ear once more in cotton-wool and carried it away with him, a disappointed man. He showed it in the clubs, and had it written about in the newspapers, but although the story became a historical matter, and rankled in the national mind, it failed to reach the dimensions of what to-day we would call a " stunt," or to inspire what to-day we would call a " slogan."

The differences, however, between English trading vessels and Spanish revenue cutters still continued. The South Sea Company had abused its privileges; and other vessels, even fleets of them, frequently put into Spanish harbours under pretence of refitting and refreshing, but with the real object of selling English goods. Off many harbours on the Spanish Main lay a line of vessels analogous to the Rum Row of modern times. The Spanish revenue was seriously affected, and an annual fair of Panama, intended as the mart for South America, once the richest in the world, became shorn of its splendour and deserted by its crowd. The Spaniards naturally objected, and were not always courteous in their methods. The English merchants began to make themselves heard, and public opinion in England was skilfully engineered. Fresh fuel was thrown on the flames by disputes on the limits of the territories which the English had recently formed in North America, and, in honour of the King and Queen, had received the names of Georgia and Carolina. The opposition in Parliament then took the matter up and made it a party " plank." The rising genius of Pitt was now enlisted in this American business. Every resource of oratory was applied to exaggerate the insults and cruelties of the Spaniards and to brand as cowardice Walpole's love of peace. It was asserted that the prisoners taken from English merchant vessels had not been merely plundered of their property but tortured in their persons, immured in dungeons, or compelled to work in Spanish dockyards, with scanty and loathsome food, their legs cramped with irons, and their bodies overrun with vermin.

It was now the year 1738, and someone remembered old Jenkins and his ear. He was soon traced, and it was found that his ear had been carefully preserved in a bottle during the last seven years. The story was revived in the House of Commons, and it seems that Jenkins, with his bottled ear, was summoned to the bar of the House and there examined. Modern research has thrown great doubt upon Jenkins's tale, and it has indeed been insinuated that he lost his ear, not on the *Rebecca*, but in the pillory. But his story, as always happens in moments of great excitement, was admitted without proof. A spirited answer which he made enhanced the popular effect, and gave just what the Press wanted

—a slogan. Asked by a member of the House what were his feelings when he found himself in the hands of the Spanish : " I recommended," answered Jenkins solemnly, " my soul to God, and my cause to my country." The words flew rapidly from mouth to mouth. Fuel was added to the general flame. An impulse, almost incredibly strong, was imparted both to Parliament and public. " We have no need of allies to enable us to command justice," cried Pulteney ; " the story of Jenkins will raise volunteers." England rushed headlong into war with Spain, and it seemed as if her goal in the New World might be South and not North America, and that Spain, and not France, might be her principal opponent. " The Jenkins's ear question," wrote Carlyle, a century later, in one of his passages of vivid irony, " which then looked so mad to everybody, how sane it has now grown ! In abstruse ludicrous form there lay immense questions involved in it which were curious enough, certain enough, though invisible to everybody. Half the world lay hidden in embryo under it. Colonial Empire ! Whose was it to be ? Shall half the world be England's for industrial purposes, which is innocent, laudable, conformable to the multiplication-table at least, and other plain laws ? Or shall it be Spain's for arrogant, torpid, sham devotional purposes, contradictory to every law ? The incalculable Yankee nation itself, biggest phenomenon (once thought beautifulest) of these ages, this, too, little as careless readers on either side of the sea now know it, lay involved. Shall there be a Yankee nation, or shall there not be? Shall the New World be of Spanish type? Shall it be of English? Issues which we may call immense."

In October, 1739, a Declaration of War against Spain was issued in London. As the South American colonies of Spain had given the first impulse to the war, so it was against them that England's chief exertions were directed. Two squadrons were accordingly equipped—one, under Anson, to sail around Cape Horn and rifle the shores of Peru; the other, under Vernon, to attack Porto Bello and the eastern coast. The capture of Porto Bello decided the English ministry to send Admiral Vernon a large reinforcement both of ships and soldiers. A further addition was at once seen to be necessary before these reinforcements sailed, owing to the hostile attitude of France. It was proposed to seize and destroy Cartagena, in the Gulf of Darien, a city in what is now the State of Colombia, on the north coast of South America. It was even hoped that the possession of this fine harbour might lead to extensive conquests in the continent. As the army had been reduced at the conclusion of Queen Anne's wars, it was now necessary to expand it again, and, as in 1914, the retired and half-pay officers, still fit to serve, were called upon. At this time the Wolfes were residing at Greenwich, having migrated from Westerham, and James Wolfe was, with his brother, attending a school at the former place kept by the Rev. Samuel

EARLY CAREER OF WOLFE

F. Swinden. Employment came at last for Colonel Edward Wolfe, who was appointed an adjutant-general, and was directed to proceed in that capacity to the camp which had been formed in the Isle of Wight. This was in July, 1740, when James Wolfe was but thirteen and a half years of age. Child though he was, a longing to be a soldier even then possessed him, and he seems to have been eager to take part in the expedition. Young Wolfe proceeded with his father to Newport, in the Isle of Wight, in that July of 1740, from which place, on August 6th, he wrote to his mother stating that he and his father were just about to embark, but that the actual departure would probably not take place for a fortnight. The letter was that of a dutiful and affectionate lad to an anxious and affectionate mother, but there is not a line in it to suggest that the young volunteer had begun to "take notice." There is not a word about the camp, or the troops, or the sailors, or the ships, or the object or the destination of the expedition of which he was a part.

The omissions are, however, of no account, for, as it turned out, Wolfe—luckily for himself—was not destined to leave England on this occasion. The expedition did not sail until November, and during the weeks of waiting Wolfe's health suffered so severely from life on board a transport that his father had no option but to send the lad home and back to school. Colonel Wolfe himself sailed in due course, and when the fleet joined Vernon, at

Jamaica, it formed by far the most powerful armament ever yet seen in those seas. The force comprised 115 ships, more than 30 being of the line, with 15,000 sailors and 12,000 land forces on board. The result was, however, a disastrous failure. There was gross mismanagement, continual bickering and jealousy, and a violent epidemic in which Lord Cathcart, the commander of the troops, himself perished. Wolfe's father survived and returned in due course to his family, with the marks of the expedition on his constitution. Years later he warned his son to avoid combined naval and military expeditions—that son whom Corbett was to call " the greatest master of amphibious warfare the world has ever seen since Drake took the art from its swaddling clothes."

While young Wolfe, back at school, was grappling with his history lessons, he little realized that a sovereign in Europe had started to make history by which the whole world would be affected, and in which the whole career of Wolfe himself was to be involved. The sovereign was Frederick II, King of Prussia, who, within a few years, was to undergo a transformation from the worst poet to the greatest soldier in Europe. His rapacity, his latent ambition, and his totally unsuspected military genius, were to spread war throughout the world. As Macaulay has said, on the head of Frederick is all the blood which was shed in a war which raged during many years, and in every quarter of the globe, the blood of the column of Fontenoy, the blood of the mountaineers who were slaughtered at Culloden. The evils produced by his wickedness were felt in lands where the name of Prussia was unknown; and, in order that he might rob a neighbour whom he had promised to defend, black men fought on the coast of Coromandel, and red men scalped each other by the Great Lakes of North America. Wolfe missed being present at Fontenoy, but he served with distinction in the campaign of which that battle was an episode. He fought at Culloden, and in that portion of the globe which appears in the vivid phrase " The Great Lakes of North America " he found death and glory. Practically speaking, therefore, the whole of his military career can be said to be included within the terms of Macaulay's indictment of Frederick the Great.

There is no more confused or dreary war than that of the Austrian Succession. But as with it, and with the greater war which soon followed, the whole future of North America came to be involved, some brief account of its origin is unavoidable. In the year 1740 there died the Emperor Charles VI, whose sway can be considered under two separate headings. On the one hand he was the Emperor, that is to say, the elective head, of that ramshackle and crazy structure which, in spite of its grandiloquent title, was neither Holy nor Roman, nor an Empire. In this imperial capacity Charles VI has little to do with the subject-matter of this volume. But, apart from his position as Emperor, Charles had crowns and possessions personal to himself.

He was the head of the Hapsburg dynasty, Archduke of Austria, King of Hungary, King of Bohemia, and his other possessions included Transylvania, Silesia, Bosnia, Milan, Mantua, and the Austrian Netherlands. Having no son, Charles had drawn up a document, called the Pragmatic Sanction, which declared that the various States which constituted his dominions as Archduke of Austria should never be broken up, but should pass on his death to his elder daughter, the Archduchess Maria Theresa. This law had been ratified by the estates of all the kingdoms and principalities which made up the great Austrian monarchy. England, France, Spain, Russia, Poland, Prussia, Sweden, Denmark, and the Empire itself, had bound themselves to maintain the Pragmatic Sanction. From no quarter did the young Archduchess receive stronger assurances of friendship than from Frederick II, King of Prussia. Yet, in order to extend his dominions, in order still more " that he might get himself talked about," as he later confessed, the King of Prussia, reviving an old claim to part of Silesia, hastily assembled an army and invaded the dominions of Maria Theresa.

France, the traditional enemy of Austria, took the same side as Prussia. Feelings of chivalry impelled England to assist Maria Theresa. Moreover, the Electors of Hanover were traditional allies of the House of Hapsburg, and George II was, therefore, her keen supporter. The pacific Walpole, in England, tried to act as an intermediary between

Maria Theresa and Frederick, while, in France, Cardinal Fleury hoped to restrain his country from espousing the cause of the Elector of Bavaria, who was a claimant to some of the possessions of Maria Theresa. But all to no purpose. In England a storm of popular indignation swept Walpole away. His successor succeeded in negotiating a peace between Frederick and Maria Theresa by which Prussia withdrew from the struggle, and then in combining nearly all the German Powers, save Prussia, against France. In England the Commons voted Maria Theresa a subsidy, and more than five millions were granted to prosecute the war, while an army of English and Hanoverians was assembled to evict the French from Germany.

Here began Wolfe's career of active service. Already he was a soldier, for soon after he had returned to school at Greenwich he had written to his father, begging to be allowed to choose a military career and asking him to exert what influence he could to secure a commission for his son. The squire of Squerryes also bestirred himself, and young Wolfe made frequent visits to Westerham about this time. Here, towards the end of the year 1741, while James Wolfe and the Warde boys were amusing themselves in the garden of the house, an official letter was brought to Wolfe. On being opened it was found to contain a commission as second lieutenant in his father's regiment of Marines. The incident was not forgotten, for the inheritor of the estate, who was present at the time, later erected a monument to perpetuate the memory of the event on the spot where it had occurred. The memorial, which still stands, surrounded by lofty trees, in Squerryes Park, consists of a pedestal surmounted by an ornamental urn. On one side of the pedestal is a record of the birth of Wolfe " in this parish," with the date. The base is covered with inscriptions, amongst which are the following lines :—

> Here first was Wolfe with martial ardour fired,
> Here first with glory's brightest flame inspired.
> This spot so sacred will for ever claim
> A proud alliance with its hero's name.

There is no evidence to prove that Wolfe ever served with the Marines, nor is it probable, seeing that his father's regiment had not yet returned to England. Sea service would not have suited Wolfe, for, although he was to make his name as a master of amphibious warfare, he was peculiarly subject to sea-sickness, a failing to which another great soldier, Moltke, was always liable. Whether it was Wolfe's dislike of the sea, or, more probably, the fact that he realized the possibilities of active service were greater on the Continent, at any rate steps were taken to have him transferred to the line. The application was successful, and on March 27th, 1742, Wolfe was appointed Ensign in Duroure's Regiment, then known also as the 12th Foot, and the Suffolk Regiment of to-day. His chance of active service now came. Of the army which existed at that date, 16,000 had been set apart as

EARLY CAREER OF WOLFE 83

an expeditionary force, and of these such corps as were ready for embarkation in the spring were collected at Blackheath. Here, on April 27th, 1742, the force was reviewed by King George II, accompanied by his sons, the Prince of Wales and the Duke of Cumberland. On parade were three troops of the Horse Guards, the Blues, five regiments of dragoons, and thirteen of foot. Included in the latter was Duroure's, and present with it on parade was Ensign Wolfe. The command of the force was entrusted to the veteran Earl of Stair, and the embarkation was carried out without delay. Here, in anticipation, it may be said that, owing to the slowness of the Dutch, no active operations took place until the following year, and till then the British forces remained in Flanders, " idle, unemployed, and quarrelling with the inhabitants." From Ostend Wolfe marched with his regiment to Bruges, and thence to Ghent, where the British troops seem to have received a cold welcome. The inhabitants, a mixture of French and Dutch, were Austrian subjects, and by no means the most loyal of Maria Theresa's peoples. " They hate the English, and *we* hate them," wrote an English officer in one of his letters home, " and the Queen of Hungary holds them like a wolf by the ears." Collisions between the citizens and the garrison were of frequent occurrence, often over absurd trifles. There was an occasion when a butcher accused an English soldier of stealing a piece of meat. The butcher attacked the soldier, one of whose comrades ran the butcher through the body. A free fight ensued, in which several soldiers were killed, and, some dragoons coming up, the mob was dispelled, but not without several casualties on its side. However, the magistrates assembled and ordered an edict to be published to the effect that whoever should offer the least affront to the subjects of King George " should be whipped, burned in the back, and turned out of the town."

Several letters from Wolfe to his mother during this period of enforced inactivity are extant. It is certain that he must have been making satisfactory progress in his profession, for his appointment shortly afterwards as acting-adjutant is clear testimony to a superiority of Wolfe over those of his own rank. At the same time it would be mere affectation to pretend that the letters show any sign of military precocity. He makes but the scantiest allusions to the military situation, and breaks off from a mere conjecture into a deprecation of the value of his opinion : " Some people imagine that we shall return to England in the spring, but I think that's not much to be relied on. However, I'm no judge of these things." Although biographers of Wolfe are wont to torture themselves by endeavouring to discover latent military genius in his letters of this period, the fact remains that they have no military interest or value whatever. They are simply the bright cheerful messages home of a lad with a ready pen and not without a sense of humour. Here is a typical one, written to his mother from Ghent, under date of September 12th, 1742. He was then only a boy of fifteen and a half, but exactly seventeen years later he was leading an army to one of the great victories of English history :—

"I got yours two days ago by Captain Guy. I'm heartily sorry to hear that the pleasure of hearing from you is now at an end. I fancy the expense is not so great as you imagine ! I'm told by several gentlemen that 'tis no more than sixpence, and that, once a month, wouldn't hurt your pocket. I answered the packet you was so good to send me by Captain Merrydan. I dined with him yesterday, and think he seems to be a very good sort of man. I'm glad you've got a house. Long may you live to enjoy the blessings of a good and warm one !—a thing not easily found in this town, but that we young ones don't mind.

"You desire to know how I live. I assure you, as to eating, rather too well, considering what we may come to. For drink I don't care much ; but there is very good rum and brandy in this place, and cheap, if we have a mind to take a little sneaker now and then just to warm us. The weather begins now to grow coldish ; we have had rain for the last two weeks, and people say 'tis likely to continue till the frost comes in. I have not begun with fire yet, neither do I intend till I know where we shall encamp.

"This place is full of officers, and we can never want company. I go to the play once or twice a week, and talk a little with the ladies, who are very civil, and speak French.

"I'm glad to hear with all my heart that my brother is better. He says he goes to the cold bath and that does him good. Pray my love to him. I hope my father is well, and keeps his health; be so good as to give my duty to him, and to my Aunt Allanson, if she is with you, and, believe me,

"Your dutiful & affectionate son,
"J. Wolfe."

"I see my friend George often; he has just left me, and desires his compliments."

In another of his letters Wolfe " prays his love to cousin Goldsmith." This was Edward Goldsmith, of Limerick, whose mother was a sister of Colonel Edward Wolfe, the father of James. The father of Edward Goldsmith was first cousin to the Reverend Charles Goldsmith, the original of Dr. Primrose in " The Vicar of Wakefield," and the father of the celebrated Oliver Goldsmith, who had been heard to claim relationship with the conqueror of Quebec. With Edward Goldsmith Wolfe was always on terms of affectionate intimacy, and left him a substantial legacy in his will. The George referred to in the letter quoted above was his friend, George Warde, of Westerham, who was now a cornet of dragoons.

Early in February, 1743, the British force was set in motion. James Wolfe had now been joined by his brother, for whom an ensigncy in the same regiment had been procured. The force was moving into Germany, and the march was made under conditions of roads, weather and food severe enough to try the strongest constitution, and of a kind to put a great strain upon delicate youngsters like the Wolfe boys. Already on February 12th Wolfe, in writing to his mother, tells her " this is our fifth day's march. We have had very bad weather all the way. I have found out by experience that my strength is not so great as I imagined." In fact, he decides to hire a horse and to do one day on horseback and one day on foot alternately during the remainder of the march. " I never come into quarters without aching hips and knees " is another extract from the same letter. The march led through Bonn, where the younger brother, Edward, in a letter to his father—who had now returned from the Cartagena Expedition—tells how provisions had run short, and how the snow had been so deep that a few days before he was walking up to his knees in snow. The billets were bad and the inhabitants unfriendly, but, on the whole, the conditions do not seem to have been unduly severe for a winter campaign, although it is clear that they took the two young soldiers rather by surprise.

The political and military situation in Europe was at this time one of extreme complexity, but, to follow the fortunes of James Wolfe, only the merest outline of the main incidents is here required. The purely Silesian war between Frederick of Prussia and Maria Theresa had come to an end ; but the War of the Austrian Succession still went on, and in it England, France, Austria, Spain, Bavaria, Sardinia, Hanover and Holland were engaged. Confusion is added to the inherent complexity of the whole matter by the fact that although

England and France were about to fight a great battle, they were not at war. Both France and England were acting merely as auxiliaries. There was still a British resident in Paris, and a French one in London. As for the purely military situation, in December, 1742, the French had been forced to abandon Prague ; and when the New Year came the French and Bavarian armies were not working in harmony. The Bavarians were defeated, and the French army, separated from them, retreated in confusion from Bavaria, harassed by the Austrian cavalry until, receiving reinforcements, it was able to make a stand upon the Neckar.

Meanwhile the British troops, under the Earl of Stair, were continuing their march from Flanders into Germany with the object of joining hands with the Austrian forces. On the way they were reinforced by some Austrian regiments, under the Duke of Ahrenberg, and by 16,000 Hanoverians, in British pay, who had wintered in the bishopric of Liège. But so tardy was the march that it was the middle of May before the Allies crossed the Rhine and fixed their station at Hochst, some twenty-five miles south-south-east of Frankfort. Here Lord Stair determined to await the arrival of 6,000 Hanoverians, in Electoral pay, and also the same number of Hessian mercenaries, who had been garrisoning the Flemish fortresses, but had now been relieved by Dutch troops. Even without any fresh accessions Stair could muster nearly 40,000 soldiers. This number was, however, inferior to the strength of a French army which, moving generally eastwards from the Rhine—about thirty miles to the west—was likewise heading for Hochst. This army, 60,000 strong under Noailles, was now but a few miles from Stair's right flank, and obviously made his original project of pushing on to join hands with the main Austrian forces out of the question until the threat was dealt with. Stair wished to force a battle, but Ahrenberg, his Austrian colleague, was unwilling, and, what was worse still, Noailles, although much the stronger, would not fight, rightly preferring to cut off the Allies from their magazines at Hanau, while at the same time preventing them from moving up the River Main, where fresh supplies might be maintained. In these circumstances Stair fell back over the river to Aschaffenburg on June 16th. Three days later King George arrived from Hanover with the Duke of Cumberland and found affairs in a critical state. The soldiers were on half-rations, the horses were in poor condition from want of forage, Stair and Ahrenberg were at loggerheads, the reinforcement of Hessians and Hanoverians had not arrived, and the army was in a very unpleasant situation, being cooped up in a narrow valley with the river on one side and the mountains on the other. After much deliberation it was decided to fall back on the magazines and reinforcements at Hanau—a forced move, as a matter of fact, for forage had run so low that the proposal had already been made to destroy all the horses.

Before daybreak on June 27th the Allies struck their tents and fell back in two columns, the river now being on their immediate left and the Spessart Mountains on their right. From the far side of the river Noailles made excellent use of his opportunities. He threw some bridges over the Main ahead of the Allies, and sent his nephew, the Duke of Grammont, with 23,000 men, to Dettingen, through which village the Allies must pass. This French detachment occupied an almost impregnable position behind a swamp and a ravine formed by a watercourse. Noailles himself, with his main body, remained on the left bank of the river, along which he posted batteries to take the Allies in flank during their retreat. Further, no sooner had the Allies evacuated Aschaffenburg than Noailles threw some French troops across the river to hustle them from behind. What between the stopper at Dettingen which they would find in front, the prodding from behind at Aschaffenburg, the cannonade against their exposed left flank, and the wooded and rocky mountains on their right, the Allies would soon find themselves in a most uncomfortable position. Noailles gleefully exclaimed that he had them in a perfect *souricière*, or mouse-trap. It was exactly the same expression that Moltke used on the eve of Sedan. But 1743 was not 1870, and the Allies had what MacMahon's troops had not : " the requisite unconscious substratum of taciturn inexpugnability, with depths of potential rage almost unquenchable."

When the Allies started on that dewy morning of Thursday, June 27th, 1743, with guns playing on their left flank, it was not known that Dettingen was in the enemy's hands. The rearguard seemed the post of danger, and the gallant, choleric little English king took command of it, wearing the same powder-stained red coat in which he had led a cavalry charge at Oudenarde thirty-five years before. About eight o'clock the advanced guard found Dettingen held in strength. When the news was brought in, King George at once left the rearguard and galloped to the front to take command. The situation was indeed alarming, but the King determined to make an immediate attempt to cut through Grammont's force. The French batteries in front having opened fire, the balls fell thick about the King. He was implored to " go out of danger." " Don't talk to me of danger," he retorted. " I'll be even with them." The Allied army was drawn up in five lines—two of foot and three of horse. Somewhere in the middle of the front line was the 12th Foot, and with the regiment were the two Wolfe brothers, James Wolfe acting as adjutant. Noailles was at the moment with his nephew, joyfully gazing at the hurried efforts of the Allies to deploy in the cramped position in which they found themselves. Satisfied with the efficacy, so far, of the mouse-trap, he then recrossed the river to give some further directions in that quarter. This was to prove the undoing of the French, for Grammont could not brook the long delay, nor see without a maddening sense of exasperation the methodical and " thrice intricate deploying, planting of field-pieces, counter-batteries; ranking, re-ranking, shuffling hither and then thither of horse and foot " on the part of the Allies. Burning to engage his adversaries, and believing that the force before him was only a detachment which he might easily exterminate, Grammont committed the fatal mistake of ordering his troops to advance. By thus quitting his ground he forfeited an immense tactical advantage and gave battle on merely equal terms. Further, by his action, the French guns on the other side of the river, which had been doing great execution in the ranks of the English—who were on the Allied left, and thus nearest the Main—were masked.

The battle consisted of three phases. The first two consisted of attacks by the French cavalry; in the third and last phase the infantry of both sides advanced to the attack. It was about one o'clock when the fight began, the Grey Musketeers of the French attacking the front line of the Allies, consisting of nine regiments of English foot, four or five of Austrians, and some Hanoverians. Part of the front line was broken, but the breach was merely local, and the French horsemen, in whose ranks rode members of the *élite* of France, were almost annihilated. Alarmed by the onrush, the King's horse bolted with its rider. George, however, succeeded in stopping it and, dismounting, remarked that he preferred to fight on foot, for he was sure, at any rate, that his legs would not run away with him. The second phase was cavalry *versus* cavalry, in which neither side effected much. This action was of short duration, and the opposing horsemen fell back to their respective armies. Then began the third and last attack made by the foot on both sides. Placing himself at the head of the British and Hanoverian infantry, King George, flourishing his sword, called out in English : " Now, boys,

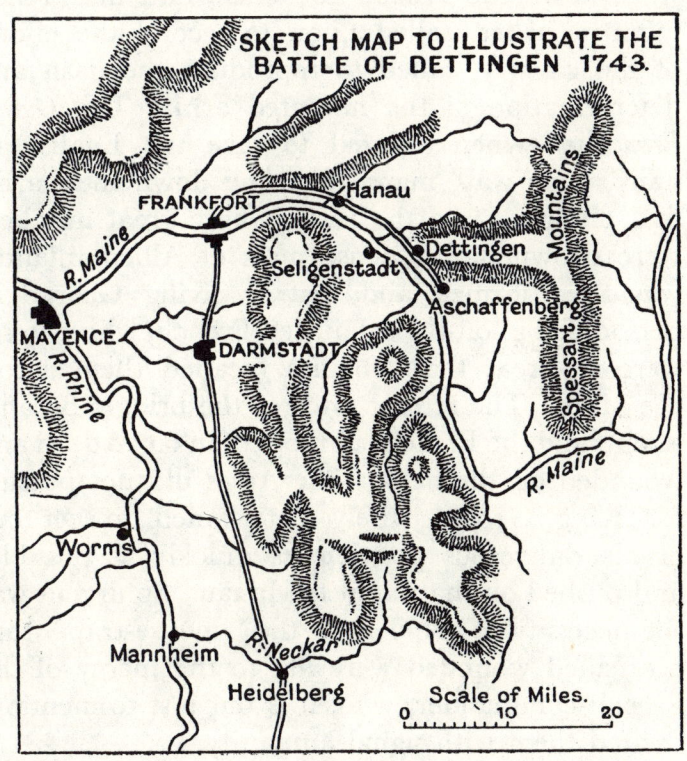

now for the honour of England; fire and behave bravely, and the French will soon run." Like his father, the Duke of Cumberland was in front, and, like his father, behaved with coolness and courage. But, notwithstanding the bravery of the royal leaders, their troops had been thrown into a temporary disorder by the impetuous charges by the flower of the French cavalry. The stubborn resistance of the Allied infantry had, however, worn down the French horsemen, and the French infantry, when called upon to second the efforts of the cavalry, failed to reproduce the dash and determination of the mounted arm. The *Gardes Françaises*, when ordered to take the English in flank, gave way, many throwing down their arms and plunging into the river, where great numbers were drowned. A dense mass of Allied infantry was then formed and, led by King George in person, fell upon the exhausted French, whose losses were so great that Noailles recalled them across the Main. The retreat towards the bridges became a rout, and the French left more than 6,000 dead and wounded on the field. The Allies did not pursue, for King George wisely determined to get out of his dangerous position as quickly as possible, and pushed on that night to Hanau. So urgent was the necessity to get clear of the "mouse-trap" that the Allied wounded were left to the mercy of the French commander, who, it is but just to mention, treated them with signal humanity.

Such was Wolfe's baptism of fire. Fortune had

indeed smiled on him. "Every man," as Lord Kitchener used to say, "gets his opportunity"; but few soldiers have had the opportunity of serving as regimental adjutant in a great battle at the age of sixteen and a half. From the battle he escaped unscathed, although his regiment suffered heavily —more heavily, in fact, than any other English unit, the casualties in it being almost a hundred, of whom twenty-nine were killed. And it was part of Wolfe's good fortune that just as the battle began he found himself close to the Duke of Cumberland, who, attracted doubtless by Wolfe's youthful eagerness, engaged the young adjutant in conversation. But if Fortune favoured Wolfe by bringing opportunity in his way, it is certain that he grasped the chance afforded him. Although his horse was shot under him early in the day, he continued to do his duty on foot with skill and coolness, and it is significant that within five days of the battle King George signed a commission appointing Wolfe adjutant of his regiment, and a few days later he was promoted to the rank of lieutenant. The fact that a mere boy was appointed to the onerous and responsible position of adjutant, on active service, is clear proof of the courage and ability he had displayed at Dettingen, and it is fairly certain that the Duke of Cumberland conveyed to the King the favourable impression he had formed of Wolfe's behaviour at a very critical moment.

The military career of Wolfe for the next three

years continued to be so intimately bound up with the question of the Austrian Succession that the course of that great European problem must be further outlined. Of the Austrian Succession, *pur sang*, the issue was now practically decided by the defeat of the French in Bavaria by the Austrians, and by the Battle of Dettingen. But the question of the territorial dominions of Maria Theresa was now being overshadowed by the question of who was to be the new Emperor. Here the interests of the people of England began to diverge from those of their King. The English people knew little, and cared less, of that purely continental abstraction—The Empire. On the other hand, King George II was also Elector of Hanover, and, as such, he cared a great deal, for he was a Prince of the Empire. As a Hanoverian sovereign—although, as such, traditionally an ally of Austria—he had no very strong wish to see the Imperial dignity permanent in the House of Hapsburg, in which it had lain, with but one short break, for three hundred years. His continental policy aimed really at the exaltation of Hanover; but this—or, at any rate, so Frederick II believed—implied the degradation of Prussia. That country, therefore, fell into the arms of France. Out of this welter grew two opposing leagues. England, Holland, Austria, Saxony and Sardinia were on one side; the most important members on the other were France and Prussia. The European contest began thus to assume a more general and intelligible form, for England and France—still "at peace," be it remembered—appeared each at the head of a great league. And, so far as those two Powers were concerned, the shadowy issue of the Imperial dignity gave place to the more concrete question of sea-power and colonial supremacy. In other words, the Pragmatic Sanction accelerated the issue of the future of America towards the solution of which Wolfe gave his life.

The Battle of Dettingen had prevented the despatch of French reinforcements to the Danube and Bohemia, and the campaign of 1743 closed with the expulsion of the French from Germany. It was now clear that the contest would be carried on in the Austrian Netherlands, for this theatre was obviously convenient to France, and was no less so to the Allies, seeing that the Dutch had at last joined them, and because the British would be brought close to their base at Ostend. In anticipation of this view, and also in order to find convenient winter quarters, the British army returned to Flanders, the 5th Division, in which was the 12th Foot, marching to Brussels and thence to Ostend. Here James Wolfe passed the winter, his brother Edward, whose health had suffered severely during the campaign, having obtained leave to proceed to England. Of the life of the elder brother during that winter of 1743-44 few details are extant, but it may safely be assumed that he devoted himself with assiduity to his duties as adjutant. Fortune smiled upon the Wolfe family in the first half of the year 1744, for in February the father was promoted to the rank of brigadier-general, and on June 3rd James obtained his commission as captain in Barrell's Regiment, the 4th Foot, now The King's Own. Edward Wolfe also returned to the 12th as a lieutenant, his father having aided him in getting the step—a necessary proceeding in those days of purchase.

The inaction, the petty jealousies and the divided councils of the Allies in Flanders at that time are the subject of a masterly survey in Sir John Fortescue's great classic " The History of the British Army." The British Government was slow to act; Wade, the English commander, was far below Marshal Saxe in talent; and there was no Marlborough to adjust the jarring claims of English, Dutch, Germans and Austrians. Shortly after Wolfe had been made a captain both his regiment and that of his brother marched to join the army of British, Hanoverians, Austrians and Dutch which assembled under Wade on the Scheldt. Wade, however, did nothing, whereas the French, under Saxe, after being concentrated at Lille, proceeded to overrun the Netherlands. The Allies remained helpless while Saxe was on the move, and in June he took Ypres. " I am sorry to inform you of so disagreeable piece of news as Ypres being surrendered after a siege of eight days," wrote Edward Wolfe to his father, but he adds later : " Our men keep up their spirits," and declares that " neither the taking of the town nor the numbers of the French does in the least deject them, but makes them only wish for a meeting." This was one of the last letters Edward Wolfe was to write. Always delicate, his health had become seriously undermined by the hardships he had undergone, and by October he was dead. He was not yet seventeen, and his youthful appearance had gained for him in the 12th the affectionate nickname of " The Old Soldier." " He was an honest and good lad," wrote James Wolfe to his mother, " and always discharged his duties with the cheerfulness becoming a good officer. He lived and died as a son of you two should, which, I think, is saying all I can." A pathetic passage occurs in this letter in which Wolfe exhibits a naïve self-reproach at finding that the natural resilience of youth has blunted his sorrow and that " time healeth all things." " There was no part of his life," wrote Wolfe of his brother, " that makes him dearer to me than that where you have often mentioned—*he pined after me*. It often makes me angry that any hour of my life should pass without thinking of him, and when I do think of him, that though all the reasons I have to lament his loss are now as forcible as at the moment of his departure, I don't find my heart swell with the same sorrow as it did at that time. Nature is ever good at blotting out the violence of affliction. For all tempers (as mine is) too much given to mirth, it is often necessary to revive grief in one's memory." This is a remarkable piece of analysis on the part of a youth of seventeen. Wolfe has sometimes been charged with being emotional and theatrical, but these manifestations did not spring from insincerity. He had ever a sensitive soul, and this letter is proof of it; no son, writing to his mother on the death of her youngest born, would descend to affectation.

This year, 1744, had in it one event, at any rate, of military importance. France and England put an end to the comedy of posing merely as " auxiliaries," and a formal if belated declaration of war was made. It was France who forced the issue by a plan which, from the military point of view, had much to recommend it. Her project was, by a maritime strategic counterstroke, to divert the English from Flanders and to compel them to take thought for the defence of their own country. This counterstroke was to be strengthened by the presence of Charles Edward Stuart, whom his partisans called the Prince of Wales. Early in the year an army of 15,000 had been assembled under Saxe at Dunkirk, and fleets were collected at Toulon and Brest for the invasion of England and to support a Jacobite rising. The Brest fleet came out of harbour and approached the English coast. The English fleet was drawn into pursuit, and for the moment the coast of Kent was unguarded. Meanwhile a considerable portion of the French army was on board the transports and had sailed. But, as in the year of the Invincible Armada, a violent storm wrecked the scheme of invasion. The open support given to the Young Pretender and the actual attempt at the invasion of England put an end to the unreality of the existing situation, and, by the end of March, France and England were definitely at war.

But the declaration of war could not galvanize the British commander into activity nor cement the flimsy alliance of British, German, Dutch and Austrian forces. Wade would or could do nothing. The year passed away in inactivity, and the Allies towards the end of it fell back to Ghent once more. Here Wolfe passed another winter, and was still there in April, 1745, when the campaign in Flanders took a new turn. The young Duke of Cumberland —he was not yet twenty-five—succeeded Wade. Whatever the military capacity of the young Prince —he certainly achieved defeat in nearly all his battles—he had many of the qualities of a commander. He was energetic, courageous, devoted to his profession and a strict disciplinarian. On his arrival in Flanders he took prompt steps to check the slackness and indiscipline which had crept over the army. Starting with the officers, he cut down the absurd amount of private transport—the hallmark of a " bad " regiment—often taken into the field. He also checked the abuse of too frequent and irregular leave. Further, he put a stop to the immense amount of marauding. So drastic were his reforms that a young officer wrote home to complain that " the Duke has become most damnably military."

The young Prince soon had an opportunity of

proving his mettle. Early in the spring a French army under Marshal Saxe invested Tournay. The Allies, consisting of the English, Hanoverians, Austrians and Dutch, determined to make an attempt to raise the siege, the force amounting to little more than 50,000 in all. With these troops the Duke advanced to the relief of Tournay, for he had been nominated commander-in-chief of the allied forces, though subject to the control of the Austrian commander, the Count of Königseck. Wolfe's regiment was not included in the force now to take the field, for it was left to form part of the garrison of Ghent. Marshal Saxe, whose forces were much superior in numbers to those of the Duke of Cumberland, was able to leave 15,000 men to continue the siege, while with the remainder he marched southward along the river and occupied a very strong position near Fontenoy to cover his operations. Strong though the position was, the allied generals determined to attack it, and on May 11th, 1745, the Battle of Fontenoy was fought. The attack made by the English and Hanoverians was carried out with surpassing gallantry, but elsewhere in the field the Allies did not show such determination, and the attempt to relieve Tournay therefore failed. But, although tactically the battle resulted in defeat for the assailants, Fontenoy, as an instance of intrepid devotion and superb discipline, has always been a source of just pride to the English soldier. No less a judge than Fortescue declares that as an example of the prowess of British infantry Fontenoy stands almost without parallel in its history. In this glorious defeat the total British loss was over 4,000, and 21 guns were taken by the enemy. After the battle Cumberland retreated to Ath and thence to Lessines. Reinforcements were summoned from Ghent and elsewhere. Amongst the regiments despatched was Barrell's, and thus, ten days after Fontenoy, Wolfe found himself at Lessines, and early next month was appointed by Cumberland brigade-major to Pulteney's brigade. Wolfe was lucky in quitting Ghent when he did, for the place was surprised early in July. The Duke of Cumberland was now in a difficult situation, for without adequate forces he had to keep an active army in the field while at the same time trying to keep adequate garrisons in Brussels, Ghent, Mons and other places. Two British regiments which had been despatched to Ghent after the Battle of Fontenoy were made prisoners.

The war on the Continent was proceeding in a manner unsatisfactory for England; before the summer was over the general situation was alarming. In the previous year the French Government had determined to force England to abandon her enterprise in the Netherlands by financing and supporting a military and political counterstroke in Scotland. This attempt, as has been told, was defeated by conditions of weather. Now, in 1745, a similar distraction was to baffle England, although, curiously enough, this venture, which made England hurriedly withdraw troops from the Continent, was made not only without the connivance but without even the knowledge of the French Government. Prince Charles Edward, failing to get the support of the French ministry, determined to go alone and unsupported to Scotland and throw himself upon the loyalty of his friends there. Scraping together what little money he could, and purchasing a small supply of firearms, the Prince, secretly and in disguise, embarked at Nantes in a privateer. It so happened that a French man-of-war, the *Elizabeth*, of 64 guns, was under orders to cruise on the north coast of Scotland, and the agents of Prince Charles Edward were able to arrange that the purchased arms should be embarked on this vessel and that she should act as a convoy to the ship conveying "Cæsar and his fortunes." The influence of sea-power, which was to be such a marked feature of the campaign which ensued, made itself felt at an early stage. On the fourth day out the *Elizabeth* fell in with the British 58-gun ship *Lion* and a desperate action ensued. After a well-matched fight of five to six hours the vessels parted, each nearly disabled. The *Elizabeth* had to put back, and though the Prince landed safely on the west coast of Inverness, he had lost the greater part of the arms and stores he had so laboriously provided.

In the campaign which was now to follow—a campaign in which it seemed at one time as if the work of the Revolution was to be undone—Wolfe gained his first experience as a staff officer. For this reason, if for no other, it is well to give briefly the course of the struggle. The early stages are not easy to realize, for Prince Charles Edward when he landed had no army, hardly even a bodyguard, few arms and but little money. He had, however, a name, although that gained him at first a cold reception. It is unnecessary here to go into a detailed description of the way in which the clans rallied to him and how the insurrectionary standard was raised in the solitary village of Glenfinnan on August 19th. It is necessary, however, to free ourselves from the illusion that the whole of the Highlands responded *en masse* and rallied to the Stuart cause. The head of the MacLeods and the head of the Macdonalds stood aloof; the Duke of Argyle's Highlanders, the Earl of Sutherland's men, the Monros and several other Protestant clans were sincerely attached to the reigning dynasty. In the Lowlands the people of Scotland were on the whole firmly attached to the Protestant succession, and were probably the most loyal subjects of the House of Hanover in Great Britain. But they had long been unaccustomed to fighting, and the disasters in Flanders, the rapid progress of the French power, and the memories of the vigour of the Highlanders under Montrose and Dundee might well have shaken them in their allegiance and have made them range themselves on the Stuart side. But at this moment the news of a fortunate event in America lightened their despondency, and the issue of the Anglo-French struggle in the New World reacted sharply on the contest in Scotland. The news of the capture of the great French fortress of Louisburg by a New England force, assisted by some English ships of war, made a profound impression in Great Britain and contributed greatly to animate the friends of the Protestant succession in Scotland. This feat of arms will be dealt with later at some length, but it is worthy of mention here as showing how the continent of Europe, Great Britain and North America acted and reacted upon each other in this War of the Austrian Succession, and how the question of hegemony in America was wrapped up in the issue of Hapsburgs, Stuarts and Guelphs.

To return to the Jacobite venture. The situation in Scotland was that the English military commander had altogether some 3,000 troops under his command, mostly in the south. In order to keep the Highlands in check some forts had been erected along the chain of lakes by which Scotland is cleft in sunder by a great valley running from Inverness in the north-east and running in a south-westerly direction to the salt-water lake Loch Eil. Where the valley reaches this loch there was a lonely post named Fort William immediately under Ben Nevis, and close to the spot where the followers of Charles Edward were first assembled. While trying to reinforce this post the royal troops came first into collison with the insurgents. Cope's plan was to march north at once and nip the rebellion in the bud. On the same day as that on which the Young Pretender had hoisted his standard at Glenfinnan, Cope left Edinburgh at the head of some 1,500 infantry. His goal was Fort Augustus, on what is now the Caledonian Canal, as a central post from which he hoped to aim a decisive blow at the rebels.

The pass of Corry Arrack, some ten miles south of Fort Augustus, was, however, in the hands of the rebels. It was a position of immense natural strength. Corry Arrack is a huge precipitous mountain, ascended by part of General Wade's military road which winds up in seventeen zigzags or traverses before it attains the rugged heights. The pass was known to the country people by the name of the Devil's Staircase. Faced by this formidable obstacle, Sir John Cope diverted his march north-eastwards to Inverness, a proceeding for which he was much blamed at the time. It is true that by so doing he uncovered the Lowlands and the capital. On the other hand, it was not improbable that the Prince's army might be lured in pursuit; and there were good military grounds for supposing that Charles Edward would not venture to push south, leaving Cope's substantial force on his left rear. The Pretender, however, took his courage in both hands, and headed for Edinburgh, entering the city on September 17th. The castle remained in the hands of the royalist garrison. Cope's move to Inverness had, however, this sterling advantage to recommend it : that it brought him to the sea, and he was thus enabled to transport his force to whatever portion of the coast-line he desired. He hurried his troops from Inverness to Aberdeen, where he embarked them, with the result that, even before Charles Edward had forced his way into Edinburgh, Cope's army was drawing near to Dunbar. The Prince had immediately to cut himself adrift from Edinburgh in order to deal with the peril caused by the advance of Cope from Dunbar westwards towards the capital. The situation was one illustrating the immense advantage of sea-power, and had the battle which ensued terminated differently, it might have achieved a noteworthy place in the annals of amphibious warfare. Actually, however, Cope was disastrously defeated at Preston Pans. Never was victory more complete : of the royalist infantry under 200 escaped, all the remainder being killed or taken prisoners.

So far, and indeed until later in the campaign, there was a strange apathy in England as to which side should prove victorious. The Government, however, took steps. The King had returned from Hanover at the news of the growing insurrection. Marshal Wade was at Newcastle with such troops as he could collect. The militia of several counties was called out ; and the influence of sea-power was revealed by the ease with which some regular regiments were brought home from Flanders. Amongst the forces collected by Wade at Newcastle were Wolfe's and Barrell's regiments, the former

EARLY CAREER OF WOLFE

being that called after the father of James Wolfe. The father, though now rather infirm, took the field as a divisional commander, the son acting as a brigade-major in another division. This office included what are now known as " Q " duties, for there is extant an order dated November 2nd, 1745, directing Major James Wolfe to be paid £930 for allowance for ninety-three baggage horses to the seven battalions lately come from Flanders.

Contrary to the advice of many of his followers, the Young Pretender had resolved to march into England, and, in order to avoid Wade's force, the route taken was through Cumberland. On November 8th, 1745, the Highlanders crossed the border, gaining possession of Carlisle with little difficulty. Wade made an attempt from Newcastle to strike the left flank of the Young Pretender's force, but, delayed by impassable roads and heavy snowstorms, was forced to return to Newcastle. The Prince passed through Preston and thence to Manchester. Here he skilfully deceived the Duke of Cumberland—who had assembled an army about Lichfield—into the idea that he was marching into Wales, and reached Derby intact. The Young Pretender was now but 130 miles from London, with nothing directly between him and the capital but a camp at Finchley on its northern outskirts. Historians, dazzled by the success of the Prince up to this point, are sometimes inclined to maintain that a continued advance would have laid all England at his feet. It is difficult to see on what military arguments this conclusion is based. From the military point of view the situation of Charles Edward was one of great peril.

His little army of 5,000 had behind it Wade, and Cumberland was racing parallel to it on the west, trying to head it off. These commanders disposed, between them, of a number of troops greatly superior to the strength of the insurgents, and if ever there was a "thruster" it was the Duke of Cumberland. Even if the Prince eluded his pursuers he would be checked outside London by the Guards, with the London train bands, who would be led by the fiery little King George himself—a monarch who would certainly not resign his crown without a struggle. Meanwhile Vernon held the Channel, and his fleet would have obstructed all supplies from France. The only hope for Charles Edward was that the English army and the English people might rally to his side. But the former, exulting in the record of Dettingen and Fontenoy, were loyal to the core to the King and his soldier son. As for the people, they had held conspicuously aloof from the Stuart cause, and, except at Manchester, the Prince had secured but a paltry number of recruits. Sullenly Charles Edward yielded to the arguments of his commanders, and, early in December, began his retreat. The Duke of Cumberland, with his cavalry, set off straightway in pursuit. Joined by a body of horse sent across country by Wade, the Duke pressed close upon the heels of the Highlanders, reaching Carlisle the day after they had left. Greatly to the surprise of the rebel garrison left in the place, Cumberland battered Carlisle with heavy artillery brought from Whitehaven and quickly compelled its surrender. Retiring ever northward, Charles Edward entered Glasgow on December 26th, having marched 580 miles in fifty-six days since leaving Edinburgh. From Glasgow, where his reception had been hostile, the Prince marched to Stirling to besiege the castle and to gain, if possible, by its capture, a constant and easy communication between Highlands and Lowlands. Reinforcements brought his army to a strength of nearly 9,000 men—the largest number which ever mustered under his banner.

The future conqueror of Quebec was now about to receive a further lesson in the art of war. Wolfe was with Wade's force at Newcastle, and Wade, reinforced by the Duke of Cumberland's cavalry, was sent into Scotland. The Duke himself was directed to return to Lichfield and to march his infantry to the south coast to guard it against possible French invasion—an interesting episode as showing that the English command of the sea was not regarded as absolute. Wade was relieved in his command by General Hawley—a ferocious disciplinarian who had gained from his men the nickname of " The Lord Chief Justice." With a force approximately equal to that under Charles Edward, Hawley marched from Edinburgh to raise the siege of Stirling, which still held out. Profoundly despising his enemy, Hawley took up a position at Falkirk without even ordinary military precaution. Here the English were attacked by Charles Edward, who deceived his opponent as to where the decisive blow was to fall. Hawley was forced back to lower ground; his artillery got hopelessly jammed in a morass, but as the Highlanders had also left theirs behind, neither side had, in that respect, any advantage over the other. The battle began with a charge of the royal cavalry on the left, in which two raw dragoon regiments, who had previously fled at Edinburgh and at Preston Pans, " being now well skilled and experienced in that military operation, repeated it on this occasion," as one historian cynically puts it. The Highlanders rushing forward now broke the royalist centre and left; but, at the other flank, the one steady cavalry regiment and the infantry made an orderly retreat. Hawley fell back on Edinburgh, having lost some five hundred of all ranks as well as three colours, and all his artillery, ammunition and baggage.

Such a battle had in it the elements of disaster for the English, especially when the aspect of *moral* is considered. It is a tribute to Wolfe's shrewdness that on arrival at Edinburgh he penned a letter to his uncle skilfully minimizing the regrettable incident in such a way as to check the feelings of alarm and despair which might well have been caused by the exaggerated rumours which always follow defeat. The letter in its composure, its skill, and its mixture of half-truth with absolute mendacity, is a remarkable composition for a lad of nineteen, and is worth quoting in full :—

"To William Sotheron.
"Edinburgh, January 20th, 1746.
"Dear Sir,
"If you have not seen the *Gazette* you will have heard of our late encounter (for 'twas not a battle, as neither side would fight); and possibly it will be told you in a much worse light than it really is. Though we can't have been said to have totally routed the enemy, we yet remained a long time masters of the field of battle, and of our cannon, not one of which would have been lost if the drivers had not left their carriages and run off with the horses. We left Falkirk and part of our camp because the ammunition of the army, on which we can only depend, was all wet and spoiled; but our retreat was in no ways molested by the enemy, as affecting our superiority. The loss of either side is inconsiderable, and we are now making all necessary preparations to try once more to put an end to this rebellion, which the weather has hitherto prevented, and, in my opinion, can at any time be the only objection.
"I am,
"Dear Sir, etc.,
"J. Wolfe."

Indignant at the defeat, and burning to retrieve the shame of it, the Duke of Cumberland secured his appointment as commander in place of Hawley. General Hawley, however, continued to serve as a lieutenant-general, and, at the Duke of Cumberland's request, he took Wolfe as aide-de-camp.

The Pretender did not follow up his success, but, from a false sense of honour, persisted in the siege of Stirling, thus allowing time for the reconstitution of the broken English army. At last, however, Charles Edward yielded to the entreaties of his advisers and retired northwards to Inverness, followed closely by Cumberland in pursuit. Again the remorseless effect of sea-power told heavily against the insurgents. The English ships prevented the arrival of any supplies from France, and soon the Highlanders were in sore straits for money and munitions. Cumberland, on the other hand, marched first to Aberdeen, having picked up 6,000 Hessians that had landed at Leith—sea-power again. Based on the sea and well supplied, he marched along the coast towards Inverness from Aberdeen, the ships keeping him company in the offing. On April 16th Charles Edward with his wearied but undaunted Highlanders stood at bay on Culloden Moor. The result of the battle is well known. The opening cannonade was wholly in favour of the English; and although the gallant Highlanders broke through the first line, the firm formation and the scathing fire of the second threw them into hopeless confusion. The Pretender fled; the insurrection was over; vengeance began. The Duke of Cumberland was hailed as the saviour of England and earned, with less justice perhaps, the nickname of "Butcher" for his work in stamping out the embers of the rebellion.

Of the part played by Wolfe in this decisive campaign few details are extant. That he carried out his staff duties with courage and skill, and to the complete satisfaction of the Duke of Cumberland, may be taken for granted in view of the fact that he was, a year later, recommended by the commander-in-chief to fill a vacant lieutenant-colonelcy. An anecdote is narrated, on the authority of Sir Henry Stuart Allanton, that riding over the field of Culloden after the battle, the Duke of Cumberland observed a wounded rebel smiling defiance at him. The Duke, turning to Wolfe, who was with him, exclaimed: " Wolfe, shoot me that Highland scoundrel who dares look on us with such contempt and insolence." To which Wolfe replied that while his commission was at his Royal Highness's disposal, he could never consent to become an executioner. A few letters written by Wolfe during the campaign are in existence, but they are detached and objective, and afford us little glimpse of Wolfe himself in the field. On the day after Culloden he wrote to a military friend at York a useful account of the engagement; but there is no need to reproduce it here, for it adds nothing to our knowledge of the battle, and, like all accounts of battles written by participants, is not impeccably accurate. It is curious, however, that Wolfe, the master-to-be of amphibious warfare, should have made no reference in any of these letters to what was the decisive factor in the whole campaign—sea-power. It was sea-power which closed the seas to French assistance for the Pretender and enabled the English to transfer troops from the Continent with ease. It was seapower which interrupted the Prince at Holyrood and forced him hurriedly to march out to engage Cope while leaving the untaken castles of Edinburgh and Stirling in his rear. And it was sea-power which kept Cumberland's soldiers well fed and well supplied while the Pretender's men were beginning to lose the cohesion of an army through lack of essential supplies.

After the Battle of Culloden the royalist army remained in the vicinity of Fort Augustus, Wolfe himself being still at Inverness engaged in minor staff duties connected with the pacification of the country. On July 18th the Duke of Cumberland left the army in Scotland and proceeded to London. Soon after the Duke's departure the forces in Scotland were dispersed, several regiments being ordered to Flanders, while others were quartered in Stirling and other garrisons. Major Wolfe remained behind and was for a time employed apparently in reconstructing the small fort at Inversnaid, on the eastern shore of Loch Lomond. Before the winter set in he left Scotland and spent some time with his parents at their house in Old Burlington Street, London, sailing early in January, 1747, with his regiment for Holland, where fighting was resumed. The rebellion in Scotland, and the consequent recall of British troops from Flanders, had left that country at the mercy of the French. In February, 1746, Saxe had taken Brussels. The large garrison became prisoners of war, and to Brussels succeeded Antwerp, Mons, Charleroi and Namur. England, however, was not disposed to abandon the cause of Maria Theresa, and King George II, enraged with Louis XV for the support given to the Young Pretender, had resolved on vengeance so soon as the rebellion in Scotland should be suppressed. Early in 1747 an allied army assembled near Maestricht, in all amounting to over 120,000 men, under the Duke of Cumberland as generalissimo, and made up of English, Hanoverians and Hessians (representing the British contingent), Bavarians, Austrians and Dutch. The force remained inactive for several weeks owing to the breakdown of the supply arrangements of the Austrians and Dutch. The French, on the other hand, were well supplied and carefully sheltered. The weather was adverse to the early opening of a campaign, and the feebleness of the Dutch enabled the French to close the southern mouth of the Scheldt below Antwerp to the Duke of Cumberland. The latter determined to bring Saxe to a general action. His last letter before beginning operations had a special interest, for it contained a recommendation that Major James Wolfe might be permitted to purchase a vacant lieutenant-colonelcy in the 8th Foot, that officer having served constantly and well during the past two years as a major of brigade, and proved himself capable and desirous to do his duty.

The manœuvres and counter-manœuvres of

Cumberland and Saxe respectively brought about the Battle of Lauffeld on June 21st (July 2nd), 1747, some three miles south-west of Maestricht. The French attacked the Allies, who held a naturally strong position, but the allied right had been so strengthened that while it could not be attacked, neither could it issue itself to the attack. Saxe's first attack was brilliantly repulsed; a second met no better success; a third, in which six Irish battalions were employed, promised good results. A counter-attack ordered by Cumberland was restoring the situation, when a panic among some Dutch squadrons brought a further change. To cut a long and confused story short, the Allies were forced to retire, the retreat of the British infantry being covered by a superb charge of British heavy cavalry. The Allies had lost some 6,000 and the French probably not less than 10,000 men. As a consolation the British had taken nine French colours and five French standards. In this battle Wolfe was wounded. He has left us no record of the engagement, and we have not even the glimpse afforded us by his letters dealing with Dettingen, Falkirk and Culloden. In a letter written long afterwards we have, however, this incident about his faithful servant Roland:—

"He came to me at the hazard of his life in the last action with offers of his service; took off my cloak and brought a fresh horse; and would have continued close by me had I not ordered him to retire. I believe he was slightly wounded just at that time, and the horse he held was shot likewise."

After a few days in a field hospital Wolfe proceeded to England and celebrated his coming of age at the house in Old Burlington Street. His career was a promising one for a young soldier. He had been adjutant of his regiment, and had served several years on the staff, earning high praise from the commander-in-chief; he was a major and had been recommended for a lieutenant-colonelcy. His experience in the field was wide, embracing four battles, of which two were crowning victories. A long spell of peace soldiering lay now before him, and we may take advantage of the interval to review the conditions in the country where his great victory was to be won.

CHAPTER THREE

THE SITUATION IN NORTH AMERICA AFTER THE TREATY OF UTRECHT. THE FALL OF LOUISBURG IN 1745 AND THE FRENCH EFFORTS TO RECAPTURE IT.

Ingens iteremus æquor. Let us cross the broad Atlantic and get away from the tangled issues of the succession to the Austrian diadem to visit a world where the problem was more clear-cut and precise. Save for participation—to be described in due course—in a futile and forgotten expedition, Wolfe had now done with European warfare. It is with North America that his name is ever linked, and there his great achievement depended not only upon his own capacity as a commander, but upon conditions which, during his youth and early manhood, had been so shaping themselves as to enable him to operate with some marked and definite factors in his favour, while other factors told against him. These conditions will be revealed by a synoptic view of the French and English settlements in America, particularly from the military aspect, which, in turn, is intimately connected with such factors as exploration, population, social conditions and relations with the Indians. And there is a still wider issue—and one with which Wolfe's great triumph is most intimately connected—that of sea-power.

In spite of the characteristically English reduction of fighting power after a victorious campaign, and the neglect of such fighting services as survived—both of which happened after Utrecht, just as they happened after Waterloo—Wolfe had the good fortune to be born in an era when English sea-power was, on the whole, assured. In a former chapter it has been pointed out how a different state of things had reacted upon the New World, and how the retention of Quebec by England was impossible owing to the abysmal state of inefficiency of her naval forces. It was in 1632 that Quebec, from lack of sea-power, was perforce surrendered, but, less than a quarter of a century later, Blake had reasserted England's naval pre-eminence so far as the Dutch were concerned. England and France then became the definite competitors for maritime supremacy in a struggle which did not actually cease until the termination of the Napoleonic Wars. It was a struggle in which the efforts of France were the more spasmodic, those of England the more sustained. Richelieu had found the French navy extinct; he re-created it and had made it an efficient service at a time when English patriots were refusing to pay ship-money. But Richelieu's establishment shrivelled after his death, and although it was raised from its ruin by the pride and policy of Louis XIV, it was neglected by his successor, Louis XV, by whose reign the whole of Wolfe's life was bounded.

Wolfe was born at a time when to Englishmen it

had come to be regarded as part of the nature of things that English troops should be transported across the Channel and Narrow Seas with impunity, and, further, when Englishmen saw nothing remarkable in the seizure of an important strategic point from an enemy by means of a naval and military expedition sent from England. The soldiers of Queen Anne had been conveyed with all their baggage and impedimenta to the war theatre in which lay the battlefields of Blenheim and Ramillies, of Oudenarde and Malplaquet; and, in the year in which Blenheim was fought, Rooke, with his fleet and some regiments acting as marines, had captured Gibraltar — an achievement not eclipsed even by Quebec itself. Throughout Wolfe's lifetime the sea supremacy of England, though often challenged, was never destroyed, and it was in the conditions of such superiority that Wolfe was enabled to play his part. Sea-power is, however, a condition which is not in evidence except in war; it is very seldom absolute, and in the eighteenth century it was liable to reversals which, even if merely temporary, were able to make a profound difference in a campaign. More stable and more easy of recognition was the influence exerted by strategic points and by geographical and social conditions. In these the French were certainly not at a disadvantage as regards the struggle for supremacy which was certain to ensue in North America.

For all practical purposes entry into Canada from

Europe could be only by the River St. Lawrence, and the interposition of Newfoundland reduced the means of entry into the gulf to one or other of the channels north and south respectively of that island. For larger ships the northern channel was not suitable. When the Treaty of Utrecht was signed, it left England in possession not only of Newfoundland but of Nova Scotia as well, and she was thus in the position of being able to hold the portals of the St. Lawrence. But this potential advantage was seriously diminished by the fact that France was allowed to retain Cap Breton Island, and that she had refused to abrogate her right of fortifying it. When Newfoundland was ceded to the English all the French officials and fishermen moved to the harbour on the eastern coast of Cap Breton Island, ever since known as Louisburg. The island itself received the name of Ile Royale, and here, in 1720, the French began the construction of the fortifications which eventually cost over two million sterling, and even then they were never completed in accordance with the original design, on account of the enormous expense, which far exceeded the original estimates. The fortress occupied an area of over a hundred acres, and was planned on the best systems of Vauban, while the fine and almost land-locked harbour was defended by batteries on an island at the entrance and at other important points. The great fortress and naval base at Louisburg would obviously fill a rôle exceeding that of a mere defence to the entrance of the St. Lawrence. It would provide great offensive possibilities against the coast-line of the English colonies. The destruction of New England was never impossible so long as the French held Louisburg and provided that command of the sea could at least be kept an open question. And Louisburg was a grave threat to New York. As far back as 1666, Talon, the *intendant* of Canada, had placed on record his opinion that France should seek on the Hudson a second entrance into Canada, and one by a route which was not blocked by ice for six months in the year. New York would serve admirably for this purpose. Its magnificent ice-free harbour, and the facilities for entering Canada by river, lake and portage routes, clearly showed to French eyes that it was one of the strategic points of North America; and not less so because its capture would cut the English strip of colonies in two and would provide the French with the possibility of attacking the Iroquois from two fronts. Further, Louisburg was the natural centre from which Nova Scotia might be recovered and the French Newfoundland fisheries might be protected. Another advantage lay in the protection which, in case of war, could be afforded to the trade route from Canada to the French West Indies, and the menace which could be exerted upon the trade route from the British Isles to the North American colonies.

From the Atlantic, communication by water exists—by the St. Lawrence and thence by the chain of inland seas known as the Great Lakes—to the very heart of the North American continent. In the eighteenth century the navigation of this route was not continuous, for the rapids between the St. Lawrence and Lake Ontario, and the Falls of Niagara, between that lake and Lake Erie, as well as the rapids between Lake Huron and Lake Superior, were not then circumvented by canals. Nevertheless, even at the period of which we are now treating, this water system had immense strategic importance, and the advantages inherent in it lay with the French. The influence latent, in the eighteenth century, in Lakes Erie and Ontario has been revealed by the occurrence of the war of 1812, when the British were in the position of the eighteenth-century French-Canadians, and the Americans took the place of the English colonists of the time of Wolfe. In that war the operations by land were conducted mainly about the two extremities of Lake Erie, command of which by a naval force was found to be the deciding factor of success. Both Americans and British had flotillas on its waters. Naval engagements took place upon it. Command of this lake enabled one side or the other to move troops and supplies by water or compelled them to resort perforce to land transport by rough tracks in sparsely inhabited country. In 1813 two squadrons, amounting to fifteen vessels in all, met in combat. Victory rested with the superior American force, and henceforth, during the war, Lake Erie remained American. Similar struggles took place for the command of Lake Ontario, where first one side then the other obtained temporary command of its waters. Working backwards from the War of 1812 to the era of Wolfe—but bearing in mind Lord Bryce's statement " History never repeats itself"—it will be seen that what was actual when the struggle lay between English and Americans was inherent and possible when the contestants were French and English. And it is no less clear that, during the earlier period, the possibility of exploiting this inland sea command lay obviously with the French rather than with the English. To begin with, Lake Erie was entirely French; and the fort at Niagara guaranteed communication with Lake Ontario and thence with Montreal, Quebec and Europe. Similarly, on Lake Ontario, Fort Niagara at the west had its counterpart in Fort Frontenac at the eastern end; and although the English colonists fortified Oswego, on the southern shore, the place was somewhat of a hostage to Fortune, and could not at first effectually interfere with French water transport on the lake.

In fortified positions the balance of advantage was with the French. There was no English fortress— for Halifax was not founded till 1749—whereas in Louisburg and Quebec the French had two strong places, one of them being a naval base. Quebec differed from Louisburg in this—that whereas the latter was designedly constructed as a fortress from definite plans, the former never really emerged beyond the stage of a fortified city; and no less an authority than Saxe wrote strongly against the folly of erecting fortifications round a city and imagining the result to be a fortress. The original choice of Quebec as a fortified settlement had nothing to do with either the question of sea-power or with the problem of defence against, or attack upon, another European race settled in the North American continent. Its selection resulted from the facilities for anchorage supplemented, as they were, by a commanding position on shore which could be defended without difficulty against Indian attacks. Its convenience of position led to its growth into the capital of New France; but the importance it came to assume on that account was to prove a serious handicap to the French—so much, indeed, as seriously to discount the advantages they enjoyed elsewhere. In case of war a double task was likely to be imposed upon the garrison of Quebec. It would have so to command the waterway as to deny passage to hostile vessels, while at the same time to keep the attackers, both on land and water, at such a distance as to ensure the safety of the city itself. To reconcile these two duties would be a difficult, if not an impossible, task, and in endeavouring to carry it out there would infallibly be a tendency to call in a field army to extend the radius of defence and thus to secure immunity for the government offices, the cathedrals, the nunneries, the shops and the private houses, which went to make up the city. To do so would, however, be to forfeit the opportunity of using that field army for its true purpose—that of offensive action, away from Quebec, against the English colonies. The whole question of Quebec is, however, reviewed at greater length in a subsequent chapter, and merely a brief reference to the disadvantages it laboured under is here required.

As for the routes by means of which the invasion of the English part of North America by the French, or conversely the French portion by the English, could be carried out, two main routes connected Canada with the English colonies, both of them great military waterways, the one running north and south, the other east and west, with the old Dutch frontier town of Albany standing at the junction of the two. Of these routes the former consisted of the Richelieu River from the St. Lawrence to Lake Champlain, which merged into Lake George. At the southern end of the latter sheet of water twelve miles of forest upland had to be negotiated, after which the River Hudson was reached, and by it a direct route to New York was assured. So curiously direct is this route that a ruler laid upon the map running due north from New York to some distance below Montreal will indicate it with sufficient accuracy. It will be noticed that the route was almost entirely by water—an important factor in a territory as yet almost entirely roadless, save for a few Indian trails, and although there were on the two rivers numerous rapids and shallows which had to be portaged, both routes were navigable in the backwoods sense. The other route, also almost entirely a water one, was from New York to Lake Ontario. Just north of the town of Albany the Mohawk River enters the Hudson. An advance from Canada could be made up the Oswego River, from the town of that name on Lake Ontario, and then into Lake Oneida. A short portage then led to the headwaters of the Mohawk, by which the Hudson could be gained and touch secured with another force moving south by the River Richelieu –Lake Champlain–Lake George route. It must not be assumed, however, that these two routes were the sole avenues through which Canada and the English portion of North America were vulnerable one to the other. We have seen in the first chapter of this book how French raiding parties worked south from Quebec and Three Rivers into English territory, and how the expedition from the former even reached the coast-line near what is now Portland in Maine. Further, as we shall see later, on more than one occasion an English commander brought an army from the coast to the neighbourhood of the present Pittsburgh—with incredible difficulty, it is true—whence there was available the route to Lake Erie by which the French kept their Fort Duquesne supplied. We can, however, regard the routes described in the previous paragraph, uniting north of Albany, as the two routes promising most chance of success to a French invasion of the English colonies, or to an English invasion of those of the French.

From these routes, and particularly from the

second, Quebec was remote. From the military point of view it would seem that the centre of gravity of New France lay at Frontenac, where Kingston now stands, and that the attempt to balance Canada on Quebec resulted in a condition of unstable equilibrium. Clearly New France was indissolubly bound up with the retention of Louisburg. But should that great water-fortress fall—and it fell twice in thirteen years—and should a naval effort to recover it meet with failure—as actually happened—then, in such circumstances, there was no gain to be obtained by the French in locking up field troops in the proximity of the cathedrals and government offices of Quebec. The base for an instant counterstroke by land, as a retort for the loss of Louisburg, was the waterway from the Richelieu to Niagara, with Albany as the first objective. It is not maintained—and the attempt to do so would be useless—that the French could ever have retained Canada, given that the immense factor of sea-power was to operate for England. But there are good grounds for believing that had an enemy attempt on Louisburg been followed by an immediate military advance, on lines carefully prepared beforehand, and had the present Kingston, not Quebec, been the military focus of the country, France at any rate would have had the opportunity of occupying territory with which to bargain at the peace negotiations, or of protracting operations until the question of sea-power could be put up for contest once again. For it must always be borne in mind that major operations on the St. Lawrence or along the Canadian frontier could not be continuous, but had to be suspended during the North American winter.

It may be urged that any military advantages which the French possessed from conditions of topography and fortified places were offset by the striking disparity in population when compared with that of the English colonies. In 1713, the year of Utrecht, the population of Canada was under 19,000, and thirteen years later it was still under 30,000. In 1739 the population had increased to 42,000, and it is estimated that in 1747 it could not have been short of 52,000 souls. An exact comparison between these figures and those for the English colonies for any given year is not always possible, but it is significant that when the French authorities in 1714 calculated that there were 4,484 males between the ages of fourteen and sixty in Canada capable of bearing arms, it was estimated that the English colonies had 60,000 in that category. We shall probably not greatly err if, during the period between Utrecht and Aix-la-Chapelle, we estimate the numerical native fighting superiority of the English colonies as about fourteen to one. Too much, however, must not be read into these figures. Events were to prove that the final decision depended largely on the number and quality of regular European trained troops placed in the field, and this factor depended not so much upon the relative increase of the inhabitants of the two sectors of North America as upon systematic military reinforcement in time of peace, and in war upon the factor of command of the seas, which was essential for the transport of troops to the theatre of operations.

Besides, it must be remembered that, in a case where the hegemony of a continent was to be fought for, a mere enumeration of heads on either side does not lead us very far. A great deal depends upon the military qualities of the inhabitants of the rival states. In courage, in self-sacrifice and in resolution, the settlers in Canada and the English colonies were equally matched; nevertheless, there did exist circumstances—as there existed in the United States in 1860—which tended to give one side an initial military advantage over the other, quite distinct from any question of mere numbers. This will, perhaps, be understood better by noting the contrast between the English and French colonist as described by Charlevoix in 1720: "There is," he says, "a wealth in New England (a general term by which the northern colonies, including New York, were often described by the French) from which it appears those living there do not know how to draw profit; and in New France a poverty concealed under an air of ease in no way studied. Trade and the cultivation of the plantations gives strength to the former; the industry of the *habitants* sustains the second, while the taste of the nations gives to their relations an inexhaustible charm. The English colonist amasses wealth, and enters into no superfluous expense. The French enjoys what he has, and often makes a show of what he does not possess. The former labours for the benefit of his family ; the latter leaves his heirs in the difficulties which he himself experienced, to extricate themselves from any emergency as may be possible. The English Americans do not desire war, for they have much to lose. They in no way show consideration to the Indians, for they do not believe that they have any requirement for them. For contrary reasons, the Canadian youth detest peace, and live with the aborigines of the country, from whom they easily gain esteem in war and friendship at all times."

It is a curious reflection that a system of government—as existing in the American colonies—which had its very roots in independence should have fostered a population mostly stay-at-home ; while a paternal—one might almost say a grandmotherly —administration—as was that of France—goaded its subjects into ranging far and wide. As has been mentioned before, agriculture was the main concern of the English settlements, the fur trade that of New France, and the wide-ranging propensities of the inhabitants of the latter are thus in part explained. Again, the geographical conditions of the two countries was entirely dissimilar. The English settler looking westward gazed upon the forbidding Alleghanies. The Canadian, looking in the same direction, saw alluring lakes and waterways promising easy routes to undiscovered territory.

These two factors alone would tend to hardihood and enterprise amongst the Canadian youth, but even stronger still, perhaps, was the influence bred from a revolt against the working of Canadian bureaucracy. The power of the Canadian *intendant* —the civil head of affairs—penetrated into every department of life. In everything his interference was obvious. He looked with disfavour at the growth of the use of the sleigh among the young Canadian fashionables, and peremptorily and in the King's name gave orders against the discontinuance of the snow-shoe. He established custom duties; regulated the current value of money; prescribed the gradients for the streets of Montreal; controlled the sale of liquor; regulated the position of militia captains in processions; in ecclesiastical matters decided in what order the consecrated bread was to be given; made rules for points of precedence in church; and drew up regulations by which the mode of leaving the church door after divine service was minutely laid down. These are but samples taken at random from a survey of the wide powers of the *intendant*, but they are sufficient to show the cramping sensation of restraint which must have been experienced by high-spirited young Canadians.

Canada, in short, was administered from Versailles, and, as a result, there was little advancement in the colony for the native Canadian. His field of action was not at headquarters but with the outposts. The political arena was closed to him. The young

Canadian of the higher class looked forward to a life of adventure, to serve as a soldier, or to abandon the artificial existence of the towns for a more stirring career in Acadia or beyond the Lakes. The attractions of the fur trade, stimulated by the revolt against bureaucracy in Quebec and Montreal, engendered a peculiar class of men—to whom reference has already been made—known as *coureurs de bois*—half-civilized vagrants, whose chief vocation was conducting the canoes of the traders along the lakes and rivers of the interior. Many of them, shaking loose every tie of blood and kindred, sank into barbarism. The wandering Frenchman of Canada chose a wife or concubine amongst his Indian friends, and in a few generations scarcely a tribe of the west was free from an infusion of French blood. In nothing (not only in the seventeenth and eighteenth centuries, but even to-day) is the difference between the Latin and the Anglo-Saxon as a colonizing race more vividly in evidence than in this question of the " colour bar." Then, as now, the overseas Englishman was marked by an intense inbred resolve in favour of race purity. There were exceptions, of course, the most notable being the union of Rolfe with an Indian " princess," from which some of the first families of Virginia are proud to trace their descent. But, on the whole, the characteristically English aversion was marked even in the early days of American settlement. With the French the case was widely different. From the beginning they showed a tendency to amalgamate with the forest tribes. The Jesuits looked to marriages between Frenchmen and Indian women as a method for the dissemination of the Faith. "The manners of the savages," wrote the Baron la Houtan, "are perfectly agreeable to my taste." Frontenac himself did not disdain to put on Indian raiment and to take part in the savage ritual of the Indian war dance. At first great hopes were entertained that, by the mingling of French and Indians, the latter might be won over to civilization and the Church. But the effect was precisely the reverse, for, as Charlevoix observed, the savages did not become French, but the French became savages.

The philosopher may muse over what would have been the future of North America had French domination become supreme, and had the destinies of the continent been entrusted to a Gallo-Indian race. Such speculation is, however, outside the scope of this volume, and the subject of the French intercourse with the Indians is alluded to merely with the idea of ascertaining what advantage or otherwise this conferred entirely from the military point of view. Undoubtedly, in this respect, France was in the better position. The slight rewards attainable by the young Canadian in civil life drove him to the wilds. The title *coureur de bois* carried with it some stigma, but when the phrase gave place—as it did about 1727—to the new term *voyageur*, a new class of recruit was secured. The majority of Canadian young men preferred the excitement of the *voyageur's* life and the risks and profits of trade, not so much for the material gain as for the assurance that in time of war their services would be required, and that a reputation for gallantry would bring distinction. The experiences they had necessarily to undergo were admirable training for the post of a partisan leader in *petite guerre*. And the history of Canada shows that—certainly until the days of Montcalm—the expeditions from Quebec and Montreal were of this nature. A select body of men, under a bold and enterprising leader, attacked a settlement or locality, committed havoc or damage according to the power he possessed, and then retired. Such method of warfare was never indeed distinguished by much military combination or skill, and by itself could exercise little permanent effect. But it called forth the qualities of fortitude, courage and endurance. It was ideal training in woodcraft and in stratagem ; in working with the Indian or in beating him at his own game. Used in combination with disciplined and trained regular soldiers, these irregular troops —Indians, with the non-commissioned and officer elements formed by *voyageurs*—would prove of inestimable value, and a force so constituted, and in the proper proportions, would be irresistible unless it were met by an army similarly composed.

The English colonists enjoyed no such advantage, or, at any rate, not to the same extent. But although they were, on the whole, certainly as compared with the Canadians, stay-at-home rather than explorers, this statement is only relatively true. The backwoodsman and the trader came into notice at an early date, and during the period which we are now considering had begun to excite the apprehensions of the French. In 1721 Longueil, the *lieutenant du roi* at Montreal, reported that on the River Chouaguen, some four leagues from Lake Ontario, he was met by one hundred Englishmen with six canoes, who made him produce his pass, showing him, at the same time, the order of the governor of New York that no Frenchman should go by without a passport. Longueil nevertheless continued his journey to the Onondaga village and obtained the consent of that Indian tribe for the erection of the fort at Niagara. There he met more than one hundred canoes engaged in carrying furs to the English to exchange for a return cargo of rum ; among them were several canoes of the Nippissing and Sault Indians from Lake Huron. So enterprising were the English at this period that they had carried their operations to within a league and a half of Fort Frontenac and seriously interfered with the trade of that place and of Niagara. But this was done, not—as was the case with the French in similar circumstances—in harmony and alliance with the Indians, but either in opposition to or, at best, during an armed neutrality with them. The borders of the English colonies displayed no such phenomenon of mingling races as characterized the outposts of New France.

The English fur traders and the white men in

their employ did, it is true, throw off the restraints of civilization, but though they became barbarians they did not become Indians. " Scorn on the one side and hatred on the other still marked the intercourse of the hostile races." With the settlers on the frontier it was much the same—with, however, a very marked exception in the case of Pennsylvania. Rude, fierce and contemptuous, they daily encroached upon the hunting-grounds of the Indians, and then paid for the injury with abuse and insult, curses and threats. The native population shrank before the English as from an advancing pestilence. On the other hand, in the very heart of Canada Indian communities sprang up, cherished by the Government and favoured by the easy-tempered people. Large bands were gathered together, consisting in part of fugitives from the borders of the hated English, and aiding in time of war to swell the forces of the French in repeated forays against the settlements of New York and New England.

It will be seen, therefore, if the factors set forth in the preceding pages are fairly considered, that, in any contest for the hegemony of North America, France had distinct and tangible assets on her side. She possessed two fortresses in Louisburg and Quebec, while, in fortified posts—to which further reference will shortly be made—the balance of advantage again lay with her. The waterway of the St. Lawrence above Montreal, combined with Lake Ontario and possibly Lake Erie, provided her with a formidable base of operations. Her population was—if inferior in numbers—more warlike and more trained in petty warfare than that of her opponent. And her relation with the Indian tribes was one which would favour her at the expense of her rival—although against this must be set the fact of the hostility of the powerful Iroquois. Parkman, in his "Half Century of Conflict," although he overlooks some important military considerations, is eminently correct when he points out that after the Peace of Utrecht, if the English colonies were comparatively strong in numbers, their numbers could not be brought into action ; while if the French forces were small, they were vigorously commanded, and always ready at a word. It was union confronting division, energy confronting apathy, military centralization opposed to industrial democracy, and, for a time, the advantage was all on one side.

In spite of the fact that the French enjoyed a military centralization, not all their work of fortification was based upon the requirements of a campaign to decide the future of North America. Trade assumed more importance than offence or defence ; and not strategy, but fur, dictated the site of several works. The origin of the fort at Niagara lay in the desire to control the trade from the west and to prevent the furs being carried to Albany, which was daily being done with impunity. It was begun in 1725 on the spot where a wooden blockhouse had formerly stood ; built of stone, it was completed in 1726. From similar motives the English had retaliated with a loopholed house of stone at Oswego, on the southern shores of Lake Ontario, hoping that the western Indians, who greatly preferred English goods and English prices, would pass Niagara and bring their furs to the new post. Trade, however, has a way of engendering preparation for war. Three officers and sixty other ranks of regular troops were sent to garrison Oswego, drawn from some unregimented companies maintained in New York at the charge of the Crown. The French on their part had a garrison at Niagara, and—what was of even greater significance—they built two armed vessels at Fort Frontenac to control the waters of Lake Ontario.

How forts and fur were interwoven will be still further clear from the work of La Vérendrye between the years 1731 and 1739. The son of an officer of the Carignan Regiment, La Vérendrye crossed the ocean to take part in the War of the Spanish Succession, and was nearly killed at Malplaquet, where he received seven wounds. Returning to Canada, he found no opening and, like so many of his class, he took once more to the woods. Starting from a small post north of Lake Superior, he set out to discover, if possible, a route to the Western Ocean, and incidentally to develop business relations with such new Indian tribes as might be met. His journeys took him—and after his death the work was carried out by his sons—to the foothills of the Rocky Mountains and to regions where the Indians spoke of men clothed in iron further to the west—Spaniards who were ranging eastwards from California. In spite of immense difficulties La Vérendrye diverted a great and lucrative fur trade from the English at Hudson's Bay and secured possession of it by eight fortified posts between Rainy Lake—west of Lake Superior—and the River Saskatchewan, including three posts on the shores of Lake Winnipeg. These various forts were merely stockade works flanked with blockhouses. The difficulty of building and maintaining them in remote wildernesses was almost incalculable. Most of them, however, were still standing during the Seven Years' War, by which the destiny of Canada was decided, but their rôle in that struggle was negligible, and, reviewing the Anglo-French struggle for North America, it seems that the military training, the resolution and the hardihood of a La Vérendrye might have been utilized with more profit to France in the domain of war rather than of trade; and had he been employed, not in a remote wilderness, but upon the frontier between the two rival nations, certainly some useful work might have been done in the construction of military roads. It was not until 1734 that a vehicle on wheels passed even from Quebec to Montreal.

Upon the great waterway from the St. Lawrence to New York the French exerted a grip at an early stage, and it is here that the centralization and solidarity of New France appear in marked contrast to the jealousies and bickerings of the English colonies. The first step was defensive—the erection of a stone fort at Chambly on the Richelieu River as a protection to Montreal against an English attack by way of Lake Champlain. Command of the waters of that lake was clearly of military importance, and in 1726 the French decided to hold the narrows at the southern end, selecting a site upon the eastern shore. This territory was claimed both by Massachusetts and New Hampshire; the western side was within the bounds claimed by New York. The French, finding the western bank equally suitable, dug themselves in at Crown Point, erecting in time a fort with a massive stone tower mounted with cannon to command the lake, which was there but a musket shot in breadth. Thus was established an advanced post of France, a constant menace to New York and New England and the parent of a still greater menace—the fort of Ticonderoga to the south of it. The erection of the fort at Crown Point was denounced as an outrageous violation of British territory, a remonstrance which the French authorities received with perfect equanimity in view of the lack of unity, indeed the actual dissension, between the English colonies.

In the west, too, France was active and alert. There her aim was to control all the waterways between the Great Lakes and the Gulf of Mexico. Niagara held the passage from Lake Ontario to

Lake Erie; similarly Detroit provided the link between the latter and Lake Huron. Michilimackinac guarded the area where Lake Huron is joined by Lakes Michigan and Superior. On the western shore of Lake Michigan a fort at Green Bay barred the way to the Mississippi by the old route of the Fox River and the Wisconsin. Other routes from the Lakes to headwaters of the Mississippi were guarded by forts on the Miami, on the site of the present Vincennes, and by a fort at St. Joseph. On the Mississippi itself were the forts of St. Louis and Chartres, the latter mounting guns and rebuilt later of stone. But the erection of these posts was far from being compatible with a military policy of conquest of the English colonies. They represented merely the opening phase of a feeble attempt to confine the English between the Alleghanies and the sea. By setting up so flimsy a cordon from the empty and over-officialed Canada to the struggling and bankrupt Louisiana, and by endeavouring to maintain a territory of which the framework was too weak, France surrendered much of the asset of centralized authority which made her positions on the St. Lawrence and Lake Ontario so strong. The political history of North America till 1763 is mainly the story of the pressure of the English colonies on the paper barrier on the Ohio and Mississippi, and the extent of France's responsibilities told against her in war.

Before quitting this subject of the relative military situation which existed in North America at this time, it is of particular interest to read the views of a Canadian viceroy. De la Galissonnière arrived in Canada in 1747, and although his memoir was written after the close of the War of the Austrian Succession and thus, in its bearing on what has been argued in the preceding pages, is somewhat *ex post facto*, yet, seeing that the struggle was reproduced in the Seven Years' War in greater intensity, his views are worthy of reproduction here. Before the memoir was written, and while he was in Canada, it may be remarked that De la Galissonnière considered that an attack on Quebec by sea was probable, and it is significant that he proposed a strategic counterstroke by means of attacks both on Hudson's Bay and Oswego. In the actual memoir, which was written in 1750 after his return to Europe, De la Galissonnière was definitely of opinion that a recrudescence of hostilities in Europe would spread to America and that an attempt would be made to invade Canada. Accordingly, as a first step he urged that Canada should secure the avenues by which such attack might be made. But that he did not contemplate merely a defensive policy is clear from the stress he laid upon the advantage Canada possessed in making war on Anglo-American territory. He instanced the number of French Canadians who lived in the woods with the Indians, qualified to lead them in fight, or themselves to attack the Indians. There were the *coureurs de bois*, or *voyageurs* as they had come to be called, whose activities have been described earlier in this chapter. A feature of De la Galissonnière's strategy was the immediate wresting of Hudson's Bay from the English on the first declaration of hostilities. This is a point of great interest, for, unlike the English, the French could approach Hudson's Bay by land, and the seizure of this great commercial zone would have given France a bargaining asset in peace negotiations. The ex-viceroy saw that Louisburg would be taken a second time unless the French seized Acadia ; which seems tantamount to urging that the English should not be given the opportunity of developing Halifax as a base of naval and military operations, but should be forced to rely upon Boston and New York. In the memoir the writer brings out another important point—and one frequently overlooked by writers of to-day—namely, that, owing to the closing of the St. Lawrence by ice for several months in the year, it was essential that communication by land between Louisburg and Quebec should be secured.

Such communication was, however, impossible so long as the English held Acadia. He therefore laid down in principle that no English fort should be built from Canseau to the isthmus—joining the New Brunswick and Nova Scotia of to-day—and that a neutral strip, seven to ten miles wide, should be provided along which the French should have right of passage. Louisburg was esteemed not only as being a naval base, but as a local protection to the island of Cap Breton, the fisheries of which made it a nursery of seamen. As regards the west, De la Galissonnière considered the development of the Ohio-Illinois sector as imperatively called for; Detroit was of primary importance, for once it contained a farming population of one thousand it would feed and defend the remaining territory. He summarized his views by dwelling on the necessity of permanently settling the country at Crown Point, Niagara, Detroit and the Illinois, recommending that emigrants from France should be despatched, especially soldiers. Some smugglers might be added, and women—even of easy virtue, if necessary—but of these latter only a few, since owing to a superfluity of women in Canada this step might not be required.

Leaving this academic discussion of the possibilities open to, and the advantages enjoyed by, either side, and contenting ourselves with the conclusion that, on the whole, France was the more favoured in both respects, we can pass to the history of what actually occurred after the Treaty of Utrecht. In the first place, France quickly repented of her bargain, and, in spite of the compact, was inclined to maintain that, with but a few local and trivial exceptions, the whole of the North American continent, except Mexico, was hers by right. In spite of the fact that England and France were now officially at peace, there was but a thinly veiled hostility between the two nations in their North American possessions, the contest dividing itself into three parts—the Acadian contest; the contest for northern New England; and the struggle for the West. The object of France was to exploit the Indians against the English, particularly the Abenakis, of what is now Maine, who were described by Charlevoix as the only Indians who were hostile to the English and Iroquois. The French policy was to prevent such enmity from becoming dormant. Two years after Utrecht instructions were sent from France to prevent the Indians accepting any benefits from the English and to retain them in the "true religion." It was the distinctly avowed principle of the Canadian viceroy in 1716 to prevent all intercourse with New England; but this prohibition extended to trade, not to hostilities. Vaudreuil connived at the seizure of English fishing boats and asked that arms and ammunition should be distributed, indirectly suggesting even what posts the Indians should occupy. Many of the latter, however, showed no desire to quarrel with the English. The Abenakis enjoyed greater commercial advantages with the English than they did with the French, and unless the latter would assist in the restoration of territory to the Abenakis they would not move. There was also the complication brought about by the fact that while the French were stimulating the Abenakis to make efforts to recover their territory, the Indians were not slow to point out that the trouble would not have arisen were it not that the French, by the Treaty of Utrecht, had surrendered Abenaki territory which was not theirs to give. The dispute seems to have had its origin in a genuine desire on the part of the Canadian viceroy to add to the power of defence of Canada against invasion from the English colonies, and on several occasions he went so far as to threaten war. But in this he was not supported by the authorities in France, whose conduct, although marked by a good deal of duplicity, was on the whole for peace. The court of France, however willing to profit by intrigue in the encouragement of Indian attack, absolutely refused to listen to the recommendation that the Abenakis should be sustained by force of arms. The question eventually became one of rival missions, and to that of the venerable Jesuit Rasles, on the banks of the Kennebec, the government of Massachusetts replied by an attempt to establish one of the Protestant faith : " Calvin and Loyola met in the woods of Maine." A war with the Indians followed, in which the English colonists were successful and in which Rasles met his death. The French had instigated, but had failed to support the Indians, and these, seeing how matters stood, concluded with the English a peace which was long and faithfully maintained. Commerce took the place of religion. English trading posts supplanted Jesuit missions. The eastern boundary of New England was established.

On the whole the long period of peace which followed the Treaty of Utrecht was undisturbed by serious hostilities in North America, and the French

Government probably considered that by the construction of the fortress of Louisburg, by strengthening the French position along the route which led from the St. Lawrence to New York, the rebuilding of Fort Niagara, and the erection of forts in the west and along the Mississippi, better work had been done than if a series of pinpricks of *la petite guerre* had been indulged in. Even the great issue of the Pragmatic Sanction, which shook Europe in 1740, left North America at first unaffected, and the nominal state of peace existing between England and France was a real one in the New World. By 1744, however, it was clear that a formal declaration of war could not be long delayed, and at this crisis the centralized and military rule in Canada gave her an advantage over the English colonies. The Canadian viceroy foresaw that hostilities could not be avoided, and he at once took proper military precautions. Crown Point was revictualled and reinforced. Niagara was placed in as good a condition as possible, and Frontenac was put in an efficient state of defence. There were at this time in Canada 600 regular troops with—the figure is given by Kingsford, but it seems an exaggeration—15,000 Canadian militia nominally available. Of the Indians who could take the field there were the Christian Iroquois of the Sault and Lake of the Two Mountains—some 400 in all. There were, too, 700 Abenakis to distress the enemy on the frontiers of New England and to join in the operations in Canada if required.

The great fortress of Louisburg, on which the French cause necessarily depended so much, was not in a very satisfactory condition. There were discontent and bad discipline in the garrison, and the workmen on the fortifications had threatened to mutiny from dissatisfaction at the fact that the extra pay which they received was less than they had been promised.

Fortune favoured the French at the outset, for the news of the definite rupture between France and England was sent out by a fast vessel to Louisburg, and was known there some weeks earlier than in Boston or even to the small British garrison in Nova Scotia. The military governor of Louisburg, Duquesnel, conceived that an opportunity existed to strike an unexpected blow for France and to recover a province wrenched from her by the Treaty of Utrecht. The possibilities were encouraging, for Nova Scotia had been consistently neglected by the English Government since its cession by France. The naval base at Halifax had not yet been formed. The garrison of the colony was absurdly small. In 1717 eight independent companies at Annapolis and Placentia (the latter place in Newfoundland) had been formed into a regiment known as Philipps's from the name of its commanding officer, later to be known as the 40th Foot. The population of Nova Scotia—amounting at the time to some 16,000 souls—was almost entirely French. The inhabitants at first did not relish British supremacy, and were constantly intriguing with the Indians. In 1723 a party of the latter had attacked the garrison at Annapolis, burnt two houses, scalped a sergeant and private, and taken several prisoners. The garrison, with a nominal five companies at Annapolis and four at Canseau (opposite Cap Breton Island), suffered extremely from the rigours of the climate and from neglect by the government at home. Annapolis was in such a state of dilapidation that its sandy ramparts were crumbling into the ditches and the garrison cows walked over them at their pleasure. As late as 1740 there were no barracks nor storehouses at Canseau, and, for want of them, some soldiers actually perished. At Annapolis there was no issue of fuel. The men could get nothing to drink but water. Meat was not issued. And when soldiers were invalided out they had to pay for their passages to England.

The little post at Canseau, with its indifferent accommodation, its wooden redoubt built by the local fishermen, and its garrison reduced to eighty-seven, of whom a third were unfit, was, of course, at the mercy of its great neighbour, Louisburg, from which a force of over 600 soldiers and sailors, escorted by two small armed vessels, was sent. The English surrendered on condition of being sent to Boston, and the little fishing station, with its miserable citadel, was burned to the ground. The recovery of the whole of Acadia was now contemplated. A surprise attack was made upon Annapolis, the garrison of which had fallen below 100 men. A proposal from the enemy that the place should surrender was rejected, and a second attempt, in which the French force was assisted by bands of Indians, was beaten off. Two more attempts were made against Annapolis—the garrison of which had been strengthened by some forty men with some officers, and by fifty Indian rangers from Boston—but without success. The commandant, Major Mascarene, a French Protestant, whose family had been driven into exile, refused to listen to any proposals for capitulation, and the British flag continued to fly over the lonely settlement, the attackers eventually returning to Louisburg.

This attempt to recover Acadia was, therefore, a failure, and the French were ill-advised to make the attempt. In the first place the operation was necessarily an amphibious one ; this was a challenge to British sea-power. Some French warships had been expected off Annapolis, but British cruisers bottled them up in Louisburg, and it was to the non-arrival of the French men-of-war that the sudden abandonment of the land operations against Annapolis was due. In the second place Duquesnel's hasty decision to act independently of the viceroy negatived the advantages of centralized military authority, which was the great asset of Canada, and, as a matter of fact, when Duquesnel directed the two men-of-war to sail from Louisburg to Annapolis, the senior naval officer had refused to take orders from a mere fortress commandant. Before the dispute was settled British cruisers were blockading the place. Again the attempt to regain Acadia almost certainly diverted French attention from the project most likely to promise success, namely, a prompt invasion of New York from Lake Ontario and the St. Lawrence. And in the fourth place—although this factor could not have been foreseen—the attempt upon Nova Scotia brought Louisburg into such prominence as to lead to its overthrow.

The existence of Louisburg during the twenty-four years since the fortress had been founded had always been a source of uneasiness to Massachusetts, and, indeed, to the whole of New England it was a standing menace. It was ever a threat to the fisheries, which were almost as vital to New England as was the fur trade to New France. It had become such a haunt of privateers as to gain the name of the Dunkirk of North America. And the recent French expedition to Annapolis, unsuccessful though it had been, had caused some alarm in Boston lest a similar attempt, but on a larger scale, might be made against that city. Louisburg, let it be remembered, was a fortress, erected from designs of a master of fortification, with embrasures for 148 guns and garrisoned by some 600 regulars, besides some 1,400 militia. Yet the governor of Massachusetts, William Shirley, listened readily to the proposal that Massachusetts should take upon herself the tremendous task of reducing the French stronghold. Shirley himself had already thought deeply on the matter, and he had been profoundly impressed by the reports on the state of Louisburg brought by the prisoners who had been taken at Canseau and, after detention at Louisburg, had been sent to Boston on parole. The matter was laid before the legislature of Massachusetts and, after a hesitation very natural in view of the audacity of this scheme, the expedition was resolved on by the majority of a single vote. Shirley now wrote to all the colonies as far south as Pennsylvania to ask for co-operation. New York sent a small supply of artillery, with provisions, powder, clothing and bedding for the troops. Pennsylvania sent provisions. New England alone furnished the men. Of these Connecticut promised 516. New Hampshire agreed to furnish 304. From Rhode Island were to come 300, but, owing to disagreement, they eventually arrived too late for active operations. The bulk of the expedition was to be furnished by Massachusetts, whose contingent amounted to some 3,000 men. That colony, as was natural from the size of her contribution in soldiers, had the right of appointing the commander-in-chief, and Shirley's choice fell upon William Pepperell, a merchant of Kittery, of Devonshire stock, who was now in his forty-ninth year, and a colonel of militia.

In almost everything which was required for the subjugation of a fortress belonging to a great military and naval Power, as France was, the New England force was woefully deficient—in numbers, in military experience, in siege material, in munitions and supplies. The sole point in which the means were adequate was that of transports, for which the shipping at Boston and elsewhere yielded sufficient tonnage. As the expedition was to be an amphibious one, clearly some strong naval protection would be required, and when the resolution had been formed to persevere with the expedition, Shirley despatched a vessel to Commodore Warren at Antigua, begging him to co-operate with such ships as could be spared from the Leeward Islands. Meanwhile, Massachusetts acted with such wonderful vigour in carrying out the preparations for the expedition that in seven weeks the transports were provided, the guns and stores embarked, and the troops assembled, formed into regiments, and held in readiness to sail. As a naval contingent the colonies were able to supply thirteen armed vessels, the largest being a brig converted into a frigate, mounted with twenty-four guns. The chance of success depended, however, very largely on the assistance to be rendered by Warren with his men-of-war; but on the eve of the departure of the expedition there came his reply regretting that without His Majesty's approval he could not co-operate. The blow was a serious one, and Shirely communicated the news to none but Pepperell and the latter's second-in-command. With indomitable resolution he determined to adhere to the scheme. On March 24th, 1745, the expedition, consisting of about ninety transports, escorted by the provincial cruisers, weighed anchor and began its voyage.

On April 5th the fleet arrived safely at Canseau

and took possession of the English settlement, which had, as already related, fallen into the hands of the French. The force remained here three weeks, the time being devoted to drilling and training the militiamen, while the little naval force ranged the sea, which it did to such good purpose as to bring in six French prizes laden with supplies for the fortress. The provincial cruisers even went so far as to chase a French frigate of thirty-six guns, which, however, got away. On land some of the time was utilized in rebuilding the blockhouse, in which eight guns were mounted and a garrison of eighty men was placed. So far all was well with the expedition. But it was now in French waters, and the task of moving it over the fifty miles which separated it from Louisburg was an extremely perilous one. But on the morning of April 22nd a large ship, flying British colours, was seen standing into Canseau. She proved to be the frigate *Eltham*, with the welcome news that Warren himself, with other ships, was on his way. On the next morning the commodore appeared in the *Superbe* of sixty guns, accompanied by the *Launceston* and *Mermaid*, of forty guns apiece. It so happened that immediately after Warren had sent, from the West Indies, his letter of refusal to Massachusetts, he had received orders from home—for Shirley had suggested an attack on Louisburg to the government—authorizing his co-operation, and he had accordingly sailed at once to Boston and thence to Canseau. Warren's squadron was an invaluable reinforcement, and when later he was joined by six more ships of war—three from England and three from Newfoundland—interruption from the sea by the French was unlikely.

Taking the provincial flotilla with him, Warren sailed away to blockade the fortress. The land force followed on April 29th, consisting of 4,070 men, of which 3,170 belonged to Massachusetts. Some hope seems to have existed of taking Louisburg by surprise, and in some very detailed, if naïve, instructions which had been drawn up, it was thought possible to seize the place " while the enemy were asleep." On the morning of the 30th the transports arrived in Gabarus Bay, a mile or so to the west of the fortress. The task which lay before Warren and the New Englanders was a formidable one. The navigable entrance to the harbour was but half a mile in width, and was under fire from Island Battery, at the entrance, and from Royal Battery, on the mainland, these two works mounting between them sixty heavy pieces. The defence of Louisburg on the land, or western side, was furnished by the conventional work of ditch and rampart, the ditch being eighty feet wide and from thirty to thirty-six feet deep, while the rampart of earth faced with masonry was about sixty feet in thickness. The number of guns mounted varies in different accounts, but actually there seems to have been about one hundred cannon. The amount of artillery available for the attackers is no less uncertain, but the exact figure seems to have been thirty-four cannon and mortars.

The landing of the troops was a difficult operation, but it was carried out with success, and on May 2nd the New Hampshire contingent established itself at the head of the harbour, where it burnt a warehouse and other buildings. So low was the *moral* of the French that, on the occasion of this raid, the garrison of the Royal Battery evacuated the work in panic, after spiking the guns, but without having fired a round from them, and without, too, having had even a bullet fired against the battery. An attempt was made to retake the battery which had been occupied by the New Hampshire men, but it failed, and the guns were redrilled and turned upon the town. The landing of the guns and stores was difficult and dangerous owing to the heavy surf, and it was a fortnight before the meagre supply of artillery was all on shore. Some mortars were placed about 400 yards from the town, and a battery was thrown up on Green Hill to the north-west of the fortress to attack the northern defences. Sallies were made from the town to interrupt the work, but without success. Other batteries were now erected between Green Hill and the harbour, the guns being dragged at night on sledges owing to the marshy nature of the ground. Soon, from the dampness of the ground and insufficient supplies of food and clothing, the troops suffered severely, but their spirit was unconquerable and their resolution undaunted. The troops made a jest of technical military terms. They laughed at proposals for zig-zags and epaulements. The men knew little of strict discipline. They were without tents, but fortunately the weather, in a region subject to thick fogs, proved on the whole fair. The men kept themselves in good condition by exercise and amusement when off duty, firing at marks, fishing, shooting game, wrestling, racing, and even chasing balls shot from the enemy's guns.

A triumph for the besiegers was the capture, by Warren's squadron, of the French ship *Vigilant*, of sixty-four guns, carrying from France munitions, stores and reinforcements of 560 men. The loss of the powder and stores was a serious blow to the garrison, and a very valuable contribution to the meagre stock of the besiegers. But this was to some degree offset by a failure in an attempt to capture the Island Battery, by which the English loss in killed, drowned and captured was nearly 200. A kind of deadlock had now set in which Warren was anxious to end by a combined operation in which the navy, having taken on board 1,600 of the soldiers, was to attack the water front, while the remainder of the army should assault by land. The project, however, was abandoned, chiefly owing to the fact that the Island Battery was still unsilenced. But against that work a battery established on Lighthouse Point—equipped with French guns which had been discovered on the beach— was doing tremendous execution. At the same time the English batteries on land were pouring shot relentlessly against the fortress. Soon the town was in ruins. Powder began to run short within the place. The French were disheartened by the loss of the *Vigilant*. The Island Battery was crippled, and the fortress batteries on the water-front were nearly destroyed. Rumours of a combined naval-military attack shook the nerves of the garrison and inhabitants of Louisburg. The desponding Duchambon—who was now the governor of the place—sent out a flag of truce. Terms of capitulation were arranged, and on June 17th, 1745, the French garrison marched out with the honours of war. The strongest fortress of North America had fallen before a force of New England farmers, mechanics and fishermen. This was the greatest success achieved by England during the War of the Austrian Succession, and in the long struggle between France and England in the New World it ranks as one of the outstanding events.

The news of the fall of Louisburg reached England during the last week in July, and was received with exultation, especially as the news of Fontenoy had aroused a feeling of despondency. In the same week Charles Edward landed in Great Britain in his second attempt for the restoration of the House of Stuart. In a previous chapter it has been told how the intelligence of the success in North America braced many waverers and bound to the Hanoverians many who would otherwise have espoused the Stuart cause. It is scarcely an exaggeration to say that, but for the confidence, the determination and the military worth of the New

Englanders in 1745, the whole subsequent history of the mother-country might have been changed. The effect of the fall of Louisburg was, of course, not confined to Europe. It was naturally more marked in North America, and it told seriously against the French, for, the initiative having been seized by the English colonists, the French were forced to conform. Instead of being able to profit by the military advantages which have been discussed earlier in this chapter, the French had to forgo all chance of an attack, on as large a scale as possible, to be pushed home from the Lakes to the St. Lawrence, and to devote their energies merely to regaining a fortress which they should never have lost. Further, the fall of Louisburg, by exposing Quebec—whose weakness now became unpleasantly evident—aroused a feeling of alarm for the capital in the bosom of the French viceroy. The defence of that city occupied his attention and ruled a vigorous offensive into New York and New England out of the question. Some operations in that quarter did take place, but they never rose beyond the level of raids and forays, and it was not by *la petite guerre* that the destiny of North America was to be decided.

The shame of the surrender of Louisburg had sunk deep into the heart of France, and a strong feeling arose as to the duty of retrieving the national honour by retaking the place. The effort made was one worthy of a proud and great nation. A total of sixty-six vessels, of which ten were ships of the line, twenty-two frigates, and thirty-four transports was gathered together at Brest under the command of the Duc d'Anville. The flagship was the seventy-gun ship *Northumberland*, captured off the coast of Portugal from the English on May 8th, 1744. On the transports were 3,000 good troops who were to be landed at Chebucto—now Halifax—where the fleet was to be reinforced by four line-of-battle ships from the West Indies, and the military force was to be strengthened by a body of Canadians. The programme to be fulfilled was an ambitious one. The troops were in the first instance to be landed at Mines, where they were to be joined by another contingent from Canada, and there await the arrival of the French ships. Louisburg was then to be recaptured; Annapolis was to be taken; Boston to be attacked; and devastation to be let loose upon the coast of New England. The elusivenes of sea-power is well illustrated by what followed. In spite of the superiority of the British navy the French fleet, leaving Brest on June 20th, 1746, reached Chebucto early in September unscathed so far as enemy action was concerned, and indeed unseen. But, as Sir Herbert Richmond has pointed out, "that element of sea-power consisting in efficient seamen, well-organized supplies and good sea-hygiene was lacking." Stormy weather was encountered; the squadron was scattered; two ships foundered; others were disabled, and pestilence broke out on board the fleet. On arrival at Chebucto only a portion of the expedition remained. The admiral died of apoplexy. The vice-admiral committed suicide. Their successor saw that, in the condition of the fleet and of the soldiers, the attempt against Louisburg was impossible. But he clung to the hope of a successful stroke against Annapolis, even although only a thousand men were left in fighting condition, and some were dying every day. The troops were re-embarked, and the forlorn hope set sail. But a storm off Cape Sable dispersed the ships, and, at a council of war held on board the flagship, it was resolved that there was no choice left but to return to France. Such was the close of this disastrous expedition, in which, without achieving anything whatever, the French are said to have lost upwards of 2,500 men.

The alarm which the viceroy of Canada had felt for Quebec, after the fall of Louisburg, was fed by rumours of a projected attack which reached the capital. Canada was wild with alarm at reports of English preparation. In July, 1746, a report came from Acadia that from 40,000 to 50,000 men were to take part in the operation, and this was followed by a rumour that there were thirty-two warships at Boston ready to sail against Quebec, and that 13,000 men were to march at once from Albany to Montreal. In these figures there was much exaggeration, but the rumours themselves had a firm basis of fact. Before even the New England force had started for Louisburg in April, 1745, the far-seeing Shirley had written to the English

Government suggesting that in the event of success a general attack upon Canada should follow. When Louisburg fell the proposal was once again put forward, and Shirley in his communication expressed the opinion, with which the whole destiny of North America was to be concerned, that "French and English cannot live upon the same continent."

The Duke of Newcastle listened to the proposal and directed Shirley to consult with Admiral Warren as to the proposed invasion. The campaign was to be a double one and to be conducted by both the colonies and the mother-country. A contingent of British troops from home was to sail for Louisburg, where it was to unite with the New England force, and the expedition, convoyed by Warren, was to sail for Quebec; while, by the Lake Champlain route, the contingents from New York and the colonies further south—aided, it was hoped, by the Iroquois—were to advance on Montreal. The eight battalions which were to come from England actually embarked at Portsmouth, but they never sailed for America. If the capture of Louisburg compelled France to shape her movements at the will of her adversary, it is no less true that the prompt effort by France to retrieve the fortress stayed the hand of England and for the moment paralysed her action. The exact destination of the French fleet assembling at Brest in the spring of 1746 was not known; the blow might, of course, be aimed at America, but it might, no less possibly, be aimed at England,

Ireland, or the Mediterranean. In these circumstances the British expedition was detained in home waters until it was too late in the year to sail, being subsequently diverted elsewhere. The result was that Shirley, who had thundered *Delenda est Canada* in the Massachusetts Assembly, had to content himself with a much more modest attempt on Crown Point. But during it astounding tidings reached New England. It was reported that a great French fleet and army were on the way to retake Louisburg, conquer Acadia, burn Boston, and lay waste the other sea-board towns. This was d'Anville's ill-starred expedition, of which details have already been given. But the tidings diverted the energies of New England from the invasion of Canada to the defence of her own coast-line, and the alarm engendered is compared by American historians to that which filled England on the approach of the Spanish Armada.

The whole of this series of incidents is worth dwelling upon, illustrating as it does the elusiveness and instability—at any rate in the conditions of communication which existed in the eighteenth century—of the thing known as sea-power. As a nation England was at the time unquestionably the superior of France at sea. When Louisburg fell, it was of enormous importance that, if the hegemony of North America were worth anything, advantage should at once be taken by England of the change in the situation and that the conquest of Canada should be immediately pressed. Similarly for

France—and in order to prevent such conquest—the immediate recovery of Louisburg was essential. From each country an overseas expedition was demanded, and each country made its preparations accordingly. But whereas the stronger naval Power was forced to hold back her expedition, the armada of the weaker not only crossed the Atlantic unscathed and reached the theatre of war, but for several weeks rode securely in the English harbour of Chebucto. From June 20th, when the fleet left Brest, to December 7th, when its shattered remnant reached France once more, no interference from the enemy had been experienced by d'Anville's fleet. But the elusiveness and instability of sea-power could not, of course, from the very nature of things, be expected always to favour the same side, as the French soon found to their cost. Undaunted by disastrous failure, the French equipped another fleet, which sailed from La Rochelle in May, 1747, for the reconquest of Louisburg. Anson, however, was lying in wait, cruising off Cape Finisterre, and, in the action which ensued, six ships of war and four Indiamen were taken. The French fought with their usual gallantry, but the defeat was a total one, and no further effort was made by sea to regain the lost fortress of France.

Earlier in this chapter, when the strategic importance of Louisburg was under consideration, it will be remembered that its value in the question of the recovery of Nova Scotia for France was stressed. That province became intimately involved in the operations concerned with the attempted recapture of Louisburg by the French in 1746. To the French, Nova Scotia—or Acadie, as they called it—was invested, apart from its military advantages of position, with the feeling of sentimental regret over a lost province, as was the case with Alsace-Lorraine more than a century later. When d'Anville left Brest in June, 1746, it was decided that the recapture of Louisburg should at once be followed by the reoccupation of Nova Scotia, and to assist in this latter operation a force of some 700 Canadians was despatched from Quebec by sea to the isthmus which joins Nova Scotia to the mainland. Advancing upon Annapolis, the commander of this force learnt of the disasters that had ruined the French fleet, and fell back to Chignecto on the neck of the Acadian peninsula, his force, including Indians, amounting at one time to some 1,600 men. Meanwhile, to the governor of Massachusetts the existence of a province on his very borders occupied by a French population—who, although nominally British subjects, were left practically to themselves—was always a source of irritation. But, curiously enough, he seems to have failed to realize that, with the capture of Louisburg, any danger from Nova Scotia had practically disappeared. Louisburg capitulated on the 17th of June, 1745, but not long afterwards we find Shirley writing to Newcastle to say " if a thousand French troops should land in Nova Scotia all the people would rise to join them, besides all the Indians." As a matter of fact, the Acadians, although they were attached to France, were by no means always ready to sacrifice their interests to her. They were exceptionally well treated by their British masters, and the mere handful of soldiers who composed the British garrison could excite no particular feeling of racial resentment. They were allowed complete religious liberty by treaty, and there seems to have been a clear understanding that they would never be called upon to take up arms against Frenchmen or Indians. Illiterate and humble, the Acadians had none of the vigour, the enterprise or the martial sentiments which distinguished the Canadians. Even if a thousand French had landed, it is by no means certain that the Acadians would have felt the frenzy of nationalism racing through their veins. They might, however, easily have been terrorized into a rejection of the British yoke, but even had this taken place, it is difficult to see—certainly so long as England maintained her grip on Louisburg, to which regular units of the British army had now been sent—what possible danger would exist for New England. The hard-bitten men who had taken Louisburg were not the men to throw down their arms at the feet of dreamy and ignorant peasants from Nova Scotia.

Reading between the lines of Shirley's vehement correspondence on the alleged danger of Acadia, it is impossible to avoid the suspicion that the military aspect of the question was overshadowed by that of religion. Acadia was priest-ridden, and over the ignorant and superstitious inhabitants some of the French priests—particularly of the type of the fanatical agitator Le Loutre—exercised a strong and terrorizing power. To the Puritan of New England Romish neighbours were intolerable, and the attack of Louisburg had sprung from a religious as well as a military bias. Parkman has placed on record how the New England soldier fancied he was doing the work of God; how the army was Israel and the French were Canaanitish idolaters, and how the ragged artillerymen of Massachusetts, battering the walls of papistical Louisburg, had flattered themselves with the belief that they were the champions of gospel truth. It was probably a touch of fanaticism which induced Shirley to despatch a force of some 500 men to deal with the French raiders, though it is but just to say that the commandant of Annapolis had written suggesting that the French detachment should be driven away and British authority confirmed. The New England force established itself at the modern Horton, but was there attacked and compelled to surrender by the French detachment, which had made for the purpose a march of seventeen days in the appalling conditions of a Nova Scotian winter. It was in expeditions of this character that the power of endurance and the patient submission to cold, privation and fatigue, were most apparent in the French Canadians. But, brilliant though the exploit had been, as a tactical

SITUATION IN 1713-1748 171

episode it was without any real or military consequence. The capitulation of the New Englanders did not even lead to the country being held by Canadian troops, for the force was immediately recalled. The event can be regarded merely as one of those exploits of *la petite guerre* in which the Canadians excelled. It would be difficult to show that this mode of warfare ever permanently gained for Canada one acre of soil. It was, however, persevered in to the last, in spite of the adverse criticisms, which have come down to us, of French military officers. In soldierly qualities, such as enterprise, resource and endurance, the Canadians had nothing to learn from New England. But there was about the attack on Louisburg a grandeur of conception and a oneness of purpose wholly absent from the pinpricks of the Canadian guerillas.

Doubtless the best reply to the expedition against Louisburg would have been an immediate counterstroke against Albany, carried out not on the lines of a foray, but as a real military operation, with provision made for retaining and fortifying the captured settlement. By this means both the Oswego and Lake Champlain routes would have been secured to the French, and a fine base for further operations against New England and New York would have been secured. In November, 1745, an attempt on these lines was made, but it was made too late ; it was half-hearted in execution, and the force employed did not exceed 600, of whom but half were white men. Saratoga was taken with the greatest ease, and Albany then lay uncovered, but it was never occupied by the French even when the English subsequently burnt the fort, which was found to be indefensible. The French in this part of the theatre of war showed activity, enterprise, and almost ceaseless energy, especially in an attack upon a settlement on the River Hoosac in August, 1746, but their operations never rose above petty warfare. The French, instead of engaging in serious military operations with a definite objective, frittered away their advantages in a futile policy of destroying outlying and unprotected homesteads. The New England borders were harried by this useless partisan warfare, but no real check was thus exercised upon the progress of English settlement. Early in 1748, when there were signs that the great European wrangle had exhausted the energies and resources of the contestants, New England could congratulate herself that, weighed against Louisburg, the French gains were but as a grain of sand. But then came a shock. When the terms of the Treaty of Aix-la-Chapelle were published, public opinion in America was stupefied to learn that Louisburg was to be handed back to France. That country had made the restitution of her lost colonial fortress an indispensable condition of peace, and in the circumstances England—who, in Europe, had met with ill-success—was forced to accept the evacuation of Flanders by the French and the removal of the menace of a French Antwerp as a *quid pro quo*. The struggle for North America would, therefore, have to be fought out later on more intensive lines. At sea, during the closing stages of the war, France had suffered fearfully at the hands of the English, and, as a naval Power, she had practically ceased to exist. But her insistence on the restoration of Louisburg showed clearly that she was determined not to let maritime supremacy go by default, and that she was not prepared to give up the struggle for North America.

CHAPTER FOUR

WOLFE'S EARLY MANHOOD. THE BEGINNING OF
THE FINAL STRUGGLE FOR NORTH AMERICA
IN 1755.

WHEN the Treaty of Aix-la-Chapelle brought a breathing space to a distracted world, Wolfe was once more upon the Continent, having recovered from his wound and having been sent to join a detachment of German troops in the vicinity of Breda. Here his duties were arduous, and existing documents show that once again he was employed on supply work—a very valuable experience for a young soldier, so soon to be a commander in the field, at a time when the service of supply was synonymous with corruption and inefficiency, and was in urgent need of supervision and reform. Already young Wolfe had been marked by his superiors as a coming man, and the Duke of Cumberland, in conversation with the adjutant-general, " had expressed great concern at not having it in his power to serve Wolfe, but that his intention was just, and he would soon take an opportunity of making it clear." All through the summer of 1748 the opposing armies rested in their respective camps during the period when the stipulations of the peace treaty were being adjusted. With the prospect of a period of inaction before him, the ambitious and far-seeing Wolfe was anxious to secure a prolonged period of absence from his regiment for the purpose of travel. Joining the army at the age of fifteen, he had spent most of his time on active service; and at a period when *ton*, deportment and address were necessary passports for success, Wolfe seems to have feared that in regimental life he might grow narrow and uncouth, lacking the ease and *savoir faire* to be acquired by travel and mixing in society. That he anticipated official opposition to his request is clear from an extract from a letter written to his mother in August, 1748, in which he says:—

"There will be difficulties in everything that contradicts a principle or settled opinion, entertained amongst us, that an officer neither can, nor ought, ever to be otherwise employed than in his particular military functions. If they could beat men's capacities down, or confine their genius to that rule (to be observed with the expected nicety, so as to exclude all other attachments) no man would ever be fitted for a higher employment than he is in. 'Tis unaccountable that one who wishes to see a good army can oppose men's enlarging their notions, or acquiring that knowledge with a little absence which they can't possibly meet with at home, especially when they are supposed masters of their present employment and really acquainted with it. In all other stations of life that method is usually pursued which best conduces to the knowledge everyone naturally wishes to have of his own profession."

Wolfe was to find his lament justified, for it was several years before he could wring from the authorities the permission to go abroad. Meanwhile he settled down for the remainder of the year 1748, his head filled with hopes of further advancement, practising economy, giving a " well-regulated attention " to chess, and " wishing nothing so much as the means of escaping from the noise and idleness " of a garrison town at the end of a campaign. By Christmas, however, he was in England again, and on June 15th, 1749, he read his name in the *Gazette* as a Major in Lord George Sackville's Regiment, later known as the 20th Foot, and now the Lancashire Fusiliers. Wolfe's new unit was then quartered at Stirling, and for the next few years he was destined to serve in Scotland.

So far little has been said of the personal characteristics of James Wolfe. In physique he was tall and thin—6 feet 3 inches in height, and of a slenderness so pronounced that he described himself as " a skeleton in motion. In short, I'm everything but what the surgeons call a subject for anatomy ; as far as the muscles, bones, and larger vessels can serve their purpose, they have a clear view of them in me, distinct from any impediment." His hair was red—aggressively so ; his eyes blue and piercing. His personal appearance, so far as the conventional proportion and disposition of features are concerned, was marred by an extraordinary retrocession of chin which has led many to describe him as unprepossessing. Sir John Fortescue frankly calls him " ugly." His profile was certainly peculiar, for, in addition to the retrocession of the chin, there was a well-marked doubling in it. His forehead sloped backward; the nose was long and slightly *retroussé*. The upper lip was attached to the nose further forward than is normal, and sloped downwards and backwards towards the mouth. His cheek-bones were high, and his complexion dull. His great height enabled him to carry off some of the disadvantages of appearance, but was negatived to a great extent by his narrow, sloping shoulders and awkward gait. His constitution was feeble, and his health almost always wretched. As a young man he suffered occasionally from ague; on several occasions he was afflicted with scorbutic trouble; often he was racked with rheumatism; and before he was twenty-five he developed symptoms of stone which, for the remainder of his life, often caused him great pain. He was undoubtedly tubercular, and there are reasons to believe that in the closing years of his short life he was afflicted with chronic tuberculosis of the kidneys and bladder. But the shard of a feeble and emaciated frame housed a spirit of unquenchable fire. Of dauntless courage, unflagging energy, and endowed with the priceless gift of vision, Wolfe was every inch a soldier and a born leader of men.

Wolfe had now reached manhood, but his early entry into the army had been at the expense of the education which was the normal lot of a youth of his class, and the years now to be described were those of development, of a self-imposed course of instruction, and the making of Wolfe the man. The life of Wolfe coincides almost exactly with the reign of George II—a period with such marked characteristics of its own as to be almost an era in itself. It was pre-eminently a period of transition —a reaction against previous influences which, in turn, and during Wolfe's lifetime and that of the King, was subject to a counteraction, if such a term may be employed. It was a period of English history which has come in for caustic criticism and even for some abuse. But it was a period which had as statesmen a Walpole and a Pitt. Among its sailors were Anson, Boscawen, and Hawke. Its soldiers were Wolfe and Clive and Eyre Coote. A reign deserves almost the title of a golden age which can show such names in literature as Swift and Pope ; as Gray and Collins ; as Samuel Johnson ; and as Smollett, Fielding, Richardson and Sterne. How clearly the period was one of transition—and, indeed, of transformation—can be seen by comparing the humiliating and ill-fated expedition to Cartagena in the early years of the reign with the triumphs of 1759 at the close. Into that most glorious year that England had ever witnessed were to be crowded the triumphs of Minden, of Lagos, of Quebec and Quiberon Bay.

But when Wolfe first reached manhood many of these great events were yet to be. His character had to receive its moulding during a time when the reaction against the dogmatism of the sixteenth and seventeenth centuries had spread into latitudinarianism which, in spite of a partial rally of the old forces under Queen Anne, was the hall-mark of the early Hanoverian age. This latitudinarianism, however, was not so much the cause as the symbol of the character of the time. If it had led to claims for the supremacy of reason by the path of earnest inquiry, it wandered also into flippant scepticism. There was an absence of enthusiasm. There was a great and growing national prosperity, but it was accompanied by a marked deficiency of disinterested principle. There was loyalty to the Throne, but much of it was a half-hearted feeling of necessity or expedience in support of a foreign dynasty. It was a period distinguished by a looseness in morals, unrelieved by even the pretence at concealment. Most people behaved badly, and nobody was ashamed of it. The ruling classes lived coarsely, spoke coarsely without any illusion of the subject. It is said, by a historian well versed in the period, that " the innocent and virtuous were little less indecent than the gross and the wicked." Good wives, and even spotless maidens, discussed, without any pretence of shame or attempt at secrecy, the nasty adventures going on around them. The age was depraved, but it was more than depraved—it was openly unclean. The Court set but a poor example in morality. Queen Caroline had now been dead over ten years; she had been a loyal, devoted, and affectionate wife, but had had no option but openly to acknowledge the King's mistresses. Who can forget her death-bed scene, when George II, in real grief, sobbed out to the Queen's advice that he should marry again : "*Non —j'aurais des maîtresses*," and Caroline's half-jesting, half-bitter : "*Ah, mon Dieu! cela n'empêche pas*"?

It was a gambling age. How far the Court here set the example it is difficult to say. Lord Mahon, on the authority of a letter of Chesterfield's, asserts that gaming was abhorred by George II, but a different impression is gleaned from Thackeray in his study of "The Four Georges." Whatever may have been the case at Court, in society in general cards were everywhere. People played for many hours a day. Among men, Brooks' and White's were especially the seats of high play ; many were the ancestral forests felled and the goodly lands disposed of to gratify the passion. Heavy drinking was almost universal, and reading was frowned on in polite society. George II was always furious at the sight of books. "Books ! Prithee, don't talk to me about books," said old Sarah Marlborough ; "the only books I know are men and cards." Even Johnson regretted that he had not learnt to play. "It is very useful in life," he says ; "it generates kindness and consolidates society."

The futility and purposelessness in high life during Wolfe's early manhood were unrelieved by any real national spirit. Various causes had contributed to the extinction of the martial spirit in England, the chief of them being probably the neglect of the militia. Prosperity had not been accompanied by a corresponding sense of responsibility; a small standing army was thought to be sufficient; and " the citizen having delivered his sword into the hands of the hireling soldier, cheerfully contributed to the expenses of government, and looked for safety to a band of mercenaries, whom he considered as dangerous to public liberty." Many motions had been made in Parliament that the militia might be put on a respectable footing, but the jealousy of the Government—dreading possibly a revival of Jacobitism—prevented any effectual step being taken for the purpose, while the peace that followed the Treaty of Aix-la-Chapelle had made the people yet less warlike. And as the small standing army, widely dispersed over the extensive dominions of the Empire, was insufficient for its protection, the unarmed and undisciplined inhabitants of Great Britain were filled—just before the Seven Years' War began—with terror and apprehension at the prospect of a French invasion. We shall see in the next chapter signs of this unmanly panic, and witness the apprehension of the ministry over the threat of France, which they had no idea of meeting except by the hire of Hessians and Hanoverians. Fortunately, however, for Wolfe, his early manhood was marked by the swing of the pendulum away from futility, coarseness, and corruption and towards a sense of dignity, sobriety, and responsibility. The latitudinarianism, the scepticism, the flippancy and unreality which had marked religion were undergoing a change from the earnest, if emotional, efforts of Whitefield and Wesley. The great evangelical revival had already begun. Clearly marked in literature is the tendency to a more sober, more serious, a more earnest and a cleaner conception of life. If there were Fielding and Smollett there was also Richardson. If there was a "Tom Jones," "Pamela" had got nine years' start of him. If "Roderick Random" was published in 1748—the year of Wolfe's majority—Gray's "Elegy in a Country Churchyard" followed but three years later. Swift died in the year in which Young finished his "Night Thoughts," and "Tom Jones" himself made his bow to a public already absorbed in "The Vanity of Human Wishes."

It was in a world revolting from coarseness and corruption that Wolfe was now to make his way. The power and influence of the great Whig oligarchy were not, however, to fall in a moment. Wealth and influence were still to do more to command success than could merit, however proved. But, fortunately for Wolfe, there were during his military career two men to whom merit appealed. The first was Cumberland, who, whatever his limitations as a commander and whatever his faults as a man, was a keen army reformer, and had his eyes always open for a promising soldier. The other was a minister, the man to be brought forth by the hour, to give England courage and to choose the right instruments for his purpose and policy. That man was Pitt.

Wolfe's character will be revealed in part by references to, or extracts from, letters written by him during the period of peace soldiering which is dealt with in this chapter, but this seems an opportune moment to correct two false impressions which have grown round his name. It is often assumed that he was a man who forced his way up to high command without any assistance, except his own merit. Actually this was not quite the case. To begin with, in those days of purchase, the promotion of an officer depended to a great extent upon the amount of money either he or his friends could lay down, and Wolfe's father had helped his son in this important respect. "If I rise at all," wrote Wolfe in a letter of 1748, "it will most probably be by means of my father's pocket." And, further, Wolfe's was an era in which influence counted for a very great deal. We know from his voluminous correspondence that throughout his career Wolfe was in close touch with men and women in high positions in the country. Further, of the two women whom he, at various times, wished to marry, one was maid of honour to the Princess of Wales and niece to the commander of an expedition in which Wolfe took part. The other was a sister of Lord Lonsdale, and eventually became Duchess of Bolton. The fact is that it was utterly impossible —until Pitt came to the head of things—for a soldier without influence, no matter how meritorious his service, to rise high in his profession.

Again, it is frequently asserted by biographers of

Wolfe that very early in his career he took a keen interest in the geography, nationalities and affairs of the North American continent, and that "there can have been little he did not know about the country when Fate took him there in 1758." The reply to these statements is that in Wolfe's correspondence between the years 1744 and 1748 there is not a single reference to the Western Hemisphere. If he even heard of the capture of Louisburg in 1745, the incident was not thought worthy of comment. Of physical geography he was so ignorant as to believe that the comparatively mild climate of the British Isles, as compared with that of Nova Scotia, was due, not to the Gulf Stream, but to the fact that "we are sheltered by the forests of Norway and Lapland from the north winds." It was not until six years after the fall of Louisburg that he makes the naïve discovery that Acadia "is near an island," *i.e.* a peninsula, and in the same letter, in which his elementary knowledge of American geography is revealed—under date of June 9th, 1751—he asks: "Is the island of St. John in the possession of the French, or do we occupy it?"

Wolfe joined the 20th at Stirling and soon found himself acting in command, for the lieutenant-colonel commanding, the Hon. Edward Cornwallis, had been selected as governor of Nova Scotia. The regiment was soon moved to Glasgow, and there Wolfe set himself to make up the leeway of his education by taking lessons from the professors of the college in Latin and mathematics.

Apart from the foresight shown by Wolfe in taking to his school-books again, his action in doing so was one of real self-denial. His pay was apparently but fifteen pounds a month; board and lodging—there were no barracks at Glasgow—horse, servants and washing came to three pounds ten shillings, and Wolfe was able to say: " I reckon myself to have a shilling a day for what they call pocket-money." No wonder that he said that he was " undone with all these expenses," even when for forty-five guineas he was able to purchase two horses, and that he had to approach his father for assistance for " the different articles of expense that necessarily attend a supreme command in such a place as Glasgow."

Wolfe's first and greatest love affair is worth dwelling on to some extent, throwing light as it does upon his character. During the winter of 1748 he renewed an acquaintance with Miss Elizabeth Lawson, eldest daughter of Sir Wilfrid Lawson and a maid of honour of the Princess of Wales. Her mother was a niece of the Earl of Peterborough, and an uncle, on the mother's side, was General Sir John Mordaunt, an old friend of Wolfe's father. Wolfe seems to have been attracted by Miss Lawson from the first, and on his return from active service, after the Treaty of Aix-la-Chapelle, he met her several times in London. Writing from Glasgow to his friend Captain Rickson, Wolfe declared that Miss Lawson " has won all my affections." The lady had a fortune of £12,000, which Wolfe, with a curious egoism, declares "is no more than I have a right to expect." His parents, as Wolfe confesses to his friend, had even bigger views—"they have their eye upon one of £30,000," a Miss Hoskins of Croydon. Miss Lawson's friends, on the other hand, were apparently not very averse from the proposed match, though they emphasized the fact that Wolfe was still very young, merely twenty-two, to be exact. Their formal consent, however, had not yet been asked, and Wolfe tells his friend : " If I'm kept long here the fire will be extinguished. Young flames must be constantly fed, or they'll evaporate." The French have a proverb that absence is to love as wind is to fire—" *il allume le grand, il éteint le peu.*" Judged by this criterion the fire of love within Wolfe does not seem to have been one which glowed with a very intense heat.

Mrs. Wolfe and her husband, the general, persevered in their refusal to countenance the match, and it is probable that some pressure—possibly of a financial nature—was exerted to make their son abandon his intention. The formal renunciation is conveyed in a curiously prolix and stilted letter from Wolfe to his father, written from Perth under the date February 19th, 1750 :—

"DEAR SIR,
"Though I have frequently given you occasion to blame either my neglect or levity, I am not, however, conscious of ever having intended to give you any uneasiness by obstinacy, or perseverance

in an error; the high opinion I have all along entertained of your just sense of things has always forced me to a proper submission to your will, and obliges me to acknowledge those actions to be actually wrong, when you think them so. Besides I am so convinced of your sincerity and secure of your friendship, that your advice cannot fail of its due weight, nor could I without the highest presumption differ from your sentiments in any of the concerns of life. As what I have said is the exact truth, I mention it by way of making a distinction between that part of my behaviour that is guided by reflection, and such steps as are the consequence of youth and inexperience, or, that have no rule to go by and are the pure effects of chance; but the main reason is to induce you not to look upon any slight omission, or inadvertency, as done with design to offend or displease. So far am I from any such intention, that my greatest satisfaction is the means of contributing in some measure to your happiness."

Without having before us the letter to which the above is a reply, it is not easy to decide definitely what Wolfe is writing about; but his biographers have agreed that the extract above quoted contains the submission of Wolfe to the wishes of his parents as to the renunciation of his suit. The whole episode is a curious one, and, even granting that Wolfe carried filial duty to an extent incredible almost in these days, is one not easy to explain. Three years later he confesses that although he had supposed himself " recovered in a great measure from my disorder that my extravagant love for Miss Lawson threw me into, yet I never hear her name mentioned without a twitch or hardly ever think of her with indifference," and, a year after that, sight of his mistress's picture, at the house of Sir John Mordaunt, "took away my stomach for two or three days, and made me grave." It is more than probable that Wolfe did not realize the depth of his affection until too late, and that it was with a feeling of bitter regret that he recognized the extent of the sacrifice which a deference to the wishes of his father and mother had cost him. Somehow the incident does not seem altogether to Wolfe's credit; and there are many who will think that poor George Osborne's was a manlier rôle. A cynic may hear, not without interest, of how the schemes of his parents miscarried. Miss Hoskins, the Croydon heiress, married Wolfe's friend, John Warde, of Squerryes, in February, 1751. Wolfe himself died unmarried, and Elizabeth Lawson preceded him by six months to the grave.

This, however, is to anticipate somewhat the chronological sequence of Wolfe's career. He never cared much for Scotland or its inhabitants —particularly those of Glasgow—the men there he found "civil, designing and treacherous, with their immediate interest always in view; the women, coarse, cold and cunning, for ever inquiring after men's circumstances." However, his opinion of the latter undergoes a change, and soon he finds "the ladies very civil, and in great numbers, and they are not so desperately afraid of a soldier as formerly." The Presbyterian divines were not much to the young major's liking—" the generality of Scotch preachers are excessive blockheads, so truly and obstinately dull that they seem to shut out knowledge at every entrance." The colonel of the regiment, Lord George Sackville, came to inspect it during its stay at Glasgow, and was apparently favourably impressed by the work of his deputy. Ten years later each was in command of British troops in a great battle, fought in different continents, but within a few weeks of each other—the one to find death and glory, the other to survive in shame.

Road-making in the Highlands formed a welcome relief from garrison duty in Glasgow. A significant light is thrown upon the efforts of the authorities to stamp out Highland dress: Wolfe's regimental orders strictly prohibit check shirts, as being suggestive of the plaid. Our heart goes out to Wolfe for his indignation at the action of the War Office in cancelling the issue of extra-duty pay formerly granted to officers when employed in superintending the road-making. The summer of 1749 was abnormally wet and cold, putting Wolfe "quite out of conceit with Scotland." Even mathematics began to pall, and Wolfe, while beginning to doubt how far they might assist the judgment, had no doubt "that they have a great tendency to make men dull." He turns from his algebra and Latin to shooting and hunting; buys a gun, and gets his horses ready to go out with the regimental pack. The vacancy in the lieutenant-colonelcy of his regiment is ever in his mind. Wires are being pulled, but Wolfe is still only twenty-two, and he admits that he cannot complain if an officer senior to himself, "and supposed to be better," is brought in. Shooting and hunting for exercise, with reading for entertainment, form Wolfe's programme. But withal he becomes desperately bored. His position was an isolated and difficult one. Acting commanding officer at twenty-two, Wolfe had, of course, many officers under him almost old enough to be his father. In a sense he was a misfit—though the incongruity was honourable to Wolfe. His officers were not quite to his liking—" few surpass me in common knowledge, but most of them in vice. I dread their habits and behaviour, and am forced to keep an eternal watch upon myself, that I may avoid the very manner which I most condemn in them." His influence, however, was a good one, and not without effect. A captain writes : " Our acting commander here is a Paragon. He neither drinks, curses, gambles, nor runs after women, so we make him our pattern."

In October, 1749, the 20th moved from Glasgow to Perth, where the news came that Lord Bury had been appointed colonel of the regiment. Apparently by this time the affair with Miss Lawson was not running quite smoothly, and Wolfe, writing to his mother, thinks that "it is now possible I might prevail upon myself not to refuse twenty or thirty thousand pounds if properly offered." The curious letter to his father, containing the submission to his parents' wishes, already referred to, was written while Wolfe was at Perth. Any lingering resentment left by this domestic jar was probably dissipated by the news that Wolfe had been promoted to the existing vacancy of lieutenant-colonel of the regiment. The promotion made little difference to Wolfe, for he had for long been acting in command, nor did it help to relieve a certain restlessness against the narrowness of regimental life. He still longs to go abroad—for two years, if possible, " to wear off the rough, unpolished coat, and give the gloss to all my future actions." Turin seemed the " best calculated to answer these ends." Wolfe, with the filial sense of duty which, admirable in many ways, seems rather far-fetched when displayed by a lieutenant-colonel commanding a regiment, begs to know if his father approves the project. Shortly afterwards a more military holiday appeals to him, and he talks of Lorraine, Metz and Thionville, but only " if you approve of the notion." It seems from later letters that the " approval " referred to was synonymous with a financial assistance which would be essential; indeed, the expression in its literal signification would be meaningless.

While at Perth Wolfe suffered in health. A scorbutic attack gave him trouble; his mother had recommended goat whey, and this Wolfe found to have " all the virtues mentioned in your letter for correcting the bad juices." This, and " a cold bath for fourteen days," gave great relief. But soon the ailment "broke out with more violence than ever," rather to the annoyance of Wolfe, who declares to his mother: "I have never drank, and do upon all occasions abstain from strong food." It is pleasant to read, a couple of months later: "It matters little what season of the year I travel in, for I am absolutely as hard as flint, and can bear all the extremes of heat and cold that are known in these climates with great ease." Possibly long days in the open with his gun did more good than the goat's whey to "the juices." Wolfe was a very bad shot, but he liked the exercise. From Dundee—his next station—Wolfe got leave to England, and joined his parents in London in the middle of November, 1750. Here, according to his own words, he "lived in the idlest dissolute, abandoned manner that could be conceived, and that not out of vice, which is the most extraordinary part of it"—till the following April, when he rejoined his regiment at Banff. From that station he wrote the usual filial letter to his father "to make you some sort of apology for every particular instance of vice and folly that has very luckily fallen under your notice while I had the honour to be near you." There is not the slightest testimony extant as to what Wolfe is here referring to, or why the Paragon should have "gone off the rails." The most probable explanation is that Wolfe had been frankly bored. He was only twenty-four, and many an austere young man—as Wolfe was—is suddenly swept from the path of austerity into a more well-trodden road. A young military man in London in the middle of the eighteenth century had many temptations. Wolfe came, saw, was conquered, and woke up with that "morning after" feeling which turns the scale in favour of austerity again. Ambitious and prudent, he conceived a sense of disgust for "life" as seen by the young man of his day.

A letter from Wolfe to his friend, Captain Rickson, at that time in Nova Scotia, is of more interest. It is in this letter that his remark about Acadia, referred to earlier in this chapter, appears. There are some apposite reflections upon the colony, and upon the local defences of Halifax, but of the larger issue of France *versus* England in North America there is tantalizingly little. "A future war with France in North America" is, however, referred to, and a reference to a report—which Wolfe hopes is true—of "a strong naval armament preparing for your assistance" seems to be the first allusion in Wolfe's correspondence to that influence of sea-power with which his destiny was to be interwoven. An interesting suggestion is that of the employment of individual companies of Scottish Highlanders, an idea which grew until eventually adopted by the commander-in-chief, to the great and lasting advantage of the British army. While at Peterhead ill-health again beset Wolfe. Stone began to trouble him, and the best physician advised soap taken internally. He confesses to an intolerance of pain, and to a lack of patience in his suffering. It is a curious mark of the buoyancy of Wolfe, which always refused to be weighed down by adversity, that the narrative of his ailments and of the remedies to be used is interrupted, in this letter to his mother, by mention of " the cheerful hours the ladies of Banff have afforded him : there were women of good understanding, others of great vivacity, and others very handsome ; so that a man could not fail to be pleased with such variety to choose out of ; and for my part I always think a pretty maid either has all the other beauties or does not want them." But, on the whole, Wolfe never seems to have been much taken by the Scots. From Inverness, in October, 1751, he writes to his father of the villainous nature of the inhabitants, and the brutality of the people in the neighbourhood, saying that the Hanoverian element was distinguished by " greater rudeness and incivility than the open and professed Jacobites."

The proximity of Culloden induced Wolfe to revisit the battlefield, and he wrote to his father a letter in which he says that he " finds room for a military criticism as well as a place for a little ridicule upon some famous transactions of that memorable day," but, unfortunately, from the point of military history, the letter contains nothing of real interest. At Inverness there was no hunting or shooting, and " when the snow falls we shall have little else to do but to eat and sleep." Wolfe wonders " how long a man moderately inclined that way would require in a place like this to wear out his love for arms and soften his martial spirit." Ten years at the outside, thinks Wolfe. The stagnation of Inverness gives him time to reflect on love and marriage, and to convey his views thereon to his mother. " I have no very high opinion of love affairs except they are built upon judgment. So you'll say, ' Where, then, would you choose? ' Why, nowhere, to men of whimsical disposition ; but otherwise, the choice reason directs is the best ; moderate fortune and sense enough to give aid in ticklish times." In the same letter he confesses to a love for children—" necessary to us in our latter days." Three months later he tells his mother that he will never marry purely for money, yet he does not believe that any infatuation of his " will ever be strong enough to persuade me that people can live without it ; besides, unless there be violence done to my inclinations, by the power of some gentle nymph, I had much rather listen to the drum and trumpet than any softer sound whatever."

During the winter Wolfe's studies went on, but apparently without much beneficial result, for, as he wrote whimsically to his father : " I have read the mathematics till I am grown perfectly stupid, and have algebraically worked away the little portion of understanding that was allowed to me." He read a great deal, with, it must be confessed, rather unfortunate results for his literary style. He sat up late at night on his twenty-fifth birthday composing a letter to his mother of such a mixture of affected moralizing and sham sententiousness that in the morning common-sense almost led him to burn it ; even the most adoring of his biographers admits that " in the morning a profound disgust seized upon " Wolfe. A few weeks later Wolfe himself confesses to his mother : " I don't always understand myself. I can't therefore wonder that I am sometimes unintelligible to others." Wolfe at this time was making the unfortunate mistake of endeavouring to write an essay every time he sent a letter. However, when spring came, " I have shut my books and am every fair day on horseback." A few weeks later, on April 10th, 1752, he packed up the bulk of the books and sent them to his mother for safe keeping, retaining but a few well-chosen ones—" a great library for a soldier." Thenceforth the change in Wolfe's letters is remarkable ; his own style—crisp, direct, informative and clear—comes into its own again.

There is a doleful note in " I was shamefully beat at chess by a Scotch laird," and Wolfe declares he must become a scholar again under Mrs. Inwood— " to make me attentive to the game and teach me to think." It is curious to reflect how few Great Captains are associated with a game said to be the image of war, and that none of them ever made any mark in it. Saxe is said to have been fond of chess and to have been a fair player, but Napoleon's attempts are described by Lord Rosebery as chess *pour rire*. Possibly an injustice is done here, for the Scotch gambit played by Napoleon against Bertrand in 1820, which has come down to us, is highly praised by experts, especially for the beautiful *coup de repos* and the subsequent smashing Austerlitz attack. But that Napoleon was sometimes an extremely unconventional player is plain from the memoirs of Madame de Rémusat, who describes him as changing at will the power of the pieces, and in this way bringing about—as can easily be understood—some remarkable positions. Moltke was fond of chess, but never approached "class." There is a legend of a remarkable game he played at Cairo, a detailed account of which appeared in an English magazine some years ago, but the veracity of the story can be impugned from several points, and not least from the vantage ground of the fact that Moltke was never in Egypt in his life. Curiously enough, Moltke was passionately fond of whist, although probably the worst player in Europe. Investigation fails to establish any connection between chess and such Great Captains as Marlborough, Wellington, and Lee. Of leading present-day soldiers, some—Marshal Foch was one— are said to be partial to the game, but in the army of chess players their place is among the sutlers and camp-followers. The real fact is that the analogy between war and chess has been very much strained. The essence of chess is that there is no concealment : everything is, in the fullest sense of the word, "above board," whereas the essence of war is guessing what is—as Wellington used to say—" on the other side of the hill," or, on the other side of the river, frontier, or sea. In the second place, no matter how difficult the position of a player at chess may be, he has time to analyse the change brought about by his opponent's last move, for during that period an enforced passivity is laid upon his opponent—a state of things so entirely different from the conditions of war as to blast into nothingness any supposed analogy between war and chess. In the third place, there is nothing in chess which even a straining of language can assimilate to "communications" in war; and strategy has been defined as "the science of communications." The outstanding feature of the relationship between war and chess, as disclosed by history, is briefly this: no great chess player has ever become a great soldier, and no great soldier has ever even approached greatness in chess.

After a visit to Ireland, where the battlefield of the Boyne led him to write that "there is not another piece of ground in the world that I could take so much pleasure to observe," Wolfe at last obtained leave to proceed to France. Luckily for him the British ambassador at Paris was the Earl of Albemarle, father of Wolfe's colonel, Lord Bury. On October 2nd, 1752, armed with letters of introduction to persons of influence, Wolfe set out for the French capital. One of his first English acquaintances there was the young Philip Stanhope, the recipient from his father, the Earl of Chesterfield, of some of the most extraordinary letters in the English language. To Mrs. Wolfe, who inquired how her son passed his time, the latter wrote, on November 25th: "Four or five days a week I am up an hour before day (that is six hours sooner than any fine gentleman in Paris). I ride, and, as I told you in a former letter, I fence and dance, and have a master to teach me French. These occupations take up all the morning. I dine twice or three times a week at home, sometimes at Lord Albemarle's, and sometimes with my English acquaintances. After dinner I either go to the public entertainments, or to visit. At nine I come home, and am in bed generally before eleven." Early in January, 1753, he accompanied the ambassador to Versailles—"a cold spectator of what we commonly call splendour and magnificence"—where he saw the King and Queen, the Royal Family, and the real ruler of France—the Marquise de Pompadour. A week later Wolfe was presented to the King and Royal Family, and "lastly to Madame Pompadour and M. de St. Coutest, the minister." The lady "entertained us at her toilet. We found her curling her hair." Although Wolfe was practising economy, this manner of living could not be indulged in for nothing, and there are several applications to his father for money. "I told you in my last letter how expensive a place this is, and, to prove it, I can assure you, upon my honour, that the articles of play and woman (the most extravagant in Paris) have not amounted to twenty Louis-d'ors, that my tailor's bill for two suits of clothes, a frock and liveries, does not exceed seventy pounds ; the ruffles that I have been forced to wear is, indeed, a considerable expense . . . I believe there are few men that live in the manner I do, and though the objects of my attentions are not in themselves the most essential, they are still such as have their use in life and may help to advance me in the Army."

Sentimental but practical, sententious at times, but hard-headed always, Wolfe was shrewd enough to see that " the fortune of a military man seems to depend almost as much on his exteriors as upon things that are in reality more estimable and praiseworthy." That he was correct in his estimate is clearly borne out by the information given by the cynical Chesterfield to his son Philip Stanhope concerning that Earl of Albemarle at whose table Wolfe had sat more than once. " Between you and me," wrote Chesterfield to young Stanhope, in 1752, " for this example must go no further, what do you think made our friend, Lord Albemarle, Colonel of a regiment of guards, Governor of Virginia, Groom of the Stole, and Ambassador to Paris ; amounting in all to sixteen or seventeen thousand pounds a year ? Was it birth ? No ; a Dutch gentleman only. Was it his estate ? No, he had none. Was it his learning, his parts, his political abilities and application ? You can answer these questions as easily and as soon as I can ask them. What was it then ? Many people wondered, but I do not, for I know, and

MONUMENT TO WOLFE IN WESTMINSTER ABBEY, WITH CANADIAN REGIMENTAL COLOURS DURING THE GREAT WAR.
(*By permission of A. E. Wolfe-Aylward.*)

To face page 200.

will tell you. It was his air, his address, his manners, and his graces." The shrewd Wolfe had seen quite as clearly as had the worldly-wise Chesterfield the value set upon airs and graces, and had determined to acquire those qualities. The commanding officer who could shut himself up in his quarters in Scotland, to wrestle with Latin and algebra and military history, was the same who fenced and danced and rubbed shoulders with people of *ton* at the gayest court in Europe. The combination of qualities required for success in both of these lines is exceedingly rare, but it was possessed to a marked degree by Wolfe. It gave to him a versatility, a nimbleness of mind, a sense of proportion, and a capacity for resource which were to stand him in good stead as a soldier.

The practical and ambitious lieutenant-colonel looked upon a gay season in Paris merely as a means to an end—the end being professional advancement. So soon as he could talk French with reasonable fluency, and his fencing and dancing passed muster, Wolfe was eager to undertake a tour to visit the French, Prussian and Austrian armies at work. His leave was, however, abruptly terminated by a letter of recall owing to the death of the major left in acting command of the 20th. Wolfe rejoined his regiment in Glasgow in April, 1753, in a condition of extreme depression, in part due to the change from Parisian gaieties to the humdrum garrison routine at Glasgow, and partly owing to the intense disappointment which he felt at having been forced to abandon the tour to the foreign armies. Certainly the homecoming, as described in a letter to his father, was not auspicious :—

"It is almost impossible to suffer more than I have done upon the road, and quite impossible to find a regiment in more melancholy circumstances than we are. Officers ruined, impoverished, desperate and without hopes of preferment; the widow of our late major and her daughters in tears; his situation before his death, and the effects it had upon the corps, with the tragical end of the unhappy man in everybody's mouth; an ensign struck speechless with the palsy, and another that falls down in the most violent convulsions. He was seized with one the first night I came to the regiment (after supper) that so astonished and affected all that were present that it was not to be described. I should have fallen upon the floor and fainted, had not one of the officers supported me and called for immediate relief; and this, as well as I can remember, for the first time in my life. Some of our people spit blood, and others are beginning to sell before they are quite undone; and my friend will probably be in jail in a fortnight. In this situation we are, with a martinet and parade major to teach us the manual exercise with the time of the First Regiment."

The second tour of duty in Glasgow was hardly an improvement on the earlier one. In May (of 1753) "We are all sick, officers and soldiers. In two days we lost the skin off our faces, and the third were shivering in greatcoats." For social recreation there were plays, concerts, balls, dinners and suppers, "of the most execrable food upon earth, and wine that approaches to poison." For the guests Wolfe had no good word : " the men drink till they are excessively drunk. The ladies are cold to anything but a bagpipe "—although showing a tendency to melt " at the sound of an estate." Road-making in the Highlands northwest of Loch Lomond was a break in the monotony of garrison life, but Wolfe seems to have welcomed the move of the regiment to England in the autumn of 1753. On crossing the frontier between the two countries, during the march south, he moralizes on the difference between the two peoples : " the English clean and laborious, the Scots excessively lazy and dirty." There is little doubt that Wolfe was a man of prejudice and moods, and that his opinions at times represent irritable comment rather than considered judgment. Later we shall find some curious, and unjust, criticisms of both English and American soldiers.

The regiment passed slowly down through England, *en route* for Dover, halting for a fortnight at Reading. The discontent which Wolfe often felt for regimental life is again shown in a letter to his father from that town, under date of October 22nd, 1753, in which he says : " If I stay much longer with the regiment I shall be perfectly corrupt, the officers are loose and profligate, and the soldiers are very devils." These words, however, and similar expressions from other letters written by Wolfe, are discounted by the fact that it is on record that his regiment was the best in the army so far as drill and discipline were concerned. The truth probably is that Wolfe's professional ideas were very high and much in advance of those of the ordinary regimental commander of his day. Dover was no more to Wolfe's liking than the stations in Scotland. The castle, where the 20th were quartered, was in a dreadful state of dilapidation : "I am sure there is not in the King's dominions a more melancholy, dreadful winter station." There was very little to do during the winter : "Our conversation from dinner till five o'clock is kept up with some difficulty, as none of us have any correspondence with the capital, nor communication with coffee houses or public papers, so that we are entirely in the dark as to exterior things. From five to eight is a tedious interval, hardly to be worked through." In the tedium Wolfe took again to his books, as did some other of the officers, the rest finding distraction in cards. Wolfe also encouraged his officers to frequent balls and assemblies in the town : " it softens their manners and makes 'em civil, and commonly I go along with 'em to see how they conduct themselves." Some relief to boredom was brought about by a captain of the regiment " whose whole happiness is made up of hunting," who imported a pack of harriers from Maidstone, but everyone was delighted when the route came to march to the west of England, the regiment arriving at Exeter in October, 1754. One of the first incidents after arrival was the drafting of a hundred men from the 20th to another regiment ordered to sail for America, and this is a fitting opportunity to pass once more to the Western Hemisphere and to take up the story of the great struggle between France and England in North America. While Wolfe's regiment had been on the march from Dover to the West Country some shots had been exchanged on a tributary of the Monongahela between a force of Virginians under a young major called George Washington and a small French party. This was on May 27th, 1754, and the shots then fired began the war which was to decide for ever the future of North America.

In the struggle which had closed with the Peace of Aix-la-Chapelle in 1748 it had been made clear that a Nova Scotia inhabited almost entirely by French settlers was a grave weakness to the English side. The conduct of the Acadians, though not entirely hostile, had been somewhat of an armed neutrality and sufficiently showed the necessity of peopling Nova Scotia with British subjects. The reduction of the navy and army after the peace left a large number of men in England without employment. The British Government accordingly offered great encouragement to all soldiers, sailors, artificers and reduced officers to settle in Nova Scotia. In addition to large grants of land, proportioned to their rank in the navy or army, the government engaged to pay the cost of their passage, to build them houses, to furnish them with the necessary equipment for agriculture and fishing, and to defray the expense of subsistence for the first year. Immunity from taxation was also guaranteed for ten years. Further, in order to establish a fortified naval station as a set-off to the restoration of Louisburg, the British Ministry selected the harbour of Chebucto. Thither, in June, 1749, came a fleet with a load of emigrants, many of whom were German Protestants, to the number of some three thousand, including women and children, all under the command of Cornwallis, the former colonel of Wolfe's regiment. In honour of the President of the Board of Trade and Plantations the new settlement received its present name of Halifax. Succeeding years brought fresh emigrants until, in 1752, the population was above four thousand.

The place was fenced with palisades and defended by redoubts of timber. Three companies of rangers were formed for the defence of the settlement, in addition to which two battalions of regular troops were detailed for the garrisons of Nova Scotia and Newfoundland. Thus was born the important naval base of Halifax, the establishment of which was to exert an immense influence in the Anglo-French rivalry. The harbour, which is open, ice-free all the year round, is six miles long by over a mile in width, and, from the upper end, a navigable passage leads to a basin of twenty-four square miles and of a depth sufficient for the largest men-of-war of the eighteenth century and later. It was of great importance that, alone of all the British colonies in the North American continent, Nova

Scotia was the offspring, not of private enterprise, but of royal authority ; that it stood outside the bickerings and jealousies of the other colonies ; and that, in case of war, the naval base of Halifax was under the direct control of the home government.

The French in Canada were alarmed by this vigorous action of the British Government, and as the limits of Nova Scotia had not yet been fixed, considerable friction existed between the two nations. The French constructed two forts on the isthmus connecting Nova Scotia with the mainland ; they incited the Indians to murder the new settlers, and spared no pains to alienate the hearts of the Acadians from the English. The priests were their instruments in this treacherous policy, and their proceedings were fully approved at Versailles. New disputes of still greater importance arose in connection with the boundaries of the British colonies to the west and south. Here the French plan was to continue the policy of uniting Canada and Louisiana by a chain of forts as a preliminary to confining the English colonies between the Alleghanies and the sea. The situation brought about by the penetration of the French from north to south carried on simultaneously with an English infiltration from east to west was one inevitably bound to result in collision. By the discovery of the Mississippi, and by the navigation of its waters to the Gulf of Mexico, the French, not unnaturally, claimed the river by right of discovery, and by the common practice of those times included in their claim the whole drainage area of the Mississippi. The eastern boundary of this vast area of Louisiana was formed by the Alleghanies. Though the British colonists had made few settlements west of the mountains, and those chiefly for the convenience of the Indian trade, the inhabitants of Virginia had always considered the extent of their country westward to be limited only by the ocean, basing this claim upon the fact the Virginia had been settled before the French had so much as discovered Louisiana. Similarly, although the extent of the claim was less, the people of the two Carolinas never doubted that they might extend their plantations to the banks of the Mississippi without encroaching on the property of any European Power.

To France, if her claim to the Mississippi were to be maintained, and the connection between Canada and Louisiana were to be a reality, the possession of the valley of the Ohio was a necessity. Already there were reports that English traders were settled on its upper reaches, and accordingly in 1749 the viceroy of Canada sent Céloron de Bienville with a force of some two hundred and fifty Canadians and a band of Indians to assert French sovereignty in the debatable region. The party reached the Alleghany from Lake Erie and, passing the site of the future city of Pittsburg, moved down the Ohio to the trading post of Logstown, driving out of the place the English traders found there. Meanwhile a company was being formed by some capitalists in Virginia for the very purpose of exploiting the country about the Ohio, and so extended were its plans that it was proposed to push on even as far as the Mississippi until suitable territory should be secured. But the divergence between French and English methods of colonization was here clearly revealed. On the latter side is a private company; on the other an emissary of Government equipped with all the insignia of Royal Arms and seals and moving about with an armed and disciplined force. In order to remedy, to some extent, such inequality, two measures seemed necessary—a confederacy between the British colonies in North America and an alliance with the most powerful Indians in the neighbourhood.

Meanwhile the French had acted with vigour and promptitude. In July, 1752, the new governor-general of Canada, the Marquis Duquesne de Merreval, arrived in Quebec and immediately took steps to prepare for the military operations implied by the instructions he had received to arrest the pretensions of the English to the Ohio, and to drive them from the territory. He began by a general review of regulars and militia. The latter amounted to 13,000 men capable of bearing arms. The new governor-general compelled all who were bound to serve to enrol themselves, and he enforced strict discipline. The military situation of Canada at this time called for reform, and in a report rendered in October, 1753, Duquesne dwelt upon the want of discipline of the provincial troops and the disinclination of their officers to active service. Duquesne describes them as *consternés* when called out. He was dissatisfied with the militia in other respects, describing them to be badly organized, and pointed out that many desertions took place. Nevertheless, Duquesne determined to act, and in the spring of 1753 he sent an expedition of fifteen hundred men through Lake Ontario to Lake Erie, where they landed at Presqu'ile, the site of the present Erie. The place had been occupied in the previous autumn; a fort of logs was now built, and Presqu'ile, easy of approach, and with an excellent harbour, served as an admirable base of operations for the French struggle for the Ohio. A road, some twenty-one miles in length, was cut southward to what was known as French Creek, a tributary of the Alleghany, and the stores, boats, ammunition, were carried to the higher level, where a second fort was constructed known as Fort le Boeuf. Sickness defeated any further operations, and the commandant died. Garrisons were therefore left at Fort le Boeuf and Presqu'ile, and the remainder of the force returned to Montreal.

Communication had now been secured by the French between the St. Lawrence and the Ohio. The menace to the growth of the English colonies was clear to Dinwiddie, the lieutenant-governor of Virginia, and he sent the adjutant-general of the Virginian militia, Major George Washington, with a summons to the commanders of the French forts to withdraw from the King of England's territory. Washington left Wills' Creek in November, 1753, with a guide, an interpreter and five men. He reached Venango, an English trading station on the Ohio, over which the French flag now flew, and was courteously received by the French officers, who, however, over their wine after supper, said plainly that they had the territory, and, "by God, they would keep it." From Venango Washington made his way to Fort le Boeuf, and delivered Dinwiddie's letter to the commandant there, who received it with courtesy, stating that he would forward the missive to the governor-general, by whose answer he would be bound, but that in the meanwhile he must refuse to evacuate his position. Washington then pursued his journey homeward, reaching Williamsburg, after a perilous passage through forests and rivers full of floating ice, in the middle of January, 1754.

Dinwiddie was determined not to be put off by diplomatic procrastination. He had already warned the home government of the danger and had urged the immediate building of forts on the Ohio, to which, in August, 1753, the King had replied, authorizing him to build the forts at the expense of Virginia, and to repel force by force. He now sent messengers to the Indian tribes inviting them to take up the hatchet against the French, "who, under pretence of embracing you, are squeezing you to death"; he wrote urgently to the governors of Pennsylvania, the Carolinas, Maryland and New Jersey, begging for contingents of men; he got his own colony to give men and a grant of £10,000; and to the more distant colonies of New York and Massachusetts he suggested that demonstrations should be made by them against Canada so as to check the French in their advance to the Ohio. His efforts to secure the assistance of the other colonies were, however, not entirely successful. In a spirit of narrow parochialism they recalled that the debatable land belonged to either Virginia or Pennsylvania, and refused to vote money to defend it. The Quakers and Germans of Pennsylvania declined to move. North Carolina alone answered the appeal and gave money enough to raise three or four hundred men. Two independent companies maintained by the King in New York, and one in South Carolina, had received orders from England to march to the scene of action, and in these, with the scanty levies from Virginia and North Carolina, lay Dinwiddie's only hope.

The £10,000 voted by Virginia had been primarily for a force to establish a fort at the forks of the Ohio upon a site which had been examined and favourably reported on during Washington's mission to Fort le Boeuf. A force was accordingly sent across the mountains in February, but during the execution of the work the backwoodsmen were surprised by the French, some 500 strong, moving down the Alleghany. Guns were landed and trained upon the half-finished fort, the few backwoodsmen being called upon to surrender. Resistance was useless, and the Virginian force was allowed to retire. The French thereupon, having demolished the work, erected a much larger fort, to which they gave the name of Fort Duquesne, on the site now covered by the furnaces and factories of Pittsburg. Obviously, unless the English colonies were prepared to submit to the erection of a cordon which would bar them from the west, the French could not be allowed to exploit their victory. It was, however, left to the lieutenant-governor of Virginia alone to champion the English cause. The force at his disposal was inadequate, consisting but of the raw regiment of Virginians and the companies from New York and the Carolinas, and even these were not all immediately available. Speed, however, was essential, and Washington, with but 150 Virginians, was sent across the Alleghanies to attack the newly-erected Fort Duquesne.

When about sixty miles had been covered, a French scouting force was encountered on May 27th, 1754, at a place called the Great Meadows, and an engagement ensued, in which the French subaltern in command was killed. Large French reinforcements were on their way, and by the middle of June there were 1,400 men at Fort Duquesne. Washington had by this been reinforced by some of the so-called regulars, maintained in the colonies at the expense of the Crown, but the assistance rendered by them was negligible. The two companies from New York came crawling up to the scene of action in a disgraceful state; they were short of establishment, undisciplined, without tents, blankets, knapsacks, or ammunition, and encumbered with thirty women and children. The troops from North Carolina were still worse—so much so that they mutinied and dispersed to their houses while yet on the march to the rendezvous. Some fifty arrived from South Carolina, but their captain, as a "King's" officer, refused to take orders from Washington, and his men, taking their cue from their commander, would lend no hand in road-making, carrying packs, or hauling guns. Washington, unable to retreat owing to the condition of his horses and men, stood at bay behind some rough entrenchments near Great Meadows, to which he gave the name of Fort Necessity. Here his force of less than four hundred men was attacked by twice that number of French, and, after a fight of nine hours, in which Washington lost a fourth of his men, he was forced to capitulate, the victors allowing the defeated garrison to march out with the honours of war and to carry their effects and one gun with them.

The defeat of Washington was a heavy blow to the lieutenant-governor of Virginia, but neither amongst his own people, and still less in Pennsylvania and New York, could he secure the determination to resist the encroachments of the French. In June, however, an assembly was convened at Albany, which was attended by representatives of the four New England colonies, as well as of New York, Pennsylvania and Maryland. The primary object was to make a joint treaty with the wavering tribes of Indians, one of whose spokesmen put the matter plainly when he said : " Look about your country and see ; you have no fortifications ; no, not even in this city. It is but a step from Canada hither, and the French may come and turn us out of doors. You desire us to speak from the bottom of our hearts, and we shall do it. Look at the French. They are men : they are fortifying everywhere. But you are all like women, bare and open, without fortifications." In these circumstances no real success attended the negotiations with the Iroquois. This assembly at Albany was marked by the famous project of union put forward by Franklin, which, however, was never put into execution, the Crown considering that it gave too much power to the colonies, and the latter asserting that it gave too much power to the Crown.

When the news of the fighting on the Ohio reached England, a decision was there taken which, although in present times it would be considered normal and obvious, in 1754 possessed a certain significance. Already, before the news of Washington's defeat, some steps had been taken, for, in July, £10,000 in specie and two thousand stand of arms had been shipped to America for service in the colonies. Now, in September, it was decided to send out to North America some regular troops composed as an expeditionary force. That the home country should thus identify herself with a colonial border struggle indicated, if not a new era, yet a certain change of policy. It had been considered, not only by Peter Kalm, the Swedish traveller, in 1748, but by many leading men in the American colonies at that time and later, that the policy of England was bound up with the desire to maintain the subjection of the colonies to the mother-country by keeping open the menace of French aggression, and in this way to repress any progress on the part of the colonies towards independence, and especially towards a commercial independence in virtue of which they would become the rivals of, instead of markets for, English trade. Actually, however, the hand of England had been forced, for France's world-wide activity had brought home to English statesmen that her efforts signified not mere local aggression for local trade advantages, but were incidents and episodes in a vast scheme for world dominion. The significance of events on the North American continent could be understood to the full only by regarding India as well. In that country, although the nations were nominally at peace, the French and English were still active rivals, vying with each other in alliances with native princes, and the successor of Dupleix and Labourdonnais, in the war which ended in 1748, had inflicted heavy blows on the English. The loss was being, to some extent, retrieved by Clive, who had already rendered his name famous by the defence of Arcot and the restoration of English power in the Carnatic, but the skilfulness with which the French had extended their influence in

India threw up into broad relief the possibilities of expansion open to her in America unless steps were quickly taken to nip these possibilities in the bud. In January, 1755, the two British regiments, the 44th and 48th, were embarked at Cork, the commander of the expedition being General Edward Braddock, a soldier of what was even then "the old school," a martinet of old-fashioned views, but not without ability, a good judge of men, of great driving power, and as brave as a lion. After a safe voyage the transports arrived at Hampton, whence they proceeded up the Potomac to Alexandria, where a camp was to be formed. There, on April 14th, was held a council at which, in addition to Braddock, were the governors of Virginia, North Carolina, Pennsylvania, Maryland, New York, and Massachusetts. Braddock laid his instructions before the council, and, after some discussion, a plan of campaign, based on those instructions, was settled. The French were to be attacked at four points at once. Working from right to left, the expeditions were to be as follows:—A New England force, under Lieutenant-Colonel Monckton, a regular officer, was to capture the French fort of Beauséjour on the neck of land between Nova Scotia and the mainland, and to settle the Acadia question once for all. Secondly, a force of provincials from New England, New York, and New Jersey, under William Johnson, whose influence over the Indians was very great, was to seize

Crown Point. Third in geographical sequence—working from right to left—was to be an attack upon Niagara, to be carried out by two new regiments just raised in the colonies and taken into the King's pay, known as Shirley's and Pepperrell's ; this column was to be commanded by Shirley himself, the governor of Massachusetts. The remaining force was to consist, in the main, of the two regiments from England ; this column was to be led by Braddock, and its objective was to drive the French from Fort Duquesne.

France, however, had been on the alert. Early in this year, 1755, the French *chargé d'affaires* in London, by judicious bribery, had got hold of Braddock's orders and had instantly communicated them to Paris on the eve of Braddock's departure. The French Government immediately sent orders to Brest to prepare a counter expedition to America, and the force detailed was much superior in strength to the meagre expedition which had sailed under Braddock. Eighteen ships of war were fitted for sea at Brest and Rochefort, and six fine regular battalions with useful war records—those of La Reine, Bourgogne, Languedoc, Guienne, Artois, and Béarn—were ordered on board for Canada, under the command of Dieskau, a German veteran who had served with Saxe. Unforeseen delays hampered the French, and it was not until the beginning of May that the expedition weighed anchor, by which time the British Government was thoroughly acquainted with the French naval and military preparations. Admiral Boscawen, therefore, received orders to capture or destroy any French vessels bound for North America. The French expeditionary force was followed, and off Newfoundland a thick fog concealed the rival fleets from each other; but two English ships, one commanded by Captain (afterwards Lord) Howe, came within speech of the French on June 10th. The foreign commander inquired if it was war or peace. The exact sequence of the events immediately following is obscure, but ere long appeared Boscawen's signal for action, and, after an engagement in which skill and intrepidity were displayed on both sides, two French ships were taken, on board one of which were eight companies of the regiments La Reine and Languedoc. The remainder of the squadron got safely to Louisburg and Quebec, and the regular troops on board were subsequently divided between Quebec and Lake Champlain. For the English the whole affair had been singularly unfortunate. It was an act of war of the most flagrant character committed while the two countries were at peace. Nothing could have justified it but complete success. The capture of a squadron and six regiments of the line would have made the enterprise worth while, but, as it was, England had put herself completely in the wrong, and had done comparatively little damage to the French.

Let us now follow the expeditions on land, beginning on the right. On the isthmus joining

Nova Scotia to the continent the French had erected at Beauséjour a regular work, with solid earthen ramparts, bomb proofs, and an armament of twenty-four guns and a mortar. The garrison consisted of fourteen officers and 150 other ranks of colonial regulars. In the neighbourhood were a number of Acadian "exiles" who had been shepherded to this part of the country by the French authorities, and particularly through the efforts of the fanatical Le Loutre, and who lived in terror both of the priest and of Vergot, the commandant of the fort. Of these so-called exiles about 1,400 were nominally available for the defence of the locality, but actually but a few, and those under compulsion, gave their assistance. The attacking force consisted of some 2,000 New Englanders and a handful of regulars from Fort Lawrence in the neighbourhood. On June 1st the expedition anchored in the bay before Beauséjour, which capitulated in a fortnight after a feeble resistance. A smaller fort called Fort Gaspereau also fell into Monckton's hands. The time had now come to put an end once for all to the continued anxiety for Nova Scotia, and the British Government announced its intention of expatriating all Acadians who refused to take a definite oath of allegiance. Many of them being unwilling to do so—probably from superstitious reasons—were sent into exile. The pathetic hexameters of Longfellow are a lasting record of the event which, whatever may be urged against it from the sentimental or humanitarian point of view, did at least rule out thenceforth the probability of French interference in Nova Scotia.

It will be convenient now to deal with the most western of the four expeditions, that under General Braddock, with its objective the capture of Fort Duquesne. On May 10th Braddock reached the assembly point at Fort Cumberland, where Wills' Creek enters the Potomac. His force consisted of about 2,200 men, of which number about two-thirds were made up by the 44th and 48th Regiments, each of which had been completed to 700 strong by the enlistment of Virginians. There were also nine companies of Virginians, each of fifty men, about a hundred from the Royal Artillery and thirty sailors, lent by Commodore Keppel. Immense difficulty had been experienced in collecting sufficient and suitable transport—a problem which would have been almost insoluble without the assistance of Benjamin Franklin, then postmaster-general of Pennsylvania. Only a handful of Indians had been got together—a serious omission in the class of warfare in which the column was to be engaged. On June 10th Braddock moved out from Fort Cumberland for the tedious march through the forest, three hundred axemen leading the way. After an exhausting march the force crossed the Alleghanies, meeting with no opposition other than sporadic attacks by French and Indian scouts. By the 18th of June the column was but thirty miles from its starting-place, and already sickness amongst the troops, the exhaustion of the horses, and the rough going had brought down the rate of progress to but three miles a day. On the advice of Washington, who was serving on his staff, Braddock determined to leave the heavy baggage under a guard, to follow on as best it could, while he himself should push forward with a body of chosen troops.

The advanced column of 1,200 men, ten guns, and the minimum of transport pushed on. Progress was still very slow, and it was not until July 7th that the force neared the mouth of Turtle Creek, a stream entering the Monongahela, some eight miles from the French fort. The disaster which ensued on the following day is well known, and need be but briefly summarized here. The French were in inferior numbers, for they could muster but 73 regulars, 146 Canadian militia and 637 Indians, but the nature of the country, which was well adapted to forest warfare, and a long experience of *petite guerre*, placed them in a situation of immense advantage. The advanced guard of the British column achieved some initial success, but the French officers rallied the Indians, and thenceforth the savages, lurking behind trees and bushy ridges, poured in a fire so rapid and deadly that the red coats, massed together, fell in heaps. Totally surprised by a system of warfare in which they could not see their enemy, the soldiers were at an immense disadvantage, and when they attempted to imitate the Virginians in the tactics more suitable for the occasion, Braddock furiously beat them back with his sword into a suicidal shoulder-to-shoulder formation. Braddock, to do him justice, performed prodigies of valour, and had four horses killed under him. Washington was twice unhorsed and had his coat riddled with bullets. The regimental officers set a noble example of fortitude to their men, but at last panic set in, and a wild retreat—covered by the Virginians, to whom the forest fighting had not come as a surprise—ensued. The survivors did not halt until the camp where the baggage had been left, sixty miles back, was reached. Here orders were given to burn everything which could not be taken back. Scores of waggons, supplies, guns and ammunition were destroyed. The relics of the column, which had suffered casualties to more than half its number, and in the fighting portion of which sixty-one officers had been killed or wounded, crept painfully back to Fort Cumberland. On the way Braddock, who had been mortally wounded in the battle, was buried, murmuring with almost his last breath : " Another time we shall know better how to deal with them." The catastrophe came as a stunning blow, not only to the colonies, but to the British Government, and its immediate effect was enormously to increase the prestige of the French in the eyes of the Indians. As a result, the western frontiers of the middle and southern colonies were exposed to merciless attacks of savages eager for scalps and thirsting for blood.

Here it may be of interest to interpolate the impression made upon Wolfe by the news of the disaster. His letter, written to his father from Southampton, under date of September 4th, 1755, gives an unpleasant picture of the condition of the army at that time, although it must be borne in mind that, with all his shrewdness and judgment, Wolfe was a man of moods and impulses. The letter runs :—

"Dear Sir,

"The accounts of Mr. Braddock's defeat are not yet clear enough to form a right judgment of the cause of it ; but I do myself believe that the cowardice and ill-behaviour of the men far exceeded the ignorance of the chief, who, though not a master of the difficult art of war, was yet a man of sense and courage. I have but a very mean opinion of the infantry in courage. I know their discipline to be bad, and their value precarious. They are easily put into disorder and hard to recover out of it. They frequently kill their officers through fear, and murder one another in their confusion. Their shameful behaviour in Scotland, at Port L'Orient, at Melle, and upon many less important occasions, clearly denoted the extreme ignorance of the officers, and the disobedient and dastardly spirit of the men.

Was there ever such a slaughter of officers as upon this expedition ? And did ever the geneva and p—— of this country operate more shamefully and violently upon the dirty inhabitants of it under denomination of soldiers ? I am sorry to say that our method of training and instructing the troops is extremely defective, and tends to no good end. We are lazy in time of peace, and, of course, want vigilance and activity in war. Our military education is by far the worst in Europe, and all our concerns are treated with contempt or totally neglected. It will cost us very dear some time hence. I hope the day is at a distance, but I am afraid it will come."

Perhaps the best comment on this letter is that ten years before it was written there was Fontenoy, and four years after it was penned there were to be Minden and Quebec. It is to be questioned whether any army can show a nobler example of discipline and devotion than was exhibited by British infantry in every one of those three battles.

Of the four expeditions against the French two have already been described; the remaining two both started from Albany with the objectives Niagara and Crown Point respectively. The former was under the command of Shirley, now a major-general, his force consisting of some twenty-five hundred men. Shirley's plan was to move by the Mohawk river to Oswego on Lake Ontario, and to make that settlement his base for the further prosecution of the expedition by water against Fort Niagara. It is difficult to see how success could have been expected, for the French held command of the waters of the lake, and even to challenge that command it would have been essential to attack Fort Frontenac at the north-eastern outlet of the lake, so as to cut the connection between Lake Ontario and Montreal, as well as to destroy the shipping at Fort Frontenac itself. The French, moreover, had been fully informed of Shirley's designs through the capture of Braddock's correspondence, and at Frontenac there was now a force of 1,400 regulars and militia. By this time Shirley's force had been reduced to about 1,500 men fit for duty, and there was considerable difficulty about supplies. The weather, too, was persistently bad, and the bateaux, made only for river navigation, were useless for the stormy waters of Lake Ontario. Shirley was but imperfectly informed by his scouts of the opposition that awaited him, but he realized clearly that the task of securing command of the lake, and of then moving down upon Niagara, was quite beyond his strength. At the end of October he returned to Albany, having accomplished no more than to reinforce Oswego with 700 men.

The attack upon Crown Point by William Johnson was marked by some success. Leaving Albany in August, Johnson, with 3,000 New Englanders and some 300 Indians, moved up the Hudson, and where the portage began he built a fort subsequently known as Fort Edward. Meanwhile the French had sent a force of 3,500 regulars, as well as militia and Indians, under Dieskau, to Crown Point. Dieskau pushed on to Ticonderoga with a mixed force of 1,500 men, whence he advanced to attack Johnson in his camp, while Johnson detached a force some 1,500 strong to work round Dieskau's rear. This detachment was very roughly handled, but, on the other hand, the attack by Dieskau was stubbornly resisted, and the inability of the attacking general to control the Canadian militia and Indians gave an opportunity for the defenders to counter-attack. The French were put to flight, and Dieskau, who was wounded, was taken prisoner. The battle was, however, followed by no important consequences, for Johnson did not think it prudent to follow up his victory, and the year closed with Crown Point still held firmly by the French.

On balance the advantage of the year 1755 lay on land with the French. Of four expeditions undertaken against them, only one had resulted in success. Of the remaining three, one had petered out, one was a victory, but a barren one, and one was disaster unredeemed. As has already been said, this disaster did not end with the precipitate retreat from the Monongahela, for the Indians at the instigation of, and sometimes led by, the French, inaugurated a remorseless and bloody campaign on the western frontiers of Virginia, Maryland and Pennsylvania. Washington, with 1,500 Virginian militia, did what he could to protect 350 miles of frontier, but the task was an impossible one. "Every day," he wrote, "we have accounts of such cruelties and barbarities as are shocking to human nature. It is not possible to conceive the situation and danger of this miserable country." The country had in past years been so peaceful, and the Indians so friendly, that many of the settlers, especially on the Pennsylvanian border, had no arms. Yet Pennsylvania would do nothing to reinforce Washington; the Quakers of Philadelphia and the Germans in the centre of the colony could not be brought to take steps to assist the settlers on the frontier, and it was not until the enemy were within sixty miles of Philadelphia that a grudging and belated permission was accorded the governor to take steps to check the Indian invasion.

It is difficult to formulate any criticism upon the campaign of 1755 unless we first come to a conclusion as to what was the objective underlying the plan of campaign of the British Government. Was this objective the expulsion of the French from North America, or merely a determination to enforce claims to territory which was, rightly or wrongly, considered to belong to England? It seems absurd that there should exist the need to ask such a question, but that it is necessary is obvious from the peculiar character of the operations, both naval and military, which have been described in this chapter. It seems, however, that we are warranted in assuming that there was no question, as yet, of a conquest of Canada, and this conclusion is based upon the fact that, with the possible exception of the leading man in the English colonies—Shirley, the lieutenant-governor of Virginia—no one in America in 1755 contemplated such an operation; and, secondly, upon the fact that, in spite of the presence of Boscawen's squadron in North American waters, no provision was made for an attack on Louisburg—an indispensable operation if the conquest of Canada had really been contemplated. Finally it may be said that the regular reinforcements sent from England to America were on a minute scale, and quite incompatible with such an objective as the expulsion of France from the New World. Moreover, the employment of such forces as were available in America in four radial columns, with the flank objectives more than a thousand miles apart, cannot be reconciled with any idea of a real attack on Canada.

By narrowing down the discussion to an examination based upon the assumption that England's objective was merely to enter into possession of what she believed to be her own, it is impossible to resist the conclusion that the projected attack on Crown Point was unwise. It is true that it tended to " fix " the French regular forces in Canada and to prevent reinforcements from these forces being sent to Nova Scotia or to Fort Duquesne. But the same result might probably have been achieved by the mere threat exercised by the presence of Johnson's force at the southern end of Lake George, without aggressive action at all. On the other hand, the attack upon the isthmus connecting Nova Scotia with the mainland seems clearly to have been justified, not because there was really more likelihood of the French regaining Nova Scotia—or, should they regain it, of holding it in the face of the new naval base of England at Halifax—but because the possession of the isthmus by the French would afford them an overland connection between their fortresses of Louisburg and Quebec. Besides, there can be no real doubt, in spite of the vagueness of treaty clauses, that the isthmus was lawfully the territory of England. The expulsion of the Acadians was the inevitable corollary to the successful seizure by England of the land entrance to Nova Scotia. The unfortunate inhabitants had proved themselves totally unable to stand up against the threats and intimidation of French agents and French priests. They were offered fair and just terms should they elect to remain, and some three thousand took this decision. About 6,000 were deported, exclusive of many who fled to French territory. It may be mentioned that those who were settled in New England, on expatriation received far more generous and humane treatment than did those who fled to their co-religionists at Quebec.

To turn now to the ill-starred expedition against Fort Duquesne, many writers—taking their cue from Parkman—have pointed out that inasmuch as the operations in this quarter were clearly directed at cutting off France from the Ohio valley, it was a needless dissemination of effort to aim both at Niagara and Fort Duquesne, and that successful operations against the former would have isolated Fort Duquesne and thus automatically have brought about its fall. There is a good deal in this contention, and it is upheld by a notable example in recent warfare. Readers of Lawrence's " Revolt in the Desert " will remember how the

Arabs, under Lawrence, designedly refrained from attacking Medina, preferring to give the Turks the trouble of trying to hold it, while the attackers harried and severed the communications leading to the town. To the Turks the place was hardly worth the effort to hold it, but fear of loss of prestige prevailed upon them to endeavour to retain it. But while it is a fair comment that an attack upon Niagara would have rendered the expedition against Fort Duquesne unnecessary, logic goes one step further and asserts that Niagara might similarly have been rendered impotent by a successful attack on Fort Frontenac. There, it is thought, was the spot where the French penetration of the Ohio valley might have been most effectively checked.

The expedition against Fort Duquesne seems to have been clearly justified from the political point of view. It is obvious, however, that Parkman is correct in pointing out the futility of adopting the policy of attacking both it and Fort Niagara simultaneously. As regards the action on the Monongahela itself, it is extremely difficult to know where to apportion the blame for the disaster. It was certainly not in the purely physical and moral qualities of leadership. Braddock was a lion in the field—though a stupid lion; his subordinate officers by their gallantry and devotion to duty have left an example of which any army and any nation might be proud. The British regulars broke and ran, but it is only the barest justice to point out that they stood fearful punishment for some time, and it was the moral effect produced by the invisibility of the enemy, added to the severity of his fire, which caused the bonds of discipline to snap. It is easy to sneer at Braddock beating back into line with his sword small parties of the unfortunate infantry who seem to have endeavoured to shake out and use cover in the attack. But it must be remembered that there had been practically no training in anything but close order formation in the British army, and Braddock may rightly have thought that to inaugurate a new school of tactics, actually in face of the enemy, was a dangerous proceeding. The real fact is that the Monongahela was not so much a French as an Indian victory, and it was Indian tactics, carried out by Indians, and in most favourable conditions, under French officers, which carried the day. Naturally the question arises, why had Braddock not Indians, too? Actually he started with but fifty, and these had dwindled to a mere handful before collision occurred. He had taken some pains to secure their aid, but with these unsatisfying results. The explanation for the absence of what was an absolute necessity in the forest warfare which was to follow is to be found in the attitude of the English colonists towards the Indians. These had been alienated by gross neglect, whereas the French, on the other hand, had always handled the natives with sympathy and tact. For this unfortunate state of affairs Braddock and his red coats paid the penalty.

All things considered, notwithstanding the defeat

of Dieskau and the expulsion of the French from Nova Scotia, the year 1755 concluded to the disadvantage of England. The disadvantage by land was, however, counterbalanced to some extent by the great number of French merchantmen captured at sea during the summer. After Boscawen's abortive effort in June the British Ministry, in order to counter the expected declaration of war by France, gave orders to make prize of all French ships on the high seas. In consequence of this order some hundred French trading vessels, many of them with valuable cargoes from the West Indies, were captured and brought into British ports. This was, of course, war in all but the name. "To men of good judgment, and watching on the spot, it was, for years coming, an ominous dubiety—the chances rather for the French, 'who understand war and are all under one head.' But there happens to be in England a Mr. Pitt, with royal eyes more and more indignantly set on this business; and in the womb of time there lie combinations and conjunctures." Parturition was not long delayed. Next year the formal declaration of war took place. There then began the great world contest known as the Seven Years' War, which was to be fought out in four continents, and by which the destiny of North America was to be definitely decided.

CHAPTER FIVE

THE SEVEN YEARS' WAR. FRENCH SUCCESSES IN NORTH AMERICA. THE TURN OF THE TIDE. SIEGE AND CAPTURE OF LOUISBURG IN 1758.

THE struggle between France and England for North America by now had reached a stage in which not only the colonies overseas, but the two mother-countries as well, were bound to be deeply involved. The year 1755 has been brought to a conclusion, so far as North America is concerned, and it is necessary now to hark back and see what effect was produced on the respective home countries by the events which have been described. In July news of Boscawen's attack upon the French transports reached Europe, and the French ambassador broke off diplomatic relations, although war was not declared for another year. In the tangle of European politics which existed at the time, neither country could quite clearly see its way. In each country there was a division of opinion. In England it was clear to Pitt that the struggle must be fought out in America, and also in India, where French prestige had been raised to a pitch never reached before, whereas the Duke of Newcastle still thought of nothing but a continental war. The King, on his part, was racked with anxiety for his beloved

AMERICA—SEVEN YEARS' WAR

Hanover, and was constantly engaged in continental arrangements to secure its safety. But the people of England by no means saw eye to eye with their Sovereign. For a maritime and colonial war with France they were eager and resolute enough, but of continental wars they were heartily tired. There was growing up in England an imperial, as against a dynastic, enthusiasm, and the instinct was recognized by Pitt. The most competent historians are agreed that the greatest inspiration of Pitt was this recognition by him of the truth and force of this imperial instinct when he came into power.

In France, although the aggression of Boscawen and Hawke upon the seas aroused a natural resentment, there was at first a hesitation to pick up the gauntlet—a hesitation due to the same tangle of European politics which was confusing England. And even when it had become clear to France that war was inevitable, there was considerable doubt as to how it should be waged. An invasion of Hanover was contemplated, but was at first rejected. Then it was proposed to attempt to carry on the war at sea and in the colonies, and to take every step to prevent it spreading to Europe. This plan was found not to be feasible, and finally, as a counsel of despair, France resolved on a daring operation—nothing less than the invasion of the British Isles, to be accompanied by a blow in the Mediterranean at Minorca. This latter operation was successful. The French captured the island in June, 1756, the

English admiral Byng failing to effect its relief. The moment it was known in London that the French had landed in Minorca, England declared war, but this quarrel *à deux*, vast and far-reaching though it was, was merged at once into one of the great wars of history in which many of the continental nations were engaged.

He who would survey the far-flung operations of the Seven Years' War must bestride the world like a Colossus. To understand its subtler points he must bear in mind that the combination of European Powers showed a striking innovation ; that the alliance between France and Austria came as an earthquake in the European system ; and that " the old lie of strata, which the diplomatic world had come to recognize as the bedrock of their art, was torn and twisted past all recognition," and this recasting of alliances ruled out of court any possibility that France might redeem American losses by the surrender of gains in Flanders. Finally, the student must visualize the whole world contest as projected on a screen on which appeared three interrogatory captions : Were the British or the French to have the mastery of the seas ? Which Power was to have the ascendency in India ? Was the Teutonic or the Latin race to be supreme in North America ? It is the answer to the last of these questions which forms the subject-matter of the concluding chapters of this volume.

In the concluding sentence of the previous chapter it was implied that by the formal declaration of war between France and England there opened the great Seven Years' War. Actually this is not quite the case, and a correcter statement would be that a long-continued struggle between France and England flowed into and mingled with a contest purely European in origin. The fight with France for North America had, even as early as 1756, been of long duration. There had, it is true, been a kind of truce for the generation which succeeded the Treaty of Utrecht in 1713, but the year 1740 marked the practical conclusion of that Anglo-French *entente* which had contributed so greatly to the peace of Europe. In 1756 the dispute with France as to the limits of our American colonies became blended with a quarrel of quite a different origin, which was to plunge Europe into general war for several years. In this European war England and France were both engaged, inevitably on different sides, but with this difference: France put out her maximum effort on the Continent and had little left for overseas engagements, while England's policy was almost exactly the reverse. With her enormous resources it might have been possible for France to be ready to contest with England the mastery of the seas and the supremacy in North America and India. Actually she allowed herself to be swayed by visions of aggrandizement in Europe, and while these visions were being shattered on the continent of Europe, Clive in India, Wolfe in Canada, and Hawke upon the seas were establishing England's predominance in the East and West.

Within a space of two years French overseas dominion was almost to perish. The year 1759 was to witness the fall of Quebec—the preliminary to the loss of Canada, whose fate was to be sealed by Hawke's crushing victory in Quiberon Bay a few months later; while, in the following year, Eyre Coote's victory at Wandewash was to mark the ruin of French hopes in India.

So much for a very general survey of the larger issues of the Seven Years' War in so far as they affected France overseas. To go a little deeper into detail and to understand how European and American affairs reacted one upon the other, it is necessary to bear in mind some factors of 1756 which are not in existence to-day. What we call " democracy " was then almost completely unknown in Europe; France, Russia, Prussia and Austria were autocracies, while in England the constitution was entirely aristocratic; secondly, what we call " nationality " had not been developed upon the continent of Europe to the same extent as prevails to-day, and, as a consequence, affairs in Europe were governed by the personal likes and dislikes of continental sovereigns to an extent not easy to imagine at the present time. In the third place, England was attached to the Continent and bound to its affairs by a chain long since broken, the very existence of which is apt to be forgotten. That chain was the connection with Hanover, of which George II, like his father, was the ruler, and from this circumstance it came about that a disturbance in Europe, while leaving England as a nation quite unperturbed, might and often did put the King of England into a state of considerable alarm, and that such alarm, given the non-democratic constitution of the country, could and often did shape the policy of England. In the fourth place, the difference of religious faith, when merely autocratic sovereigns had to be considered, had an influence greater than could be the case to-day, when such difference is diffused amongst millions of nationals. And, in the fifth place, the morality of the day tolerated the exercise of power near the throne of a kind and in a manner which would not be tolerated in the present century.

Of the sovereigns of Europe in the middle of the eighteenth century those who counted for most in any matter affecting the Continent were the Kings of England and Prussia; the King of France —though actually the real ruler of that country was his mistress, the Marquise de Pompadour; Maria Theresa of Austria, the Empress-Queen; and Elizabeth, Czarina of Russia. The mutual relationships amongst them were that Frederick of Prussia and George of England—nephew and uncle—hated each other. The Empress-Queen hated Frederick, too. She had never forgotten nor forgiven the conquest of Silesia, nor the perfidy and treachery by which its conquest had been achieved. A sincere and devoted daughter of the Church, her piety burned to wrest that Catholic province from heretic hands. The dislike experienced by Madame de Pompadour for the King of Prussia was of a more virulent kind. On the receipt of a greeting of friendship from her he had drily remarked : " I do not know her. This is not the land for swains and shepherdesses." He scoffed at her in public, gave the name of Pompadour to one of his favourite lap-dogs, and forbade his ambassador in Paris, by the most positive directions, to visit her. In Russia the Czarina Elizabeth was an amiable kindly sovereign who, however, was believed to have shown an indiscreet amiability to many of the grenadiers of the guard who had wrought the sudden revolution which had placed her on the throne. Against the Czarina's frailties Frederick loved to point the shafts of his venomous wit. An exhaustive study of treaties, despatches, political and diplomatic correspondence of the period, will bring the reader no nearer to the truth than will the simple statement that the European situation in 1756 was one largely brought about by the indignation of three great ladies, two of whom were sovereigns, and one sovereign in everything but in name, and that the indignation of two of the ladies was caused by the mocking sallies of a ribald king.

The result was that a formidable confederacy was brought into being against the King of Prussia. The impetus to it had been provoked originally by his unprincipled ambition, but the resentment had been animated and sustained by his wanton and mocking wit. Ten years before, as early as 1745, Maria Theresa had entered into some sort of arrangement with Saxony for curtailing what they regarded as the undue pre-eminence of Prussia. After the War of the Austrian Succession the Czarina Elizabeth was approached and induced to enter into a similar project. Now, in 1756, even France was induced to detach herself from her traditional policy of hostility to the House of Austria, owing to the fact that Madame de Pompadour was thirsting for vengeance against Frederick, and listened readily to the friendly approaches of Maria Theresa, who stooped to address the mistress of Louis XV as " *Ma chère cousine,*" and by the bait held out to France in the shape of promised concession of part of the Austrian Netherlands. The rapacity and caustic wit of Frederick of Prussia had brought it about that in 1756 five European Powers—France, Austria, Russia, Saxony, and Sweden—were leagued against his small and solitary kingdom. The schemes of the confederates had been kept carefully secret, but Frederick had means of securing accurate information, and at the first rumours he had hastened to draw closer to England. England, on her part, being already embroiled with France and at differences with Russia, was glad of support which would distract France from her colonial possessions. The personal antipathy of the Kings of England and Prussia towards each other gave way to the political exigencies of the times. King George II realized that Hanover could not be left exposed wholly without friends, and a convention was concluded between the two monarchs. Frederick, on his part, finding that his enemies were unprepared, and knowing that he was ready, determined to strike the first blow, and by October had begun the Seven Years' War.

The formal declaration of war by England against France made little difference to North America, where hostilities had for over a year been in full swing, but the mother-countries now began to intervene in earnest. Both nations had, indeed, anticipated events, for in England, early in 1756, Parliament had sanctioned the formation of ten new regiments, and a Bill was brought in to enable the King to grant commissions to foreign Protestants in America. The origin of this measure was a proposal made by a Protestant refugee named Prevost to raise four battalions of Swiss and provincials in America, with a British officer for colonel-in-chief, with a fair number of foreigners holding other commissions. On March 4th the order was given for the enlistment of four battalions on these lines, to be recruited in Pennsylvania, with the Earl of Loudon as their colonel-in-chief. These battalions were the Royal Americans, later the 60th Foot, and to-day the King's Royal Rifle Corps—a regiment in which the numerical designation still persists. Owing, however, to the panic aroused in England by the threat of a French invasion, not a man was embarked to America for several months. Up to the end of March the only step taken had been to despatch Colonel Webb to supersede Shirley—who had succeeded Braddock on the latter's death—as commander-in-chief. Webb's appointment was, however, to be merely a temporary measure, pending the arrival of General Abercromby, who was also under orders for America; and Abercromby, in his turn, was to give way to the Earl of Loudoun. At last, towards the end of April, the 35th Foot and the 42nd Highlanders were embarked and reached New York late in June, and a month later Lord Loudoun arrived and assumed command. For the moment, however, a vigorous offensive was out of the question. Of the Royal Americans hardly one battalion was yet raised, and the levies of the various colonies, besides being late in assembling and ill-supplied, were jealously kept by the respective colonies under their own orders and control.

On the French side the situation was scarcely better. The campaign of the previous year, necessitating as it did the employment of Canadian militia, had rendered the gathering in of the harvest a difficult matter, and the harvest at best had been an indifferent one. Something like a famine prevailed. English cruisers watched the mouth of the St. Lawrence with such vigilance that when the breaking up of the ice freed the navigation of the river, France found it difficult to supply Canada with bread. Corruption, too, was rampant. Bigot, the *intendant*, practised peculation on a scale of extraordinary audacity. A favourite method was to confiscate to himself enormous quantities of the King's stores, to enter them up in his books as issued in various quarters, and then cynically to sell the same stores back to the government at enormous prices. Naturally such a state of affairs bred a swarm of lesser swindlers, and the command of a fort or detachment was eagerly sought for as a means of swindling the Crown by dishonest returns. France, however, did not wholly neglect Canada at this time. In the spring of 1756 she despatched a distinguished soldier to take over military command, and with him were 1,200 men from the regiments La Sarre and Royal Rousillon. The new commander-in-chief was Louis Joseph, Marquis de Montcalm-Gozon de Saint-Véran, now in his forty-fifth year, a veteran in European warfare, who had already been twice wounded. Cultured, religious, brave, honest, devoted to his country and to his family, Montcalm represented the highest type of a French gentleman of the eighteenth century.

Montcalm was accompanied by Lévis and Bourlamaque as second and third in command respectively, and by Bougainville as aide-de-camp —all three excellent soldiers. With the arrival of the new commander-in-chief there began a new era in the history of Canada, particularly from the military point of view, for regular and scientific operations began to take the place of *la petite guerre*. Montcalm's first task was to reorganize the army— an undertaking which was not without difficulty owing to the feeling which prevailed between the regular troops from France and the colonial infantry. The latter were descended from the three companies of *infanterie de marine* which landed in Canada in 1684, and came to form a veritable colonial unit imbued with Canadian traditions. This force was much more popular with the Canadians than were the regulars from France, and it is said that in some quarters to-day the name of Montcalm is far from being as esteemed as that of Vaudreuil owing to the fact that the former was a Frenchman and a regular soldier, while the governor-general was of Canadian birth and had served in *la marine*. In principle this *infanterie de marine* was recruited, both as to officers and men, in the mother-country, but actually the number of Canadians in the commissioned and other ranks came to be considerable, and this quota was reinforced by many Frenchmen who enlisted in the corps with the idea of settling in Canada when their term of service should be finished. A good deal of the ill-feeling which existed between the French and the colonial soldiery was due to the fact that the former were inclined to look down upon the Canadians, and to treat them as provincials and *arriérés*—a state of affairs which prevailed to some extent over the frontier between English and Americans.

The army in Canada at this time consisted of some 6,400 soldiers, made up of 4,400 regulars and 2,000 colonials, or *de la marine*. Of the regulars,

1,400 formed the garrison of Louisburg. All these were excellent troops, particularly the newly arrived regular regiments, who came with a brilliant record of continental service. In addition to the above was the militia, composed nominally of all Canadian civilian males fit to bear arms. On paper the militia had a strength somewhere in the neighbourhood of 20,000, but in practice it was found difficult to maintain more than 1,000 in the field at one time unless the occasion was one of extreme urgency, or unless the service was carried out near the militiamen's homes. These troops are described as having been useful in Indian warfare and capable of enduring great hardship, but restless under military discipline. Montcalm clearly realized the faults and virtues of these troops, stating to a correspondent that he proposed to stiffen them with an adequate supply of regulars, and that he did not propose to entertain *la malheureuse confiance de M. de Diskau*. The Canadian militia was clothed and armed by the State, receiving no pay, but issues of rations, etc., in kind. An exception was, however, made in the case of those militiamen engaged on transport duties, to whom a money wage was paid.

On the whole, in effective military force the English were at a disadvantage as compared with the French at the opening of the campaigning season in North America in 1756. To the 6,400 regular and colonial troops of France there were, on the other side, merely the shattered remnants of the 44th and 48th Regiments; the 35th and

42nd newly arrived ; what was left of Shirley's and Pepperell's ; four independent companies from New York, and a recently formed battalion of the Royal Americans. As for the various provincial militias, in the actual number of males available for service Canada could not compare with the American colonies, but the separate identity of the latter was a serious handicap. There was no lack of zeal, but there were jealousies which would not tolerate any central system of organization. Discipline was indifferent ; there was peculation and corruption in the services of transport and supply ; and in camp a neglect of the most ordinary sanitary precautions. Each colony insisted on retaining in its own hands the transport and maintenance of its forces, and each watched its neighbours narrowly lest their burden of labour and war contributions should be below the proper share. In comparison with this system the centralized authority which existed in Canada shone brightly. Its efficacy can, however, be considerably overrated. The French Government neglected Canada just at the moment when assistance was urgently required, and if the administration of the colony itself be carefully examined, the much-vaunted centralization of authority will be seen to exist in name rather than reality. There was intense friction between the governor-general and the commander-in-chief, appalling corruption in the government service, and a sentiment of ill-will between the local and the regular army.

While Shirley was exercising his brief tenure as commander-in-chief he drew up plans for a double operation, one being on Lake Ontario with Fort Frontenac and Niagara as objectives, the other an attack against Crown Point. The Earl of Loudoun, on his arrival in America, considered the scope of such operation as too extended, and decided to concentrate upon an effort against Ticonderoga and Crown Point. For this operation some 7,000 men, nearly all New England troops, were assembled at Fort William Henry and Fort Edward, and, while waiting for Loudoun, were engaged in strengthening the fortifications, clearing the forest, and improving the road over the *portage* between the two places. Fort William Henry was in an indescribably filthy state. Graves, slaughter-houses and latrines were mingled together, and the discipline of the troops was poor. Thousands were carried off by sickness due to lack of sanitary precautions. No fighting took place other than the horrors and atrocities committed by scalping parties from both sides. At Ticonderoga the French had some 6,000 men strongly entrenched, with Montcalm himself in command, and Loudoun, who arrived at Albany in August, although by the end of the summer he had 10,000 men under him, considered that the effort against Ticonderoga was impossible.

A much more experienced soldier than Loudoun, and a far more brilliant commander, Montcalm had seen that, with the deadlock south of Lake Champlain, the hour had come for a rapid counter-

AMERICA — SEVEN YEARS' WAR 249

stroke elsewhere. For the prosecution of the French great scheme of maintaining communication with the Ohio and Mississippi the security of Lake Ontario was vital. But so long as the English were left in possession of Oswego the French command of the lake was never assured ; the forts at Frontenac and Niagara were constantly menaced, and the loss of even one of them would cut the French off from the west. Montcalm had, therefore, determined by a rapid stroke to fall upon Oswego and destroy it, thus depriving the English of a base of operations so full of menace to the French. Already, in July, an attempt had been made to capture a convoy of supplies proceeding up the Mohawk to Oswego, but without success. Now, early in August, Montcalm, leaving Lévis in command at Ticonderoga, started at full speed for Fort Frontenac, arriving there in little over a week. The blow against Oswego was to be no effort of *la petite guerre*, but a regular military operation on European lines, supplemented moreover by a sufficient quota of local assistance. Of the 3,000 men composing the force, 2,600 were furnished by the three line regiments of La Sarre and Guienne, forwarded to Fort Frontenac from Montreal, and that of Béarn brought from Fort Niagara. Montcalm had also a strong force of artillery, including some guns captured from Braddock on the Monongahela, the remainder of the force being made up of Canadian militia and some Indian auxiliaries.

Oswego was at this time in no condition to

resist a determined attack. The forts protecting it were in a poor state, and the garrison, through sickness and neglect, was in a shocking condition. The number available for the defence of the place was apparently about 1,400, but many of these were merely labourers and boatmen, the effective fighting strength of the place consisting of Shirley's and Pepperell's regiments, both much reduced in strength, and about 150 New Jersey militia. During the previous winter the privations of the garrison had been terrible. There was actual starvation, and scurvy and dysentery were rampant. The garrison was then so weak that in Shirley's regiment the strongest guard which could be mounted was but a subaltern and twenty men, and half of them had to parade with sticks to support them. Supplies and recruits—the latter often of very poor quality—had been forwarded to Oswego during the spring and summer, but in spite of these reinforcements the place was scarcely tenable.

During the night of the 4th-5th August Montcalm embarked at Fort Frontenac with the first division of his force, reaching what is now Sackett's Harbour —then called Niaouré Bay—early on the 6th. The second division followed with supplies, hospital, and eighty artillery boats. On the 8th the force had reunited, and on the following day a combined movement by land and water was made against Oswego. When once the French artillery was in action the fate of the place was sealed, for the defences were flimsy, and the English artillery had been posted in expectation of an attack, not from the east, but from the west. Colonel Mercer, the soul of the defence, was killed by a cannon shot, and despair seized the defenders, who till then had fought with resolution and spirit. On August 14th the garrison surrendered practically unconditionally, the number, including soldiers, sailors, labourers and children, being about sixteen hundred. In the forts and vessels were found more than a hundred pieces of artillery with a large quantity of ammunition. The victors, before marching away, burnt the forts and vessels, destroyed all such supplies and stores as they could not carry away with them, and wiped Oswego off the face of the earth. With the destruction of Oswego the regular military operations of 1756 in North America came to an end. There was, however, an outburst of partisan warfare on the western border of the English colonies, in which these suffered severely. New York, New Jersey, Pennsylvania, Maryland, and Virginia were specially affected, and even with a chain of frontier forts and blockhouses the border was incessantly harassed by French and Indians. At Ticonderoga and Fort William Henry the French and English faced each other until November without undertaking any serious operations, for the French were satisfied with having secured their communications with the west, and the English, though outnumbering the French at Ticonderoga, were not in a condition to attack a formidable enemy occupying a strong defensive position. Early in November the French began to move off towards Canada, leaving merely a few companies at Ticonderoga, and similarly, on the other side, the provincials marched for home, and of the regulars, some 400 strong were left to garrison Fort William Henry. Although no major operations had taken place, there had been much fighting between scouting parties. The French had here an advantage in that they had more Indians working for them than had the English. But the latter were splendidly served by rangers, chiefly from New England, of whom Robert Rogers, of New Hampshire, was a heroic figure.

The year 1756 was one of misfortune for England, and Macaulay hardly stated the case too strongly when he said that the war began in every part of the world with events disastrous to England, and even more shameful than disastrous. The most humiliating of these was the loss of Minorca in May, for not only did it involve the cession of a naval base valuable as a constant menace to Toulon, but was a severe blow to the prestige of the British Navy. " *Quae regio in terris nostri non plena doloris ?* " wrote Pitt on the news of Byng's retreat : " I dread to hear from America. Asia may perhaps furnish its portion of ignominy and calamity." He was not to be undeceived. In June, in Asia, we lost Calcutta, captured by Surajah Dowlah, and the conduct of the military authorities in that disaster which led to the horror of the Black Hole deserved, and received, severe comment. In North America the capture and destruction of Oswego was the greatest feat yet achieved by French arms. By their victory the French had recovered the undisputed command of Lake Ontario and secured their communications with the West ; further, the surrender of the place inevitably led to a diminution of English prestige in the eyes of the Indians—an important feature, even though the struggle for North America was more and more becoming an issue to be fought out by regular forces.

In this year 1756, as a result of the defeats experienced, England was in a state of angry and sullen despondency almost unparalleled in her history. Since the days of William III the people had been so led by their rulers to believe that no war could be undertaken without a strong force of mercenaries to back them that they had almost begun to lose confidence in themselves. In the panic of a French invasion most of our ships were kept in home waters, and, to supply the military deficiency of the country, large bodies of Hessian and Hanoverian troops had been brought over to England. In this year appeared Brown's " Estimate "—a book universally read and believed. The author, in the words of Macaulay, " fully convinced his readers that they were a race of cowards and scoundrels ; that nothing could save them ; that they were on the point of being enslaved by their enemies ; and that they richly deserved their fate."

If ever it were true that the hour brought forth the man, the statement can most justly be applied to England in her hour of despair in 1756. Pitt had become inevitable. The Duke of Newcastle, struggling to the last to cling to office, was forced to resign, and on November 15th, 1756, Pitt became Secretary of State on terms which were practically his own. He " came in as a conqueror," and was regarded by his countrymen as the only saviour of England. Of him it has been well said that he loved England as an Athenian loved the City of the Violet Crown, as a Roman loved the City of the Seven Hills. He saw his country insulted and defeated. He saw the national spirit sinking. Yet he knew what the resources of the Empire, vigorously employed, could effect, and he felt that he was the man to employ them vigorously. His policy was to awaken the enthusiasm of Englishmen for England ; to appeal direct to the people on the question of the country's foreign policy ; to teach England that it was on her sons and not upon hireling Hessians and Hanoverians she should rely ; and to make plain to court and King that the one object of the war was not the defence of Hanover, but the defeat of " the most ancient enemy of these kingdoms," and that the war should be waged where her aggressions had been most dangerous—in America. It was with this change of policy in England that the year 1757 was ushered in, a year which was to be one of outstanding importance in the history of North America. The system of

Pitt was introduced, but was soon temporarily suspended owing to the dismissal of the Great Commoner from office as the result of political intrigue at home. France reached the zenith of her success in America, but lost, and for ever, a chance vouchsafed to her. And Wolfe at last was given an opportunity of showing, although in a feeble and futile expedition in Europe, that capacity of generalship which was soon to affect the destiny of the New World.

To make up for the loss of the Hessian and Hanoverian troops who were to be sent home, steps were taken to increase the efficiency of the militia, and estimates were submitted for an increase of the regular forces. In the closing days of 1756 Pitt called a cabinet, at which it was resolved to send "an expedition of weight," not less than 8,000 men and a fleet, to America. The beginning of 1757 was marked by an innovation for which Wolfe has, and perhaps justly, been given sole credit, namely, the raising of Highland regiments from the clans which had been in arms against the reigning dynasty. Two regiments were thus formed, these being in addition to the existing Highland regiment, the 42nd, then in America, which had been raised in 1739, and had done fine service on the British side at Fontenoy.

Such was the energy and activity of Pitt that by the first week in February he was able to forward his ideas about the campaign to Loudoun and the American governors, so that they might know what preliminary preparations to put in hand, and on the 19th he had ready instructions to Admiral Holbourne and General Hopson, commanding the sea and land forces of the expedition. The plan adopted by Pitt was one based upon representations which had come from Loudoun, namely, that the bulk of the available force should be concentrated against Louisburg, for which operation, on the arrival of reinforcements—in April, as Pitt hoped —Loudoun would have 17,000 regular troops in America. By employing the bulk of these against Louisburg, while holding the New York frontier, chiefly with provincials, it was hoped that the fortress could be taken not later than the end of May. In June the St. Lawrence would be ice-free, and the capture of Louisburg was then to be followed up by a dash upon Quebec. Loudoun, however, was not tied down by any hard-and-fast rules, and should he consider that the attack upon Quebec should precede that on Louisburg he was at perfect liberty to alter the programme accordingly. The plan, however, broke down owing in part to weather conditions, but chiefly owing to the elusiveness and cleverness of French naval squadrons from Europe. Seven battalions to reinforce Loudoun had been embarked on March 17th; they had been detained by contrary winds, and did not reach Halifax until July, nearly two months after the date by which it was hoped Louisburg would be taken. Meanwhile Loudoun, at New York, was chafing at the delay,

AMERICA — SEVEN YEARS' WAR 257

and was naturally perturbed by the reflection that the frontier of the colony was denuded of much of its resisting power against the French at Ticonderoga. Week after week passed by without any news of the fleet under Holbourne, or of the transports he was convoying. The British naval force at New York consisted of but one line of battle ship and four cruisers—a squadron wholly insufficient to convoy the troops from New York to Halifax. It was essential, however, that the risk should be taken if the season for action was not allowed to slip away, and although the most unwelcome news came in that a French convoy had been sighted, on June 20th the expedition sailed from New York, and by the end of the month was safely in Halifax. The risk it had run had been very great. Not only had a French convoy reached Louisburg from the West Indies but squadrons from Toulon and Brest had also arrived, so that while Loudoun was making for Halifax with a weak escort, the French admiral in Nova Scotian waters had at his disposal five frigates and eighteen of the line.

It was not until July 9th that Holbourne appeared. The troops were landed, and four frigates were sent to examine Louisburg. At the end of the month news was brought back that there were in the place ten of the line and a garrison of 3,000 men, and it was then decided to proceed with the attack on the fortress. Hardly, however, had the troops begun to embark, when a frigate came flying into Halifax harbour with startling news. A complete list of the French vessels at Louisburg had been obtained from a prize taken off Newfoundland, and the number was seen to be eighteen of the line, of which three were of eighty guns. In these circumstances it was decided to cancel the whole project. The expedition was therefore abandoned, and the bulk of the troops sailed away to New York. Freed from the necessity for escorting Loudoun, Holbourne proceeded to Louisburg in the hope of tempting the French admiral to come out and give battle, but without avail. A terrible storm then forced the British fleet, which suffered severe damage, to bear away for Halifax, and when the gale had blown itself out, the French admiral emerged and brought his fleet safely back to Brest.

A commander like Montcalm was not likely to let slip the opportunity afforded him in the summer of 1757. The bulk of the British troops in North America were, in August, at Halifax. With the capture of Oswego and its destruction, Ontario had become a French lake, and Montcalm was relieved of any immediate anxiety for his communications with the West. The concentration of British troops for the Louisburg venture had left the frontier but weakly guarded. There was thus a fine opportunity for dealing a stunning counterstroke aimed at Albany, and thus threatening New York. Montcalm was particularly desirous of carrying out a formal military operation, chiefly by regular troops, instead of indulging in what he regarded as the profitless futilities of *la petite guerre*. There were, as has been referred to earlier, two military schools of thought in Canada at the time, partisans respectively of these two kinds of warfare, the protagonists being *la marine* and *les " terriens "* respectively. The cleavage had the effect of dividing the commander-in-chief from the governor-general, and the difference extended even to the mother-country, where the Ministry of Marine and the Ministry of War were often at loggerheads on the defence of Canada. The colonial party had succeeded in inducing the governor-general to sanction a *petite guerre* expedition in March against Fort William Henry, to the command of which the governor had appointed his brother, Rigaud de Vaudreuil. The force was some 1,400 strong, of which but 250 were regular troops; there were the same number of colonial troops (*de la marine*), 600 militiamen from Three Rivers, and more than 300 Indians. The expedition was excellently equipped, and the march over the frozen lakes and across deep snow was carried out in a manner worthy of the tradition of Canadian warfare. With this, however, success ended, for the attack on the fort was a complete failure, and nothing whatever was achieved by an expedition which had cost a million francs. The casualties on each side were negligible.

After this feeble termination to an expedition on " colonial " lines, Montcalm set himself to the task of organizing one upon a more European model. Owing, however, to the numerical weakness of the regular element in Canada, he was obliged to employ some militia units, in which he reposed very little confidence. The objective was the same as before—Fort William Henry—and at the end of July Montcalm had a force of over 8,000 men assembled at Ticonderoga for the purpose. In round numbers the regulars and militia each contributed 3,000 men; there were 1,800 Indians, and some 200 artillerymen. With his experience of the conventions of European warfare Montcalm had little liking for his Indian allies. To say the least of it, they were difficult people to work with. Those from the West had no idea of discipline: they would consume a week's rations in two or three days, and then come clamouring for more; they had a perpetual craving for brandy, and when mad with drink, would tear each other with their teeth like wolves; some of them were cannibals, and on one occasion the French officers were unable to interfere when an English prisoner was killed and cooked, while eight or ten other English prisoners were forced to look on while their comrade was being devoured.

On July 30th 2,500 of the French force, under Lévis, started to march to North-West Bay, on the western shore of Lake George, while Montcalm, with 5,000 more, embarked in bateaux on Lake Champlain. On the following day both divisions united near the objective, and Montcalm, convinced of the futility of *petite guerre*, opened

AMERICA—SEVEN YEARS' WAR

trenches and laid siege to the place in due form. Fort William Henry was an irregular bastioned square, formed by embankments of gravel, surmounted by a rampart of heavy logs. The lake protected it on the north, a marsh on the east, and ditches with *chevaux de frise* on the south and west. The garrison—which had been recently reinforced from Fort Edward—consisted of some 2,400 men, of whom the bulk were provincial militia. Besides the militia there were 607 of the 35th Regiment, 122 of the Royal American, 30 Artillerymen, and 95 mounted rangers, the remainder being made up of a few sailors and mechanics. Fourteen miles away, at Fort Edward, was a force which, by the addition of troops summoned hurriedly from New York, and by calling in posts from the Mohawk river, numbered about 4,000. The commandant at Fort Edward did not feel justified in despatching any reinforcements to Fort William Henry, and, indeed, sent word to the officer in command at that place advising him to surrender.

The siege was vigorously conducted, and by July 8th the situation of the garrison was desperate. The French artillery, firing from covered positions, was doing tremendous damage at close range, while of the English guns many had burst and only about half a dozen were fit for service. Smallpox had broken out among the garrison and was spreading rapidly. Terms were offered by the French, which were at first refused, but twenty-four hours later a council of war was held in the fort, at which it was decided to surrender. The garrison was to be escorted to Fort Edward, and to remain on parole until an equal number of French prisoners should be given up, and, in recognition of the gallant defence made, the garrison were allowed to carry away one gun with them. The fort was evacuated at midday on July 9th. On the march to Fort Edward the Indian allies of the French got out of hand and massacred eight of the British, maltreating many more, in spite of the efforts of Montcalm and his officers to check the atrocities. The Canadian militia disgraced themselves by looking on unmoved and, indeed, in some cases, actually taking part in the treacherous slaughter. Montcalm was eager to march forthwith against Fort Edward, the last English fort in that region, but the season was far advanced, and it was essential to allow the militiamen to return to their homes in order to get in the harvest. In these circumstances Montcalm contented himself with the destruction of Fort William Henry. Immense bonfires were lit, and the place was soon reduced to ashes. The year 1757 in North America closed therefore to the advantage of the French. Their navy had frustrated the blow against Louisburg, and their army had laid Fort William Henry in ruins.

These misfortunes unfortunately did not complete England's dismal catalogue for 1757. In Europe there was failure, too. In July the Duke of Cumberland, at the head of Hanoverian troops, had been

AMERICA—SEVEN YEARS' WAR 263

soundly beaten by the French, and was later forced to agree to the humiliating convention of Klosterseven, by which he was forced to evacuate Hanover. Pitt, as a result of political intrigue, had been dismissed from office three months earlier, but the country rose in fury at the prospect of a reversion to the corrupt and feeble administration which had held the reins of government. Pitt was reinstated as Secretary of State again on his own terms. He was eager for the fray and confident of the success of the system which he advocated. " I am sure," he cried, " I can save this country, and that no one else can."

His first venture, after resuming office, was not crowned with success. Indeed, it was an abject failure, and, regarded as a combined naval and military expedition, might be dismissed within a few lines. But the stroke that miscarried deserves something more than passing mention, seeing that Wolfe was employed in the operation, and the knowledge he there gained of how a scheme may be wrecked by want of co-operation between the navy and army, and to what depths of inefficiency feebleness of purpose and lack of moral courage can depress a project, was to stand him in good stead. Pitt's policy had been, and still was, to win America in America, but the season was now too far advanced for the despatch of any force to that continent. At the same time it was essential, seeing that France had devoted most of her energy to the war in Europe, to keep her to that theatre, and not to allow her leisure to arrange for succour to be sent to Canada. Further, Pitt had to put heart into England and to allay the invasion panic, and he had, as well, to keep Frederick of Prussia—who had just been defeated at Kolin—from making peace and thus freeing France from her continental entanglements. All these purposes might be served by using a substantial portion of the home defence force and of the home fleet to strike at some unguarded portion of the French coast. It was known that the exterior commitments of France had depleted any forces that she might have retained for home defence. An intelligence statement had asserted that there were only 10,000 men on the coast from St. Valéry to Bordeaux, while the French fleet was blockaded in Louisburg by Admiral Holbourne. Circumstances, therefore, appeared favourable for a descent on the French coast, and Pitt's conviction was strengthened by a report received from a young Scotch officer, Robert Clark by name, who had travelled in France, that the fortifications of Rochefort were easily assailable, and that the garrison was weak. The chances of success in this quarter seemed enhanced by the hope that the large Huguenot population of that district might prove half-hearted in their measures of defence, and finally Pitt was convinced that the expedition would prove of value, as Rochefort contained an important dockyard, arsenal, and foundry. Pitt's urgent orders for the preparation of the fleet staggered the Admiralty, who, however,

AMERICA — SEVEN YEARS' WAR 265

eventually performed what had first been regarded as impossible. The secret of the destination of the expedition was well kept, the King and one privy councillor alone being cognizant of it. Pitt favoured Conway for command, but the King insisted on the appointment of Sir John Mordaunt, who had shown merit in the past, but who had lost his nerve, and was conscious that he had lost it. He also appears to have been broken down in health. Pitt bowed to the King's will, and Conway went as second in command; the next senior was Cornwallis; the post of quartermaster-general was filled by Wolfe.

The necessity of relating the main points of the struggle between France and England in North America has had the effect of keeping Wolfe in the background. Since October, 1754, when he marched into Exeter with his regiment, he had been continuously on service in England, moving with his regiment from the west to the Kentish coast, when invasion was considered probable. Many letters written by him during this period are extant, but their contents are of no especial importance except where they now and then give a record of his personal opinion on military affairs or national policy. His passion for soldiering —even peace soldiering—is revealed in a letter to his mother of October, 1754, where he says: " I know nothing more entertaining than a collection of well-looking men, uniformly clad, and performing their exercises with grace and order. I should go further; my curiosity would carry me to all parts of the world, to be a spectator at these martial sights, and to see the various produce of different climates, and the regulations of different armies. Fleets and fortifications, too, are objects that would attract me as strongly as architecture, painting and the gentler arts." The reference to "fleets" at a period when the army and navy knew and cared little of the apparatus of each other, shows the "amphibious" strain now developing in Wolfe's mind. A pen picture of himself between the years 1753 and 1755 can be made up from two quotations from his letters, in the first of which he refers to his "meagre, consumptive and decaying figure . . . stripped of my bloom . . . brought to old age and infirmity, and this without any remarkable intemperance"; and in the second he tells his mother: "This is the state of my affairs—I am eight-and-twenty years of age, a lieutenant-colonel of foot, and I cannot say that I am master of fifty pounds." We get, in a letter from Wolfe to his mother, dated November 8th, 1755, an indication of the reputation he had won for himself as a regimental commander: "Dear Madam," he writes, "The officers of the army in general are persons of so little application to business, and have been so ill-educated, that it must not surprise you to hear that a man of common industry is in reputation amongst them. I reckon it a very great misfortune to this country that I, your son, who have, I know, but a very modest capacity and some degree of diligence a little above the ordinary run, should be thought, as I generally am, one of the best officers of my rank in the service." Wolfe, in 1756, ridiculed the possibility of a French invasion as a military undertaking, but it is clear that he had a poor opinion of the *moral* of the country or the capability of its rulers.

We have a very interesting description of Wolfe about this period from the pen of William Fitzmaurice, later Earl of Shelburne, who joined the army in 1757, his father, by the advice of Mr. Fox, placing him in Wolfe's regiment, the 20th. " He was handsome in his person "—this is, however, not borne out by most of the portraits of Wolfe— " thin, tall, well-made, with blue eyes, which marked life rather than penetration. He asked me what allowance my father gave me, and, upon finding it did not exceed £600 a year, he told me I must borrow, and not touch my pay, but give it among distressed officers as occasion required. . . . He was always reading Pope's ' Homer,' ' Marcus Aurelius,' etc. . . . He behaved very nobly, forgave and preferred his enemies, and bore their ingratitude afterwards with great manliness ; he did not regard money ; he was animated and agreeable to a great degree in his conversation ; he criticized himself very freely, and laid bare his failings ; he used to harangue the regiment with good success, and had great arts of popularity. . . . His principal talent was forming of troops. His manners were calculated for it. I was much beholden to him. He made me read not only military books, but philosophy; he gave me liberal notions of every kind; he unprejudiced my mind; he advised me in everything, so particularly as to make me lists of company to ask to supper, which, with other such friendly hints, made me popular in the regiment and gained me friends who never quitted me."

Wolfe did not neglect his books during these years, and the extent of his reading is shown in the formidable list of works he recommends for perusal by a young officer whose brother appealed to Wolfe for advice. Owing to the low state of military knowledge in England, all the works recommended are of foreign origin, including the King of Prussia's Regulations, Folard, Montecucculi, Vauban, La Sieur Renie " for all that concerns artillery," Davila, Giucciardini, and many others. " Of the ancients, Vegetius, Cæsar, Thucydides, Xenophon's 'Life of Cyrus' and 'The Retreat of the Ten Thousand Greeks'—with, of course, Polybius. Besides all these ' There is an abundance of military knowledge to be picked out of the lives of Gustavus Adolphus and Charles XII, King of Sweden, and of Zisca, the Bohemian." These are but extracts from a long list which, although it must have been terrifying for the young officer concerned, is clear proof of the extent of Wolfe's reading. There is, however, little of outstanding interest connected with Wolfe in these years. He was anxious to obtain the colonelcy of a regiment—an appointment the perquisites of which would have made a great difference to his financial advantage, but his youth was against him. There is an artless acknowledgment by him, in one of his letters of this time, of the extent which high birth counted, to the detriment of mere professional qualifications : " I persuade myself they will put no inferior officer (unless a peer) over my head, in which case I cannot complain." But if " a soldier " is so posted, then Wolfe is determined to quit the service the moment peace is declared. The bracketed qualification about the peer tells a good deal of the social condition of England in the middle of the eighteenth century. In 1756 Wolfe's father's old friend, the Duke of Bedford, applied for James Wolfe to go to him in Ireland as quartermaster-general, but this appointment he never took up owing to his selection for duty with the Rochefort expedition, to which we can now return.

On September 8th, 1757, the expedition set sail from Spithead. The fleet consisted of 16 men-of-war, 6 frigates, 6 bomb-ketches, 2 fire-ships, 2 hospital ships, 6 cutters and 42 transports. The transports carried about 9,000 men, there being 10 regiments, a few light horse, numerous artillery, elaborate siege apparatus (but no siege guns), and abundant stores. The destination of this armament was a mystery to those on board until September 14th, when the fleet bore away for the Bay of Biscay. It then became evident that a descent on the French coast was its aim. Wolfe at this time was experiencing all the horrors of being a bad sailor, and he writes: "If I make the same figure ashore, I shall acquire no great reputation by this voyage." About eight o'clock in the evening of the 19th, when the fleet stood off the coast, to the surprise of everybody Sir Edward Hawke signalled to his ships to lie-to at a time when the wind was fair and the night clear; the islands of Ré and Oléron were then some twenty leagues distant. Between the two lay the entrance to the Basque Roads, with Rochelle lying facing the gap, and to the right the mouth of the Charente, guarded by the Island of Aix. Some few miles up the course of the winding river lay Rochefort.

On the 23rd the island of Aix was captured. There is no need to do more than summarize briefly the humiliating operations which followed. The military commander was past his work. Hawke was an able naval commander, but was not at his best during this expedition. The initial success was not followed up. Vacillation reigned supreme, and friction between the naval and military commanders increased. Councils of war were held, whilst the French were obviously strengthening their defences. Wolfe saw that if a blow was to be struck, it must be struck at once. He had no official part in the direction of operations, but his was not the spirit to stand by when something could be done, and only waiting for the man to do it. He induced Sir John Mordaunt, who was an old friend of his, to allow him to make a reconnaissance off the coast on his own account. This being granted, he went and brought back word that he had discovered a point midway between Rochelle and Rochefort where a landing was possible.

The admirals and generals considered the scheme and unanimously adopted it, after the pilots and naval officers had declared that navigation to the landing point was feasible. But once again hesitation supervened. Fort Fouras, lying on the mainland opposite Aix, was the stumbling block. The military said it was too dangerous to attack by land, and Admiral Knowles stated that it was impossible to get close enough (after rather perfunctory soundings had been taken) to shell it effectively. Wolfe's hopes were shattered, as this new obstacle caused the original plan to be condemned by a council of war. After the expedition was over, Wolfe, referring to this time, stated that he was convinced that if a landing had been made, Rochefort would have been taken in twenty-four hours. On the 28th, two days later, after two distinct and new encampments had been seen from the sea, fresh plans were made, by their inception fully proving that Wolfe was right and the council wrong. Orders were given that 1,200 men should be in the ships' boats by midnight. It was intended that this small force should be landed and maintain its positions for some six or seven hours, while the boats were reloading and fetching the second contingent. Even to the private soldiers the folly of the scheme was apparent, but they saw that something was going to be done at last, and were only too ready for action. For four hours they sat in the boats on a cold night with a rough sea and an off-shore wind, and then they were incontinently ordered back into their ships; Wolfe says " to the astonishment and disgust of all." Nothing remained now but to hold another council of war and to blow up the fortifications on the island of Aix. In this performance some of the men were injured. Hawke refused to attend the council, and shortly informed the generals " that if they had no further military operations to propose, considerable enough to authorize him detaining his squadron, he would immediately return with it to England." Nothing being proposed, on October 1st the fleet, with the army on board, sailed from the Basque Roads.

The real interest in the unfortunate Rochefort expedition consists in the impression it made upon Wolfe and in the lessons which he saw were to be drawn from the incident. There are numerous and lengthy references to it in his letters. To his mother he says: " As to the expedition, it has been conducted so ill that I am ashamed to have been of the party. The public could not do better than dismiss six or eight of us from the service. No zeal, no ardour, no concern or care for the good and honour of the country"; and to his uncle, Major Walter Wolfe: " The true state of the case is, that our sea-officers do not care to be engaged in any business of this sort where little is to be had but blows and reputation; and the officers of the infantry are so profoundly ignorant that an enterprise of any vigour astonishes them to that degree that they have not strength of mind nor confidence to carry it through." But it is in another letter to his friend Major Rickson that we can discern more fully how Wolfe had drawn benefit even from participation in failure: "I have found out"—so his criticism began—"that an admiral should endeavour to run into an enemy's port immediately after he appears before it; that he should anchor the transports and frigates as near as he can to the land; that he should reconnoitre and observe it as quickly as possible, and lose no time in getting the troops ashore; that previous directions should be given in respect to landing the troops, and a proper disposition for the boats of all sorts, appointing leaders and fit persons for conducting the different divisions." Then follow these remarkable words: " Nothing is to be reckoned an obstacle to an undertaking of this nature which is not found to be so on trial; that in war something must be allowed to chance and fortune, seeing that it is in its nature hazardous and an option of difficulties; that the greatness of an object should come under consideration as opposed to the impediments that lie in the way; that the honour of one's country is to have some weight, and that in particular circumstances and times the loss of a thousand men is rather an advantage than otherwise, seeing that gallant attempts save its reputation and make it respectable, whereas the contrary appearances sink the credit of a country, ruin the troops, and create infinite uneasiness and discontent at home."

A commission of inquiry, followed by a court-martial on Sir John Mordaunt, were the sequel of the expedition, and Wolfe, who gave evidence at both, was the solitary participant in the affair who emerged with credit, the members of the commission testifying of Wolfe's plan that had it been adopted it " certainly must have been of the greatest utility towards carrying Your Majesty's instructions into execution." At the court-martial Pitt himself appeared, nominally to authenticate his own orders, actually to make an imperious speech. The court, however, deprecated the whole plan of the expedition and honourably acquitted Sir John Mordaunt. The affair, disastrous though it had been, favoured Wolfe, for Pitt, in his mortification over the business, was attracted by the young officer whose plan had been so commended. He marked down Wolfe as a soldier to be selected for the next stroke to be launched. It was not only Pitt who had noted Wolfe. Of him Horace Walpole wrote in his diary : " Wolfe, a young officer who had contracted reputation from his intelligence of discipline, and from the perfection to which he had brought his own regiment. The world could not expect more for him than he thought himself capable of performing. He looked on danger as the favourable moment that would call forth his talents." Walpole gives also an interesting reference to the "amphibious" strain in Wolfe, where he says that Howe—one of the naval captains of the expedition—and Wolfe "contracted a friendship like the union of a cannon and gunpowder."

Pitt spent the closing months of 1757 in organizing the machinery of war for a great blow in North America. The time was favourable, for France had made the fatal mistake of turning aside from the sea and allowing herself to be entangled in a new and extraordinary alliance in a Continental war. In 1756 the French navy had 63 ships of the line, of which 45 were in fair condition, but equipments and artillery were deficient. England, on the other hand, had 130 ships of the line. There was the chance that France—as actually happened—might draw in Spain as an ally, but even so the disparity would not be completely remedied, for Spain could dispose of but 46 vessels of the line, and from the previous and subsequent performances of the Spanish navy it may well be doubted if its worth was equal to its numbers. Losing control of the sea, France was to surrender one by one all her colonies and all her hopes in India, and when later she drew in Spain as her ally, it was but to involve that country in her own external ruin.

The details of the great plan by which Pitt proposed to put the future of North America to the test are revealed in the letters written by him at Whitehall on December 30th, 1757. The first was a letter recalling the Earl of Loudoun and directing him to hand over all orders, instructions and similar documents to General Abercromby, who was to relieve him as commander-in-chief in North America, a second letter in corresponding terms being despatched to Abercromby. The recall of Loudoun was a paramount necessity if the enthusiasm of England for the struggle in North America was to be aroused; for his failure during the year to proceed with the attack on Louisburg had come as a fresh humiliation to the country, whose resentment over Byng's failure to relieve Minorca had not been fully appeased by the judicial murder of that unfortunate admiral. To-day capable naval historians are inclined to the belief that Loudoun was, in the circumstances in which he found himself, justified in abandoning the attempt against Louisburg, but the people in England at the close of 1757 were not in a position to form so accurate a judgment. In any case, Loudoun had shown in America a great want of tact, and his withdrawal would not be regretted there. Since his arrival he had been out of touch with the colonists, and even on terms of open disagreement. He had been involved in a dispute with the colonial authorities as regards the quartering of his troops in New York, Boston and elsewhere, and although his demands were not unreasonable in themselves, they had been peremptorily made and enforced by threats.

The third letter was a circular one to all the governors in North America, informing them of the change in the high command, and directing them to obey the new commander-in-chief, and that "you will, from Time to Time, give Mr. Abercromby all the Assistance and Lights in your Power, in all Matters relative to the command, with which the King has honoured Him." The governors were also strictly to comply with all orders of the commander-in-chief as to an embargo on ships and to assist the naval commander-in-chief in all his requests for seamen and artificers, for the letter informed the governors of "The King having resolved to send a Considerable Squadron of Ships of War the ensuing Year to North America."

This circular letter was accompanied and supplemented by two others, giving further details to the northern and southern colonies respectively, and each opening with the statement that "His Majesty having nothing more at Heart, than to repair the Losses and Disappointments, of the last inactive, and unhappy Campaign ; and by the most vigorous and extensive Efforts, to avert, by the Blessing of God on His Arms, the Dangers impending in North America." Of these two letters one was to the governors of Massachusetts, New Hampshire, Connecticut, Rhode Island, New York and New Jersey ; those colonies were asked to raise each as many men as possible, so as to provide a total of not less than 20,000, who were to be ready to assemble at Albany in time to participate in an "Irruption into Canada," in conjunction with British forces, all under the commander-in-chief, beginning on May 1st, 1758. The objectives of the "irruption" were to be Montreal, or Quebec, or both places successively, these directions, however, to be subject to such alteration as the commander-in-chief might see fit to make. The King would supply arms, ammunition and tents, and would be at the charge of the necessary artillery, provisions, and boats and vessels. All that the colonies were, therefore, asked to do was to raise, clothe and pay the men called for, and the King promised to recommend Parliament in its next session to award compensation for such outlay.

The second of this brace of letters was addressed to the governors of Pennsylvania, Maryland, Virginia, South Carolina and North Carolina. In preamble it was identical, and in contents similar, to the letters to the governors of the northern colonies summarized above. Each of the southern colonies was asked to raise as many men as possible —although no definite total was mentioned, " several thousand " taking the place of the 20,000 indicated for the northern colonies. The southern contingents were to be ready to assemble at such place as might be indicated by Brigadier-General Forbes, so as to be ready to begin by May 1st " such offensive Operations, as shall be judged by the same Commander of His Majesty's Forces in those parts most expedient for annoying the Enemy, and most efficacious towards removing and repelling the Dangers that threaten the Frontiers of any of the Southern Colonies on the Continent of America." There was in this letter the same indication of the limitation of the duty of the southern colonies to levying, clothing and pay, and the same hint about a grant of compensation for outlay incurred. An important concession in both letters was the royal sanction that the system by which regular officers outranked all provincials was to cease, and that the latter would, up to the rank of colonel inclusive, enjoy precedence according to the date of their provincial commissions.

The lengthy letter of instructions sent by the same packet to Abercromby—supplementary to the one notifying him of his succession to Loudoun's post—is a remarkable one. While treating Abercromby with all the formality due to a commander-in-chief, the letter leaves him in no doubt that the plan of campaign has been elaborated at Whitehall, and it is with the carrying out of such plan, and not the formulating of any of his own, that Abercromby is directly charged. The duty of the commander-in-chief is personally to take command of the "irruption" (in this letter called "invasion") into Canada by way of Crown Point; he is to appoint Forbes to take command of the expedition mentioned in the letter to the governors of the southern colonies. The primary duty of Abercromby was, however, to see that all the siege material got ready for the operations against Louisburg last year was to be kept intact for a renewed operation against that fortress. For this purpose, including reinforcements to be sent from England, 14,000 men are to be concentrated; the operation was to begin by April 20th, under the command of an officer to be detailed by the King. It was made definitely clear to Abercromby that, even though he was commander-in-chief, he was not to interfere with the Whitehall-made plan of campaign by making any reduction in the forces to be employed against Louisburg. The very names of the regiments which he was to detail, from the forces in North America, were given. Abercromby was permitted to make alterations only in case of some extraordinary inconvenience which might be found to arise from an exact compliance with the order; but in such case the alteration was not to involve any reduction in the numbers against Louisburg. The instructions were emphatic on this point. Included also in the letter were such comparative minutiæ as the selection of the officer to be left at Fort Edward, Albany, or New York, to "have care of the Frontiers," while Abercromby should be invading Canada, and also instructions regarding the formation of a company of eighty carpenters to be raised for service at Louisburg under a Mr. Meserve, a shipbuilder of great ability and energy.

This important batch of correspondence closes with a letter addressed personally to De Lancey, the lieutenant-governor of New York, directing him to provide and cause to be built with all possible despatch boats sufficient to carry towards Canada by the Lake Champlain route at least 20,000 men, and, further, to construct one or more armed vessels for the convoying of the flotilla. The boats and armed vessels were to be constructed on Lake George, but should the military situation prevent this, then all the material was to be collected at a suitable place ready for conveyance to Lake George with the least possible delay. By this letter Abercromby—who, in the letter addressed to him, had been informed of the arrangement—was relieved of all negotiations essential for the provision of water transport for the invasion by way of Crown Point.

These remarkable letters, all of them signed by Pitt, are worth attention for three reasons. In the first place it is now clear that the question is no longer one merely of checking French trespass upon English territory; the conquest of Canada is clearly indicated. Secondly, the mother country practically takes upon herself all the expense to be incurred in this vast operation. And in the third place the home government lays down the plan of campaign to be adopted, and makes provision for details inseparable from the carrying out of such campaign. So much stress has been laid by historians upon the advantages which centralization of authority had, in the past, conferred upon Canada—when compared with the jarring elements of the English colonies—that it is well to remember that the centralization which was now—and in 1759—to govern the operations of the English, was much more marked than any previously exerted by France over Canada. Centralization had very obvious drawbacks; but when directed by a statesman of genius, like Pitt, and when carried out by seamen of the calibre of Boscawen, Saunders and Hawke, and when the military element included soldiers like Amherst and Wolfe, the benefits of centralization of effort and oneness of purpose would override all the inherent drawbacks.

Louisburg was to be the first operation of the campaign, and Pitt was determined that the humiliation of Rochefort should not be repeated. New and better men were to be placed in command. Admiral Boscawen was to command the fleet. The choice of Abercromby to succeed Loudoun was not altogether to Pitt's liking, for the new commander-in-chief was old, and had shown no signs of great capacity, but the King would not appoint young officers to high command. To neutralize the mediocrity of Abercromby, Pitt tied him down by precise instructions and sent young Lord Howe, elder brother of the commodore, and "the best officer in the army"—as Wolfe called him—as one of his brigadiers. For the paramount task of taking Louisburg the choice fell upon Colonel Jeffery Amherst, then commissary of the Hessian troops in the pay of England. Amherst had seen a good deal of service on the Continent; he was now forty-one—much too young, in the King's eyes, for high command, and Pitt secured his appointment only by threatening to abandon the Louisburg expedition unless he had his way. Three new brigadiers were appointed to serve under Amherst: Lawrence, Whitmore, and James Wolfe.

Contrary winds delayed the start of the expedition.

Wolfe chafed a good deal at the delay, and found little to give him satisfaction at Portsmouth— "an infernal den," where "the condition of the garrison (or rather vagabonds that stroll about in dirty red clothes from one gin-shop to another) exceeds all belief. There is not the least shadow of discipline, care or attention. Disorderly soldiers of different regiments are collected here; some from the ships, others from the hospital, some waiting to embark—dirty, drunken, insolent rascals, improved by the hellish nature of the place, where every kind of corruption, immorality and looseness is carried to excess; it is a sink of the lowest and most abominable of vices." And, in another letter, he declares that "the necessity of living in the midst of the diabolical citizens of Portsmouth is a real and unavoidable calamity. It is a doubt to me if there is such another collection of demons upon the whole earth."

On February 19th Boscawen sailed with twenty-three ships of the line and several smaller vessels, with his convoy of transports. There was to be no question this time of finding Louisburg guarded by a strong French squadron: Pitt had seen to it that the French navy was bottled up either in the Mediterranean or at Brest. It had been Pitt's hope that the siege of Louisburg should begin by April 20th, but the elements were against him. "From Christopher Columbus' time to our days," wrote Wolfe to his old colonel, Lord George Sackville, "there perhaps has never been a more extraordinary voyage. The continual opposition of contrary winds, calms, or current baffled all our skill and wore out all our patience." Boscawen's flagship did not arrive until May 9th, and Amherst, who had not started till March 16th, had a voyage almost as long. Wolfe, who was always a voluminous correspondent, profited by the delay at Halifax to write several letters home, including two to Lord George Sackville. In one of these are some interesting remarks on the military situation. Wolfe considered that the two most important points in America were Halifax and Oswego— "one of which we have already lost, and the other we must lose in twelve hours, whenever it is attacked." Wolfe clearly recognized the necessity for regaining Oswego, and of obtaining command of Lake Ontario by a squadron of armed vessels on its waters. He waxes indignant over the service of supply, especially at the perpetual issue of salt meat ; even for the sick and wounded there was " not an ounce of fresh beef or mutton contracted for, which, besides the inhumanity, is both impolitic and absurd." Already some regiments had between three and four hundred cases of scurvy. Wolfe thought that a free issue of meat was against the interests of discipline, as leaving the men—who, he thought, were also grossly over-remunerated on paid fatigues—too much to spend. " Too much money and too much rum affect the discipline of an army. We have glaring evidence of their ill-consequence every moment. Sergeants drunk upon duty, two sentries on their posts, and the rest wallowing in the dirt."

On May 28th the expedition, 157 sail in all, with nearly 12,000 troops, all of which were British except 500 colonial rangers, left Halifax, entering Gabarus Bay immediately west of Louisburg on June 2nd. The weather was so unfavourable, and the surf ran so high, that for five days no landing was possible. On the 8th the violence of the surf had somewhat abated, and it was decided to land the troops, there being three feint landings, with the real attack to be carried out by Wolfe's brigade at Freshwater Cove—the furthest landing spot from the fortress. Shortly after daybreak the boats pushed off, Wolfe's party consisting of five companies of grenadiers, 550 marksmen drawn from different regiments and known as the Light Infantry, some of the American Rangers, with Fraser's Highlanders, and eight more companies of grenadiers in support. The landing, although covered by the guns of the fleet, was an extremely difficult operation. So soon as the boats came within range the enemy opened a very heavy fire of grape and musketry, and the surf still beat so strong upon the shore that a place could hardly be found where the troops could be landed with safety. Wolfe actually gave the signal to withdraw, but his order was misunderstood, or ignored by three subalterns in charge of boats filled with men of the Light Infantry. These pushed on, followed by the others, and a landing was made. Some of the grenadiers were the first to get ashore, then the Light Infantry, Rangers and Highlanders. Some loss was here incurred, for many boats upset; several were broken to pieces, and in some cases men were actually crushed to death by the boats being driven over them on the return of the raging surf. Wolfe, who was armed only with a cane, leaped into the surf and scrambled over the crags with the foremost. A French battery was quickly carried at the point of the bayonet. By noon the whole of the attacking force was ashore, and the French, abandoning over a score of guns, fled into the woods in rear of their entrenchments, the British following them up until they were checked by the fire of the guns from Louisburg itself.

The weather continued to be so unfavourable that for the moment any attempt to land stores was out of the question, and it was not until the 10th that some of the tents, baggage and provisions were set on shore. More than a week passed away before all the artillery was landed, and on occasions it was necessary to raft the guns on catamarans, the surf being too heavy for boats. Until the stores and guns were ashore the attackers were in a perilous position, and had a well-directed sortie been made they might have had difficulty in holding their ground. The French, however, were more concerned in making the fortress capable of resisting attack.

The security of Louisburg depended less on its fortifications than upon the rocky, surf-beaten shore on which it looked, and upon the supposed difficulty of effecting a landing under a heavy fire from the batteries on shore. Now that the attacking force, with the siege material, had been landed, the ultimate surrender of the place was almost inevitable. The total strength of the defenders may be set at about 3,800 men, in which were included three regular regiments, excellent troops, a regiment of *Volontaires Etrangers*, two companies of artillery, and twenty-four companies of colonial infantry. The male inhabitants were also organized into companies. In the harbour were five ships of the line and seven frigates carrying 544 guns and manned by 3,000 men. On the ramparts of the fortress itself and its outworks were over 200 guns and mortars. The strongest front of the fortress was on the land or western front, which was furnished with several bastions. At both extremities of the line there was high ground favourable for the works of a besieging force, and it was towards the northern extremity, from a hillock at the edge of a large marsh, that Amherst resolved to push his first attack.

Louisburg held out for fifty-two days—a creditable record, seeing that the mother country could not get out a fleet to challenge the blockading squadron, and that Montcalm could stage no diversion, confronted as he was by the peril of the "irruption into Canada" by way of Crown Point. The chief hopes of the defenders were based on the chance of a tempest which might shatter Boscawen's fleet; of disagreement between the naval and military commanders ; or of an outbreak of sickness amongst the besiegers. But none of these things happened. The weather, in spite of some hard gales, was generally kind. There was harmonious co-operation between the sailors and soldiers. On the whole, except for an outbreak of smallpox amongst the provincial troops, the health of the attackers was satisfactory. The siege wore to an end without many dramatic occurrences. The French sank some of their ships to block the harbour ; three of those left afloat were set on fire by the shells of the attackers ; one French vessel escaped to France. A small attack was made upon the rear of the besiegers by some Canadian militia and Indians, but was easily repulsed ; there was nothing, and could be nothing, in the nature of a Balaclava or an Inkerman. There were no great sorties ; there was no assault ; the navy had little scope for action other than a brilliant operation towards the end of the siege, when 600 sailors rowed silently into the harbour and captured the two last survivors of the French line of battleships.

Wolfe landed at Louisburg, sharing with Howe the reputation of being the best soldier of his years in the army, and such reputation he enhanced by his conduct during the siege. His work there may be divided into three periods. The first, that of making the initial landing, has already been described. On June 12th he was sent with a detachment of 1,200 men and artillery, by the north end of the harbour, to Lighthouse Point, which had been abandoned by the French, to fire upon the Island Battery and upon the ships in the harbour. The battery was soon silenced, with the help of the guns of the fleet, and the French men-of-war were driven under the guns of the fortress. Recalled to the land front, Wolfe broke ground in the regular siege operations, and, despite a fierce sortie made by a party from the garrison, pushed his works steadily against it. There is extant in a journal kept by one of the besiegers a reference to Wolfe's conduct during an engagement with a party of some 200 of the garrison, who came out at night to collect wood. " General Wolfe was in this skirmish, and, as usual, in the most danger." On the 16th Wolfe made a rush forward and fortified a small elevation some 300 yards from one of the bastions, drove out the French, and held the newly gained position in spite of a very heavy fire. Everything that lion-hearted courage, unflagging energy, unremitting toil, combined with a knowledge of the theory and practice of war, could do to help on the operations was done by Wolfe. His favourite Light Infantry had been highly trained by him, and during the sorties by the enemy these would instantly retire behind some sand dunes for shelter. One of Wolfe's officers remarked to him one day that these tactics reminded him of Xenophon's description of the tactics of the *carduchoi*. " I had it from Xenophon," replied Wolfe, " but our friends here are astonished at what I have done, for they have read nothing."

As July wore on, the condition of the fortress became more and more desperate. The batteries of the besiegers had done terrible execution, and the masonry of the fortress had suffered from the concussion of the guns of the besieged. By the 26th a practicable breach had been made, and on that day the governor, Drucour, made overtures for capitulation. Amherst replied that the garrison must surrender as prisoners of war, and within an hour Drucour sent back a letter of defiance, but, moved by the entreaties of the civil authorities, he sent a second emissary to overtake the first, accepting Amherst's terms. The victors entered the fortress next day. Eleven stand of colours were taken. The number of prisoners who surrendered was 5,637. Over 220 cannon, 18 mortars, 15,000 stand of arms, 14,000 shot, 5,000 barrels of powder, and a considerable quantity of supplies formed part of the booty. Thus fell the Gibraltar of North America, to be razed to the ground within a few years, whose site is marked by grassy mounds and heaving rows of turf similar to those which, in England of to-day, recall the forts and barracks of the Roman legions.

The very day on which the victors entered the captured fortress there flew round a rumour of a set-back to the column acting under the commander-in-chief. The report was true. At the beginning of July, thanks largely to the elaborate preparations arranged by Pitt, Abercromby was ready to embark his 9,000 provincials and 6,000 regulars in 1,200 boats upon Lake George. The sight was an impressive one as in perfect weather the flotilla moved in orderly formation along the glassy surface of the lake with bands playing and colours flying. At daybreak on July 6th the force disembarked at the narrow channel leading into Lake Champlain by the headland of Ticonderoga. The plan of the attackers was to move overland along the western bank of the channel, and to fall upon the French fort at Ticonderoga from the rear. The route lay through thick virgin forest, in which the guides lost their way, and, during the confusion which ensued, collison took place with a French advanced force which had also lost its bearings. A sharp skirmish resulted, in which Lord Howe was killed. He was an officer of immense ability and remarkable personality, and by his death " the soul of General Abercromby's army seemed to expire." Next day Abercromby fell back to his landing-place.

Montcalm had arrived at Ticonderoga on June 30th, and was able to dispose of but 4,000 men to the 15,000 of his opponent. He was therefore compelled to act upon the defensive, and within a week he had formed outside Fort Carillon, on the land side, a huge breastwork, protected by an abatis of forest trees. On July 8th Abercromby —who had brought his force meanwhile to within two miles of Ticonderoga—sent his engineers to reconnoitre the French position, and, misled by an inaccurate report sent in, resolved to attempt to rush the enemy's entrenchment with infantry alone, his guns being left at the place where they had been landed. The assault on the French work, which lasted the long summer day, was nothing but a carnage, without superior direction—for Abercromby never came near the fight—and redeemed only by the superb gallantry of the attackers. Time after time the British and Americans hurled themselves desperately against the French stronghold, only to be spitted on the protruding spikes or shot down at point-blank range. Four attacks were made in this five hours; in the fifth venture some men actually hewed their way right up to the breastwork, and the fate of the day hung in the balance, but swung towards the French. At six o'clock a supreme effort was made, but to no purpose. Abercromby then drew off his exhausted troops and hurriedly re-embarked them, moving back to the head of Lake George, where he remained inactive for the remainder of the season. The casualties suffered were about 2,000, by far the greater part being incurred by the regular battalions, among whom the 42nd Highlanders had lost 500 officers and men. The failure of Abercromby's attempt put the combined movement on Quebec out of the question until the following campaigning season. But the defeat had something on the credit side. The provincials had been shown the mettle of which the British army was composed. The reputation which had been lost on the Monongahela was more than regained at Lake Champlain. Of the regiments which covered themselves with glory at Ticonderoga one had endured the mortification of precipitate retreat in Braddock's ill-fated enterprise.

Unfortunate though the set-back to Abercromby's column had been, it was in part redeemed by a subsidiary operation carried out by a detachment from it. Colonel Bradstreet, one of the ablest of the provincial officers, begged to be allowed to lead a force against Fort Frontenac. Permission was given, and, moving up to Mohawk river and then down the Onandaga, Bradstreet, whose force of 3,000 consisted entirely of provincial militia except for 200 regulars, 300 boatmen, and a few Indians, safely reached the site of Oswego, where he launched out on the lake on August 22nd. By an extraordinary negligence on the part of the French their gunboats were not cruising on the lake, and the necessity of having the maximum of force at Ticonderoga had reduced the garrison at Fort Frontenac to a mere handful of men. Little resistance was made, and Bradstreet gained almost a bloodless victory, the place surrendering on August 27th. The fort was dismantled, and the entire naval force of the French upon Lake Ontario, consisting of nine vessels, mounting between them over a hundred guns, fell into the hands of the victors. Sixty pieces of artillery were carried away besides an immense amount of stores and supplies. Command of Lake Ontario was thus lost to the French, and communication with the west, if not actually severed, was rendered extremely insecure.

Success, too, attended the task set to Forbes of defending the frontiers of the southern states. His idea of defence was to attack the French post at Fort Duquesne, which had already been the cause of two battles. Starting from Philadelphia at the beginning of July—after a long delay, due to the slowness in getting the provincial contingents together—Forbes advanced with 1,500 regulars and 4,500 Americans, choosing the Pennsylvania route as shorter and less open to attack. He was ill when he started, and during most of the march had to be borne in a litter. Through an almost unknown country the force had to climb ranges of mountains and hew a path through dense forests, carrying with them quantities of supplies for posts which were to be established on the line of communications. When towards the end of the long march, a reconnoitring detachment, 800 strong, was cut up by the French; but such success could avail the French little, for the loss of Fort Frontenac had decided the fate of Fort Duquesne, and when Forbes with his main body came up on November 26th, the garrison had moved down the Ohio towards the Mississippi. Leaving a detachment to hold the work, to which he gave the new name of Fort Pitt, Forbes fell back to Philadelphia. The campaign of 1758 had, therefore, on the whole, been very successful for England. The capture of Louisburg unlocked the St. Lawrence, and the fall of Forts Frontenac and Duquesne had not only cut France off from the west, but had rudely shaken

AMERICA—SEVEN YEARS' WAR 295

the faith of the Indians in her prowess. So much so that at a great council held in the autumn several leading tribes decided to join the Iroquois in making treaties of neutrality with the English.

To return now to Louisburg : after the surrender of the fortress Wolfe was soon busy with his pen, giving his parents, his uncle, Major Walter Wolfe, and Lord George Sackville brief accounts of the siege, and his views and criticisms thereon. He considered, curiously enough, that the attempt to land was rash and ill-advised, and that it was only " by the greatest of good fortune imaginable that we succeeded." On the other hand, he felt that, with a better knowledge of the terrain, the attackers could have acted with more vigour and have cut off half the garrison. The actual conduct of the siege he thought erred on the side of prudence : " our measures have been cautious and slow from the beginning to the end, except in landing, where there was an appearance of temerity." He comments on the " great harmony, industry and union " which marked the relationship between Boscawen and Amherst—a state of affairs which must have seemed to Wolfe in striking contrast to the half-hearted co-operation at Rochefort. Wolfe was extremely disappointed that the fall of Louisburg was not followed by an immediate attempt by sea against Quebec—a project which Boscawen, in view of the lateness of the season, did not consider feasible ; failing that, Wolfe was amazed that reinforcements should not be sent immediately to Abercromby. That Wolfe felt very strongly on this point is clear from a note he sent on the matter to Amherst, in which he says: "This d——d French garrison take up our time and attention, which might be better bestowed upon the interesting affairs of the continent (*i.e.*, of America). The transports are ready, and a small convoy would carry a brigade to Boston or New York . . . I beg pardon for this freedom, but I cannot look coolly upon the bloody inroads of those hell-hounds the Canadians, and if nothing further is to be done, I must desire leave to quit the army."

Wolfe seems to have been unfortunate in his first experience of American soldiers, and the rangers who took part in the siege must have been of a class different from those provincials who covered the disaster to Braddock, from those who marched to victory under Bradstreet and Forbes, and from those who were still rendering splendid service under Rogers and Putnam. Of those at Louisburg Wolfe wrote: " The Americans are, in general, the dirtiest and most contemptible cowardly dogs that you can conceive. There is no depending on them in action. They fall down dead in their own dirt and desert by battalions, officers and all. Such rascals as those are rather an encumbrance than any real strength to an army." It will be remembered that Wolfe had, but three years earlier, described the infantry of his own country in terms hardly less scathing. More pleasant is it to turn to his prophecy of the future of America: " These

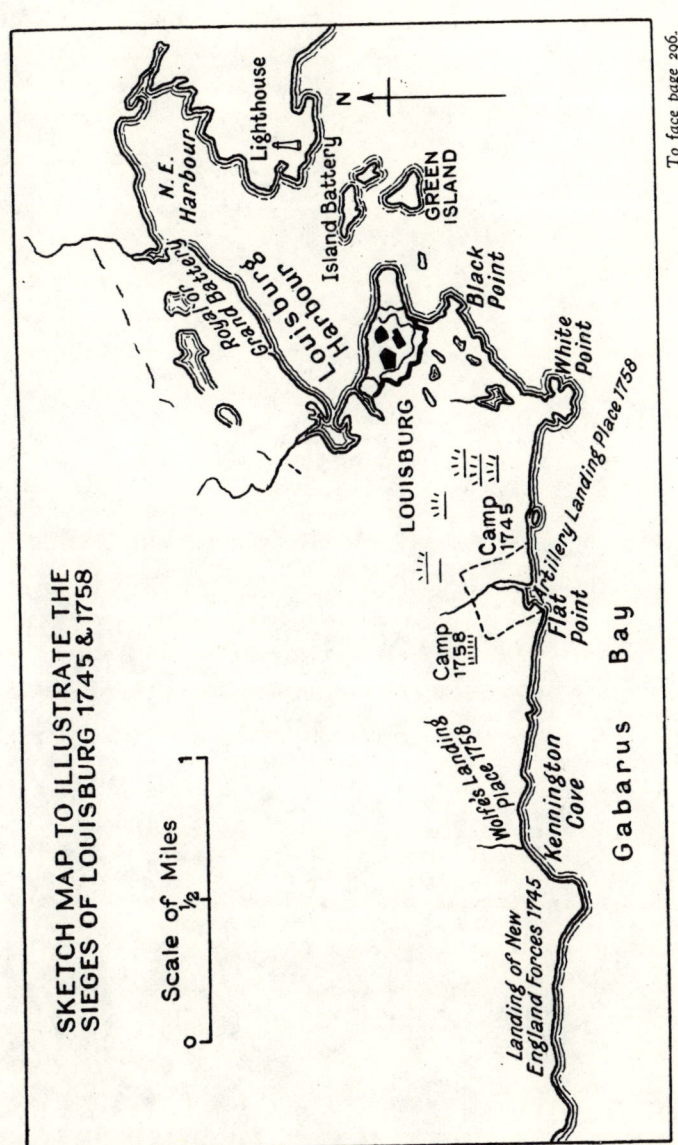

colonies are deeply tinged with the vices and bad qualities of the mother-country; and indeed many parts of it are peopled with those that the law or necessity has forced upon it. Notwithstanding these disadvantages, and notwithstanding the treachery of their neighbours the French, and the cruelty of their neighbours the Indians, worked up to the highest pitch by the former, this will, some time hence, be a vast empire, the seat and power of learning. Nature has refused them nothing, and there will grow a people out of our little spot England, that will fill this vast space and divide this great portion of the globe with the Spaniards, who are possessed of the other half."

From these criticisms and reveries Wolfe was summoned to active duty. Leaving four battalions to garrison Louisburg, Amherst sent three expeditions to complete the subjugation of Prince Edward's Island, the Bay of Fundy, and the Gulf of St. Lawrence, the last mission falling to Wolfe with a force of three regiments, carried in seven ships of the line and three frigates. The work was distasteful: "We have done a great deal of mischief, spread the terror of His Majesty's army through the whole Gulf; but have added nothing to the reputation of them," wrote Wolfe in his report. The duty done, Wolfe proceeded to England on sick leave, unaware that it was Chatham's intention that he should remain in North America to carry out a great stroke for the mastery of Canada.

CHAPTER SIX

THE CAPTURE OF QUEBEC AND THE DEATH OF WOLFE.

THE news of the fall of Louisburg was brought home by Captain William Amherst, brother of the general in command. At 1 a.m. on the night of August 17-18 he was taken into the presence of Pitt, who embraced him, saying : " This is the greatest news. You are the most welcome messenger that has arrived in this kingdom for years." Amherst next went to Ligonier, the Commander-in-Chief, and "gave him great joy," and was then hurried to Kensington, where he kissed hands. Pitt declared " General A. will make nothing of Quebec after this," and said many handsome things of him. The Duke of Newcastle, the nominal head of the government, was next visited. His Grace " in great joy, kept repeating that he had sent orders for two corporations to be made drunk."

The great news about Louisburg came as a climax to a succession of heartening reports which did much to sweep away the bitter memories of the preceding years, when the loss of Minorca, the disaster to Braddock, the Black Hole of Calcutta, the humiliating surrender of the Duke of Cumberland, and the failures at Rochefort and Louisburg in 1757 had caused profound depression in England.

Now Senegal, then Crevelt, the destruction of a nest of privateers at St. Malo, the sack of Cherbourg, victories at sea won by Osborne and Hawke, and a great victory won on land by Frederick the Great, were happily rounded off by the capture of the French " Gibraltar of the West." All England went wild with delight. The colours taken from the French were, by His Majesty's command, carried in procession, with kettle drums and trumpets sounding, from Kensington Palace to St. Paul's Cathedral, and there deposited amid a salute of cannon and other public demonstrations of triumph. Nor were such rejoicings confined to London. In towns and villages all over the country bonfires were lighted, and addresses of congratulation were forwarded to the King. In America the joy was as deeply felt and as vigorously expressed. Governor Lawrence, in Halifax, celebrated the great victory by fêtes attended by the heroes of the siege, and it is said that 60,000 gallons of rum were drunk in honour of the occasion. At Boston the celebrations took the form of an immense bonfire and of services of thanksgiving. New York and Philadelphia were not behind, and in Abercromby's army the chaplains gave praise for the blow inflicted on the servants of the Scarlet Woman.

Late in November Parliament reassembled, and the Commons were practically unanimous in allowing a free hand to Pitt, although the minister himself was frankly startled when brought face to face with the estimates. Pitt had, however, found an unexpected ally in the King, who had suddenly become as eager for conquests in America as he had previously been indifferent, and had remarked to Newcastle: "We must keep Cape Breton, take Canada, and drive the French out of America." The American campaign was to be on even more extended lines: both in the south and the north the offensive was to be undertaken. As for the former, Pitt wrote on October 16th, 1758, to the governors of Barbados and the Leeward Islands to give every assistance to General Hopson in connection with an attack to be made on the French island of Martinique. As regards the prosecution of the campaign during the coming year on the American continent, Pitt had already been busy, and was planning a triple operation on the lines of 1758, with the exception that Quebec was to take the place of Louisburg as an objective. Following the precedent of twelve months earlier, a change was made in the higher command, for on September 18th, 1758, Pitt wrote, recalling Abercromby, and directing him to hand over all orders and other documents to Amherst, who was now appointed commander-in-chief. The next important step was to communicate with the colonial governors in North America, acquainting them with the fact that it was the intention of the home government to resume operations vigorously against the French in 1759. Once more the northern colonies were asked to raise—between them—20,000 men to co-operate with the King's forces; once

THE QUEBEC CAMPAIGN, 1759

more the colonies from Pennsylvania inclusive to the south were asked for "several thousands" for the same purpose; once more it was shown how that all that was expected from the colonies was that they should levy, clothe, and pay their men, but again—as twelve months earlier—the King promised strongly to recommend to Parliament to make a grant in compensation for the expenses incurred.

The plan of campaign was, as before, drawn up in Whitehall, and was communicated to the new commander-in-chief in a letter from Pitt under date of December 29th, 1758. As in the previous year, three lines of attack were laid down, and just as had been the case in the instructions issued to Abercromby, so now Amherst was told practically in so many words that his duty was to carry out a plan laid down for him, and on no account to tamper with it except in minor details. He was told that a direct attack would be made by water from Louisburg on Quebec. This attack would be under Wolfe, with the local rank of major-general. No troops would be sent from England for the purpose, but Amherst was to make over ten battalions to Wolfe, and was also to see that the necessary artillery, stores and local shipping were got together at Louisburg, whence, it was hoped, that the expedition would sail for Quebec early in May. Amherst himself was to invade Canada by way of Ticonderoga and Crown Point, and then to attack Montreal or Quebec, " or both of the said places successively," so as either to join Wolfe at Quebec, or, at any rate, to create a diversion in his favour. At the same time Amherst was, if possible, to establish the important port of Oswego, on Lake Ontario—and it was hoped that any operations on Lake Ontario might be pushed as far as Fort Niagara—while the force under Forbes was to be employed in such offensive operations as might seem to Amherst most efficacious "towards removing all future Dangers from the Frontiers of any of the Southern Colonies of the Continent of America." As a result, possibly of conversation with Wolfe on the question of rations, Pitt laid stress on the importance of supplying the troops in America with fresh meat. The batch of correspondence of this date, December 29th, 1758, closes with a very important letter to Admiral Durell on the North American station, informing him of the projected attack upon Quebec, and directing him, immediately the navigation of the Gulf and of the River St. Lawrence should be practicable, to proceed up the river as far as the Isle de Bic, and to stop all French reinforcements or supplies passing up to Quebec. Durell was to remain in that position until receipt of further orders from Admiral Saunders, the newly appointed naval commander-in-chief in North American waters.

These instructions were supplemented by others in January and February, 1759, by which Forbes was to restore Fort Duquesne (as Pitt still called the work to which his name had been given) or, if that were not possible, to erect another fort on the site, so as to bring the Ohio into His Majesty's possession, and also to push on to Presqu'ile, or even to Cayahoga—the present Erie and Cleveland. And, further, Pitt looked ahead to the autumn, when the St. Lawrence should be closed by ice, directing that Saunders and Amherst should put their heads together and have ready betimes a scheme by which a combined naval and military expedition might, if the idea were found practicable, make a descent on the French posts in the far south, on the Mobile and Mississippi Rivers. Pitt also, in a letter to Amherst of date January 13th, 1759, showed his anxiety for the health of the troops, in instructing the commander-in-chief to obtain molasses to make spruce beer (a reputed specific against scurvy) and rum in sufficient quantities to serve the troops for six months.

Although the highly centralized system of conducting operations in America, directed from London, had produced results in 1758 which were an enormous advance upon the dismal record of the preceding year, it must be admitted that the plan for 1759 was not without serious danger. Any real co-ordination between the three major operations of which the campaign was to be composed was out of the question, and the plan, in this respect, was a more dangerous and complicated one even than that of the year before, seeing that it would be obviously more difficult for Amherst, working up from Ticonderoga, to keep in communication with Wolfe at Quebec than it had been for Abercromby, in the former position, to communicate with Amherst at Louisburg. And in the prosecution of the 1759 campaign it was hardly likely—given the practical impossibility of intercommunication—that Amherst and Wolfe should arrive at Quebec at the same time. The first who reached it, far from being in a condition to undertake the siege of Quebec, would run the risk of being engaged and defeated by a covering army, in which case the other force must be exposed to imminent hazard of destruction, and might find itself so circumstanced as to be caught in the midst of an enemy's country, with considerable difficulty about a line of retreat. This is, of course, merely to show the advantage of a defending force acting on what are called "interior" against an invading force operating on "exterior" lines. There is nothing in the least original in the view set forth above; as a matter of fact, it is very much that taken by the historian Smollett in his thoughtful survey of the campaign, which appeared in his "History of England" a few years after the actual operations. Smollet goes on to point out that had these disasters happened (and, he says, according to the experience of war, they were the natural consequences of the scheme), the troops at Niagara would in all probability have fallen an easy sacrifice, unless they had been so fortunate as to receive intelligence in time enough to accomplish their retreat before they could be intercepted. Smollett was led to conclude—but what immediately follows does not seem altogether sound—that the plan of campaign would have been " more justifiable, or, at least, not as liable to objection," if Amherst was to leave " merely a detachment " to protect the frontier of New York, and had been empowered to unite the remainder of his force with that of Wolfe in the expedition up the St. Lawrence to besiege Quebec, although even in that case Smollett thought that the total force would have been insufficient, according to the practice of war, to invest the place and cope with the covering enemy. Smollett was not a soldier—and no soldier could believe that " merely a detachment " would be able to defend the frontier of New York—but it is probable that in reviewing the campaign he had discussed the problems connected with it with military men, and it should not be forgotten that he had himself taken part in an amphibious expedition. That he had a quick eye to detect errors and to describe their results is obvious to anyone who has ever read " Roderick Random." In any case his opinions, even if they are those of a layman, are of interest as showing contemporary criticism of one of the most important campaigns in English history.

It will be noted that, in spite of his amphibious experience of war, Smollett has practically nothing to say of the naval aspect of the question. While recommending that the expedition up the

St. Lawrence be more than doubled in size, he does not stop to consider the extra tonnage involved, nor even whether such tonnage could have been made available. It may be mentioned that from the naval point of view the superiority of England over France in 1759 was by no means so well marked as it had been three years earlier. In the previous chapter it was stated—on the authority of Captain Mahan—that in 1756 the superiority of England in ships of the line was 130 to 63 ; but in March, 1758, France had 92 ships at sea or ready to sail, against 106 in commission on the part of England. Since then the Louisburg campaign had led to a certain decrease in the number of French ships, and it is not known to what extent the wastage had been made good by the following year, but probably the superiority of England by sea was not so great as it had been in 1756. Seeing that Wolfe's expedition was to be entirely dependent on sea-communications, this point is an important one and worth mentioning in a survey of Pitt's scheme. Captain Mahan has pointed out that if the French admiral in West Indian waters, when he found himself unable to relieve Guadaloupe in the spring of 1759, had taken his squadron to the harbour of New York, he would have put Amherst on the defensive and might well have rendered the campaign by the classic Lake Champlain and Richelieu River route impossible, or he might have threatened Halifax and Louisburg, in which case Saunders would have been forced to divide his fleet and deprive Wolfe of effective naval support. Another naval point of interest is that neither in the instructions of December, 1758, nor in those of February, 1759, does it seem that Pitt or his advisers contemplated an occurrence which actually happened, namely, that although Quebec should fall, the co-operating army under Amherst might not be able to join hands with it until the next campaigning season. In this case the victorious army at Quebec must—as actually happened—remain marooned there for over six months, for of course the fleet must necessarily leave the St. Lawrence before it became ice-bound. About the beginning of the following May navigation would become open once again, and there was always the chance that a French squadron, with strong military reinforcements, might—by taking great risks—slip through the patches of loose ice before the blockading fleet was properly at work. Actually, in 1759, this was what happened, although, unfortunately for France, she was unable to send an adequate reinforcement of soldiers at the time. Still, the stores and supplies, thus brought up the St. Lawrence, were of immense assistance to the garrison at Quebec, and the task of Wolfe and Saunders was greatly and unexpectedly increased.

The diversion against Niagara suggested to Amherst—and eventually adopted by him—may seem at first sight an unwise dissemination of force, seeing that the capture of Fort Frontenac by Bradstreet had completely isolated Fort Niagara, the fate of which might therefore be regarded as sealed. But Bradstreet, unfortunately, had not held Frontenac; after destroying everything, including the French gunboats, he had withdrawn, and it was only a matter of time before the French would rebuild their lake navy, which—certainly until the English reoccupied and restored Oswego—would once again obtain command of Lake Ontario and make Fort Niagara reasonably secure. Another reason for aiming a blow at Niagara was due to the fact that the fort, in addition to facilitating communication between Canada and the west, might also be of assistance in reinforcing Canada from the south. The passage up-stream of the Mississippi and movement thence to Lake Erie would be long and difficult; but it would not be impossible, and already, it was believed, French troops had been brought up the river into the Illinois country.

The selection of Wolfe to command the venture against Quebec came as a surprise to many, although, as a matter of fact, immediately the news of the fall of Louisburg had been received in London, orders were sent him from home to remain in America with a view to the assumption by him of command of the projected expedition up the St. Lawrence in the following year. These orders crossed Wolfe during his passage to England, where his arrival rather annoyed Pitt and led to something like a reprimand for Wolfe. When the minister's expectations had been explained to him at a dinner with some military friends at White's, Wolfe wrote at once to Pitt under date of November 22nd, 1758, stating that he " had no objection to serving in America, and particularly in the River St. Lawrence, if operations are to be carried on there," asking, however, for the favour of some sick leave " to repair the injury done to my constitution by the long confinement at sea." That Wolfe was not particularly attracted by the prospect of further service in America is clear from an extract from a letter begun by him to his friend, Colonel Rickson, immediately after he had written to Pitt : " I have this day signified to Mr. Pitt that he may dispose of my slight carcase as he pleases, and that I am ready for any undertaking within the reach and compass of my skill and cunning. I am in a very bad condition both with the gravel and rheumatism, but I had much rather die than decline any kind of service that offers. If I follow my own taste, it would lead me into Germany ; and, if my poor talent was consulted, they would place me in the cavalry, because nature has given me good eyes and a warmth of temper to follow the first impressions." Less than a week later he declares to one of the captains of his old regiment, the 20th, then serving on the Continent : " It is my fortune to be cursed with American service, yours to serve in an army commanded by a great and able Prince, where I would have been if my choice and inclinations had been consulted." Wolfe, however, was of an impulsive nature, and in very many of his letters it is clear that he wrote under a momentary stress of nervous irritability, due to his chronic ill-health. A man afflicted with gravel and rheumatism—and one to whom the prospect of a third Atlantic voyage within twelve months must have been a nightmare—must not be taken *au pied de la lettre* in everything he wrote. It is worth noting that just before he left Louisburg he wrote Amherst a farewell letter, in which he concluded with the words : " If you will attempt to cut up New France by the roots, I will come back with pleasure to assist."

During December Pitt and Wolfe consulted together, and on December 24th Wolfe wrote to the minister a letter which shows how he was interesting himself in the naval side of the problem given him to solve.

"In a packet of letters from North America there are two which contain some interesting circumstances, as they throw a light upon the state of men's minds in those parts. They are a confirmation to me of the thorough aversion conceived by the marine of this country against navigating in the river St. Lawrence . . . I will add from my own knowledge that the second naval officer in command there is vastly unequal to the weight of business ; and it is of the first importance to the country that it doth not fall into such hands. Mr. Caldwell, in autumn, proposed to attempt bringing off pilots from the Isle aux Coudres, after the French fleet came down, or was supposed to come down the river. The seeming danger of the enterprise, and other causes, put a stop to so great an undertaking.

"What Caldwell observes in regards to the fleet's anchoring at the Isle Bic is certainly very proper. A squadron of eight or ten sail stationed there in the earliest opening of the river would effectively prevent all relief; and it would be a very easy thing for the remainder of that squadron to push a frigate or two, and as many sloops, up the river, even as nigh as the Isle of Orleans, with proper people on board to acquire a certain knowledge of the navigation, in readiness to pilot such men-of-war and transports, such as the commanders should think fit to send up, after the junction of the fleet at Isle Bic. Nor does there appear any great risk in detaching the North American squadron to that station, as it is hardly probable that a force equal to that squadron could be sent from Europe to force their way up to Quebec, because it is a hundred to one if such a fleet keeps together in that early season; and if they were together, it is next to a certainty that they would be in a very poor condition for action. Besides, it would effectually answer our purpose to engage a French squadron in that river, even with the superiority of a ship or two on their side, seeing that they must be shattered in the engagement, and in the end destroyed.

* * * * * *

"If the enemy cannot pass the squadron stationed in the river and push up to Quebec, a few ships of war would do to convoy the transports from the Isle Bic to Quebec, and to assist in the operations of the campaign; and, in this case, the gross of the fleet remaining at the Isle Bic is at hand to prevent any attempt upon Louisburg or Halifax; whereas, if the whole went to Quebec, intelligence would be long in getting to them and their return in proportion. You must excuse the freedom I have taken, both in writing and sending the enclosed papers. If you see one useful hint in either, my intent is fully answered; if not, I beg you will burn them without any further notice."

[The Caldwell referred to was a junior staff officer at Louisburg.]

" The second naval officer in command " was Rear-Admiral Durell, whose inactivity justified—as we shall see—Wolfe's poor opinion of him, though it is but right to say that Durell's subsequent conduct in the campaign was to be marked by great enterprise and vigour. Wolfe's letter is of great interest, revealing, as it does, his appreciation of the naval issues bound up with his expedition. It may be mentioned that long before he knew that he had been selected for command he had written, while at Louisburg, urging the necessity of finding pilots for the St. Lawrence. On July 28th, 1758, he wrote to William Amherst : " Put the General in mind of *pilots*. I dare say there are plenty in Louisburg ; their names should be known, in order to their being carried on board the men-of-war a day or two before we sail." It is worth while dwelling on this attention by Wolfe to details outside his immediate profession as a soldier. For many years the navy never received adequate recognition for its great work in the Quebec expedition, and even to-day the name of Admiral Saunders is practically unknown when compared with that of Wolfe. But the reaction of late years has led to a violent swing of the pendulum, and there is sometimes a tendency to extol the share of the navy at the expense of Wolfe, insinuating that his share of the success was merely the soldiering part, and that in other respects he was what sailors might call a "passenger." The letter above quoted will dispel that illusion and show that Sir Julian Corbett was not far wrong when he declared that Wolfe was the greatest master of amphibious warfare since the days of Drake.

Wolfe's commission as a major-general was signed on January 12th, 1759. It is said that the rank was made "temporary" owing to the expostulations of some of the senior officers of the army, to whom the idea of substantive promotion to a grade so exalted of an officer so young in years as Wolfe was came almost as a shock. It was even hinted to the King that Wolfe was mad, to which George II, an experienced soldier himself, made the famous retort that if Wolfe were mad, it was to be hoped that he would bite some of the other generals. Just over a century later Lincoln played on this repartee when Grant's detractors brought the latter's indulgence in liquor to the notice of the President. But in spite of the surprise which Wolfe's appointment seems to have caused in some military quarters, there is little doubt that the selection of him was approved by the people of England. As news concerning the successful operation at Louisburg was diffused, it was felt that much of the success had been due to Wolfe, and in England his reputation had grown so high that a common toast associated "the eye of a Hawke and the heart of a Wolfe." A very significant tribute to Wolfe's ability is that his services were specially asked for by the army in America. About the time when Wolfe returned from Louisburg to England a letter was sent to Pitt signed by three of the most capable and successful of the colonels who had mastered American warfare: Monckton, the governor of Halifax, Murray, of "Amherst's," and Burton, of "Webb's." After detailing a plan of attack by the St. Lawrence, and the forces it would require, they recommend that as Amherst, in virtue of his new appointment, must remain on the continent of America, Colonel Wolfe should have the command with the temporary rank of brigadier.

Wolfe was allowed a free hand, to a certain extent, in the choice of subordinate commanders, and he selected as two of his brigadiers Murray, son of Lord Elibank, and Monckton, son of Lord Galway—two soldiers who had won distinction in North America. The third brigadier was another peer's son—Pitt's friend Townshend, who had given up the army for politics, but had returned after the fall of the Duke of Cumberland, and now asked to be allowed to serve under Wolfe. In a letter written to his uncle on January 29th, 1759, Wolfe modestly deprecated his own appointment by saying: "I am to act a greater part in this business than I wished or desired. The backwardness of some of the older officers has in some measure forced the Government to come down so low "; but he is confident of success, declaring : "If the Marquis de Montcalm finds means to baffle our efforts another summer, he may be deemed an able officer ; or the colony has resources we know nothing of ; or our Generals are worse than usual."

The King's Secret Instructions to Wolfe were issued on February 5th. We have on the authority of Lord Mahon an account of " a slight incident connected with these times, which is recorded by tradition, and affords a striking proof how much a fault of manner may obscure and disparage high excellencies of mind." The story, as given by Mahon, who had it at second hand " from a near and still surviving relative," is as follows :—After Wolfe's appointment, and on the day preceding his embarkation for America, Pitt, desirous of giving his last verbal instructions, invited him to dinner, Lord Temple being the only other guest. As the evening advanced, Wolfe—heated, perhaps, by his own aspiring thoughts and the unwonted society of statesmen—broke forth into a strain of gasconade and bravado. He drew his sword, he rapped the table with it, he flourished it round the room, he talked of the mighty things that sword was to achieve. The two ministers sat aghast at an exhibition so unusual from any man of real sense and real spirit. And when at last Wolfe had taken his leave, and his carriage was heard to roll from the door, Pitt seemed for the moment shaken in the high opinion which his deliberate judgment had formed of Wolfe; he lifted up his eyes and arms, and exclaimed to Lord Temple: "Good God! that I should have entrusted the fate of the country and of the administration to such hands!"

Historians have commented at length upon the incident. According to Lord Mahon himself: "It confirms Wolfe's own avowal: that he was not seen to advantage in the common occurrences of life, and shows how shyness may, at intervals, rush, as it were for refuge, into the opposite extreme; but it should also lead us to view such defects of manner with indulgence, as proving that they co-exist with the highest ability and the purest virtue." As to this, a modern historian quite rightly remarks: "It is hard to believe that a man who dined and conversed freely with such men as the Duke of Bedford, Lord Shelburne, Lord George Sackville, and Lord Blandford, who was regarded with prodigious favour in numerous drawing-rooms, and had just courted successfully one of the handsomest and most fashionable young women of the day, could have been quite overpowered and abashed even by a prime minister."

The truth probably is that some incident betraying Wolfe's earnestness and enthusiasm did actually take place, but—just as in the more well-known legend of his recital of Gray's "Elegy" while moving down the St. Lawrence to the great venture at Quebec—the framework of fact has been so overlaid with grotesquely inaccurate detail as to be distorted almost beyond recognition. That Wolfe surprised the two statesmen is probably true ; just as Nelson surprised and shocked Wellington. Shortly before Nelson embarked for the enterprise which ended at Trafalgar he met Sir Arthur Wellesley in an ante-room of the Colonial Office. Nelson was at first unaware of the identity of the other visitor, and in Wellington's words : " entered at once into conversation with me, if I can call it conversation, for it was almost all on his side and all about himself, and in really a style so vain and silly as to surprise and almost disgust me." But, fortunately, the Secretary of State kept the pair long waiting, and before the conversation closed, Wellington was so impressed by the good sense, the wide knowledge, and the statesmanlike outlook of Nelson as to declare later : " I don't know that I ever had a conversation that interested me more." Wolfe and Nelson resembled one another in more ways than that of their deaths : each was apt to convey a false impression by a certain impulsive enthusiasm. Wolfe, however, seems to have been quite free from the touch of vanity and love of flattery which were certainly characteristics of Nelson.

The handsome and fashionable lady whom Wolfe had successfully courted was Miss Katherine Lowther, daughter of Robert Lowther, who had been governor of Barbados. Her brother was Sir James Lowther, who later became first Earl of Lonsdale. The development of their love affair cannot be traced, but it is evident that there was no engagement until after Wolfe's return from Louisburg. About six years after Wolfe's death Miss Lowther married Lord Harry Poulett, a post-captain in the navy, who later became the last Duke of Bolton, and who was the original of Captain Whiffle in "Roderick Random." The Duchess of Bolton died in 1809, thus surviving Wolfe by half a century.

On February 14th, 1759, Wolfe sailed from Spithead on board the *Neptune*, flagship of Admiral Saunders. There are few officers who have been so scurvily treated by fame as this admiral, for his name has been allowed to sink almost into oblivion. Even to-day, in spite of the fact that every writer who deals with the Quebec campaign is at especial pains to see that due credit is given him for his great share in the success, it is scarcely too much to say that of every ten thousand people who have heard of Wolfe, to all but a mere handful the very name of Saunders is unknown. He was one of Anson's own men—one of the brilliant band who had been with him round the world. In Hawke's action off Finisterre Saunders had justified the high opinions held of him, and after Byng's failure at Minorca he had been sent out to the Mediterranean to help redeem that disaster. We would give much to have some record of the conversations and deliberations which must have taken place in the admiral's cabin between Saunders and Wolfe during that eleven weeks' voyage, but practically

THE QUEBEC CAMPAIGN, 1759   319

nothing has come down to us. It is clear, however, that Saunders did not take the soldier entirely into his confidence, for, just before sailing from Louisburg to the St. Lawrence, Wolfe, in writing to his uncle, mentioned that he was unaware what disposition the admiral intended to make in the St. Lawrence, " but I conclude he will send four or five of his smallest ships of the line to assist us at Quebec, and remain with the rest at an anchor below the Isle aux Coudres, ready to fight whatever fleet the enemy may send to disturb us." Actually, as the narrative will show, Saunders did a great deal more than this—luckily for Wolfe, who certainly could not otherwise have achieved the great victory he did. But the admiral, not unwisely, perhaps, refused to commit himself too much in advance. He had, however, given Pitt a hint the day before he sailed. Ordered, at the last moment, to detach two ships to the Mediterranean, he kept one of them, the *Stirling Castle*—sending a substitute in her place—to be his flagship in the St. Lawrence, stating laconically that " she was very handy for rivers."

Even Wolfe must have had some occasional respite from the horrors of perpetual sea-sickness, and we may be sure that he spent many hours, with map and chart beside him, pondering over the Secret Instructions with the royal initials " G. R." at their foot. He had also in his possession an excellent plan of, and a report upon, the fortifications of Quebec made in 1757 by Major

Mackellar, who was to be chief engineer of the expedition. Wolfe's task was " to attack and reduce Quebec "—or, as it was worded in the first paragraph of the instructions proper, " to attack and endeavour to reduce." This operation was to be carried out as early " as the Season of Year will admit of operations "—it being hoped that the expedition would be able to leave the rendezvous at Louisburg on May 7th—and the fleet, under Saunders, would " act in Conjunction and co-operate with our said Land Forces." Should Wolfe on arrival at Louisburg find that everything was not ready for the expedition, he was strictly charged " to make the most pressing Instances " to Amherst and Saunders to take all steps to put this matter right without a moment's delay. Should Quebec be taken, a garrison was to be left there, and Wolfe and Saunders were then to determine what operations, if any, might be carried out further up the St. Lawrence, and in this case Wolfe was to do his utmost to get into touch with Amherst, and in this event he was to come under the latter's orders, if circumstances allowed. The instructions closed with some very sound advice as to the necessity of a good understanding between the land and sea officers; Wolfe was to allow his soldiers to man the ships should their services be so required, and should the men be available; while Saunders was similarly enjoined to allow his sailors and marines to assist the land forces and man the batteries.

The task which confronted Wolfe and Saunders was one of no ordinary difficulty. There was no precedent for guidance. To carry an expedition hundreds of miles up a distant river, the navigation of which was notoriously difficult, through a hostile country, against a fortress defended by regular troops, was an operation beyond all experience. Fortune, however, was doing her best to assist Wolfe. It was a great—an inestimable—advantage for him that in each of the two preceding years he had been allowed to take part in an amphibious operation. In one he had served as a staff officer, and had been behind the scenes ; in the other he had held a fighting command. The dismal failure of Rochefort could be compared with the brilliant success at Louisburg, and from a survey of the two invaluable lessons must have been learnt by such an eager student of war as was Wolfe. The advantage of daily conferences and consultations with his naval colleague has already been referred to, and it is one the importance of which requires no stressing. Again, this long voyage—the third trans-Atlantic passage within little over a year— inevitably gave Wolfe the opportunity of observing the sailing and manœuvring power of warships ; and Wolfe was not the man to neglect the opportunity of learning as much as he could about the service in conjunction with which he was to work.

Then, too, Wolfe was spared all the onerous preliminary spadework of assembling his troops and collecting his stores. All this was being done for him by his commander-in-chief on the far side of the Atlantic. It must have been clear to Amherst that, in Pitt's eyes at any rate, he himself was to play second fiddle in the campaign ; but whatever may have been his opinion of the arrangement, he behaved with generous loyalty to his subordinate. All the high talent for administration which he possessed he devoted heart and soul to the preparation of Wolfe's force, and no expedition had ever been better equipped than that which Wolfe eventually found at his disposal, when, to the material and stores collected by Amherst, were added the ordnance and stores sent out with the empty transports from England. Finally, Wolfe, unlike the unfortunate Braddock, was not to be called upon to take the field with raw soldiers from home : the troops which would accompany him were experienced in American warfare, and most of them flushed with victory. Wolfe had an important game to win, but he held some very good cards. Let us precede him across the Atlantic and scrutinize the hand which Fortune had dealt out to his great opponent.

Montcalm was under no illusion about the fact that, on balance, the advantage of the fighting during the previous year lay wholly with the English. They occupied the Ohio valley and had made themselves masters of the entrance to the St. Lawrence. Creditable though the French resistance at Ticonderoga had been, the result was but negative ; nothing really had been gained save that the further invasion of Canada had been delayed. So clearly did Montcalm realize the unfavourable condition of affairs that on September 1st, 1758, immediately after the loss of Fort Frontenac, he wrote to the Minister of War in frankly pessimistic terms. " The situation of the colony is most critical ; peace is necessary," is how he began. He pointed out that the English had 30,000 men available as against the eight regular battalions and 1,200 colonial infantry at his disposal. As for the Canadian militia, their great drawback was the necessity of letting them return home to get in the harvest. They were useful for raids, but could not be kept long in the field, and this was also the case with the Indians. Montcalm declared his intention of finding his grave, if required, in the ruins of the colony, but this did not prevent his cry of despair, *la paix est nécessaire ou le Canada est perdu.*

So critical was the situation that the governor-general felt it necessary to bow to the wishes of the civil and military authorities in Canada, and to send emissaries to France to beg for assistance. Doreil, the commissary of war, and Bougainville, Montcalm's aide-de-camp, were chosen for the mission, bearing credentials from Vaudreuil, who, however, with characteristic treachery, wrote privately to the Ministry of Marine to say that the emissaries "did not understand Canada, and that they were merely creatures of Montcalm." On arrival in France, Bougainville at once set about seeing the proper authorities, and to such a state had "centralization" come in France that he considered himself very fortunate in having gained the ear of Madame de Pompadour and in having got that lady to interest herself in Canada. To the Ministry he presented four documents. The first was a comparative table of the strengths of the French and English, the figures of the former agreeing with the figures quoted above from Montcalm's letter, but the number of English and provincials who might be expected to make the campaign in 1759 was raised to 60,000. The second and third papers were concerned with the requirements of Canada should it be decided to continue the war in America. An important statement was that *Québec est sans fortifications et n'en est pas susceptible.* This was possibly an exaggeration, but it is worth bearing in mind, since popular accounts of the campaign of 1759 are apt to give the impression that Quebec was a frowning mass of impregnability, belted round with battlements and bastions, and bristling with heavy ordnance. Bougainville frankly declared that he realized the impossibility of sending reinforcements sufficient to achieve equality with the English, and suggested that Canada should be regarded *comme un malade qu'on soutient par des cordiaux;* the sick man might be in danger of starvation, but, seeing that nourishment could not be introduced into his system, the best plan was to endeavour to keep life in him by homœopathic doses of stimulants. In this way Bougainville considered it not impossible that if the crisis of 1759 could be safely tided over, Canada might yet be saved—a metaphor which but half-concealed the truism that the closing of the St. Lawrence by ice would end the critical period, and that, after a refreshing sleep through the winter, the patient might be in a position to begin the struggle of life once again. The stimulant immediately required was merely a few technical experts for the artillery and engineers; some guns, with a great quantity of ammunition; a thousand recruits, and four merchant vessels, whose hulls could be sunk to block the way to Quebec and the crews and gear of which could be utilized upon the lakes. The fourth memorandum proposed a retreat into Louisiana in the event of defeat on the St. Lawrence. There was also mention of a naval counterstroke against the southern states.

The reply from the French Crown was, briefly, to the effect that Canada must be left to her own resources. Any project of assisting her which implied naval reinforcement in the North Atlantic was, for the moment, out of the question. There was, however, to be no question of capitulation or of abandoning Canada by a retreat down the Mississippi; at all costs a foothold must be maintained in the colony in order that the eventual peace negotiations would have to deal with a Canada nominally at least under the French flag. As for reinforcements, these could only be very small—a mere 300 recruits and a handful of artillerymen and engineers. Ammunition and provisions would, however, be sent. Bougainville returned to Canada bearing the instructions and information given above. He arrived at Quebec on May 12th, after a delay of over three weeks caused by drifting ice, and with him came the fleet, carrying the supplies and the scanty reinforcements granted by the court. Bougainville bore also a despatch which gave warning of a great expedition fitted out in English ports for the attack on Quebec, and—what was more important—an intercepted letter from Amherst, with detailed information. This intelligence came as a thunderclap, for it had been an accepted article of faith in Canada that Quebec, owing to the difficult navigation of the St. Lawrence, was unassailable by water. Both Vaudreuil and Montcalm—for once in agreement—had been convinced that the main attack on Canada was to be made by Lake Champlain, although it was thought possible that the Ohio and Niagara might be the scene of secondary operations. Now the secret information brought out in Bougainville's pocket necessitated a complete recasting of the plan of defence of Canada.

Fortune, ever fickle, had by now begun to hamper Wolfe. To begin with, she sent weather so unfavourable that, although April 20th had been the date fixed for the concentration of the expedition at Louisburg, that date had already passed before the *Neptune* even sighted Cape Breton. Nor was this all. So severe had been the winter that the ice made it impossible to approach the coast, and Saunders had to bear away for Halifax. Here came the second disappointment; for, to their dismay, Saunders and Wolfe found Durell's squadron still riding at anchor. His ships had been ready for sea for over a month, but he had thought it prudent to wait until he heard that the ice would permit him to enter the Gulf of St. Lawrence. Wolfe had clearly realized the necessity of sealing that river; he had a fairly accurate idea of what the military resources of Canada were before the St. Lawrence became ice-bound, but now, of course, his calculations went by the board inasmuch as he was in doubt what reinforcements had managed to slip into Canada owing to Durell's delay. Actually, as we have seen, the personnel was negligible in quantity, but a large amount of food had got up to Quebec. What was worse, Bougainville had brought with him correct information concerning Wolfe's expedition, and Montcalm was thus in a position to take prompt measures to meet it.

Saunders immediately ordered Durell to sea with strict injunctions to push up the St. Lawrence as high as the Isle of Bic, and from thence to detach some small ships, if possible, to the Basin of Quebec. Here, again, Fortune proved herself unkind, for, owing to foul winds, it was not until May 5th that Durell got clear away, having borrowed from Wolfe, to complete his crews, 300 soldiers, who could ill be spared. For here Fortune played her unkindest trick. Wolfe had based all his calculations on the understanding that his force would amount to 12,000 of all ranks, but the total proved to be considerably under 9,000—a serious matter, seeing that not only had the time-table of the expedition been upset, but also the St. Lawrence had been left open owing to Durell's inactivity. Wolfe, however, did not allow himself to be discouraged, for although he wrote at once to Pitt pointing out the deficiency in numbers, he added : " Our troops indeed are very good and very well disposed. If valour can make amends for want of numbers we shall probably succeed." Writing to his titular chief, however, the same day, he put the matter rather more frankly, saying that he had little hope of success " unless we get into the river first. However, trust me, they (the French) will feel us." Another worry was that the military chest was empty. " There is a great siege to be undertaken, and not a farthing to pay the workmen. I am not possessed of a single dollar of public money." Not until May 13th were the troops at Halifax able to leave for the rendezvous at Louisburg. On arrival there Wolfe found a letter announcing the death of his father, who had passed away, while Wolfe was crossing the Atlantic, in the seventy-fifth year of his age. At Louisburg, as at Halifax, the troops were landed daily for drill and manœuvre, and we have a glimpse of Wolfe's views as to the subordination of mere drill to fighting qualities. Some commanding officers who expected to have their regiments inspected informed Wolfe that their units unfortunately had not had the opportunity of learning the most recent movements, to which Wolfe replied : " Poh ! Poh ! new exercise —new fiddlesticks ! If they are otherwise well disciplined and will fight, that's all I require of them."

A letter from Louisburg written by Wolfe to his uncle, Major Walter Wolfe, has some interesting passages dealing with the prospects of the campaign. He considered that the French would concentrate their chief attention on Quebec—" as the loss of the capital implies the loss of the colony " —a statement not strictly true, but of which Wolfe did not live to see the refutation. At Quebec he expected to find six battalions, some companies of marines, four or five thousand Canadians and some Indians ; but it seems clear that he expected to find the bulk of these in Quebec itself, and that a landing of his force near Beauport, east of Quebec, would be a feasible operation. His object would then be to move westwards, across the St. Charles River —where he expected a smart action—and then, making a left wheel, he intended to establish himself on the Heights of Abraham with his right on the St. Lawrence and his left on the St. Charles. Wolfe's plan was that he should place his army opposite the west side of the fortress, so that he might then complete the investment, the waterfront part of which would be undertaken by the navy. In this way Quebec would be isolated from the rest of Canada. Emphasis must, however, be laid on the fact that, even before he left Louisburg, Wolfe clearly visualized the forcing of the narrows at Quebec, and of operations above the city. "It is the business," he wrote, "of our naval force to be masters of the river, both above and below the town," and later in the letter he mentions the possibility of "stealing a detachment up the St. Lawrence and landing them three, four, five miles or more above the town." As for himself, Wolfe informed his uncle : "You may be assured that I shall take all proper care of my own person, unless in case of the last importance, when it becomes a duty to do otherwise."

On June 6th the entire fleet was clear of Louisburg, the movement out of harbour lasting six days. The expedition was an imposing one—twenty-two line of battleships, five frigates, eighteen sloops, and an immense fleet of transports, storeships, victuallers, traders and other attendants. The troops were in high spirits, and the prevailing toast amongst the officers was "British colours on every French fort, port and garrison in America." Two days out at sea Wolfe wrote his will. The first bequest was that Miss Lowther's picture should be set in jewels to the amount of 500 guineas, and returned to her. "In remembrance of his guest," he left to Saunders "my light service of Plate." Substantial legacies were left to four of his friends ; and to six more a 100 guineas each "to buy swords and rings in remembrance of their Friend." Some bequests to servants followed, and "Everything over and above these legacies I leave to my good mother, entirely at her Disposal." Later, during

THE QUEBEC CAMPAIGN, 1759   331

the Quebec campaign, he added a codicil bequeathing £1,000 each to his uncle, Major Walter Wolfe, and his cousin, Captain Edward Goldsmith. Another document, signed by Wolfe during the period of embarkation, is of more military interest—the "state" of the expeditionary force. The total, exclusive of headquarters and staff, amounted to 8,535, the bulk of which was divided into three brigades as follows :—Monckton's Brigade, 15th, 43rd, 58th, and Fraser's Highlanders ; Townshend's Brigade, 28th, 47th and 2nd Battn. 60th ; Murray's Brigade, 35th, 48th and 3rd Battn. 60th. In addition there were three grenadier companies from the regiments left in garrison at Louisburg, and known as the Louisburg Grenadiers ; six companies of rangers ; a *corps d'élite*, known as the Light Infantry ; and just over a hundred artillerymen. The transports sailed in three divisions under Monckton, Townshend and Murray respectively, each brigadier flying a distinguishing pennant from his frigate.

Owing to thick fogs, it was a week before the fleet could enter the St. Lawrence, and ten days before it was off the Isle of Bic, and here was met a frigate of Durell's squadron, which gave unwelcome news. From a prize taken by Durell that admiral had learnt of the passage up the river of three frigates and a score or so of storeships from France, these being the fleet which had got safely across at the time of Bougainville's return, while Durell was delaying his departure from Halifax.

Durell, however, had done much to retrieve his error of judgment, for he had now pushed up the river with his squadron as high as the Isle aux Coudres, some sixty-five miles below Quebec. Nevertheless, the blow to Wolfe was a serious one when added to the disadvantage of his late start and the discovery that the force with which he was expected to reduce Quebec was little more than two-thirds of what he had been led to expect. On the other hand, the situation had taken on an aspect which Wolfe had scarcely dared to hope for. Saunders, who could have fulfilled the letter of his instructions by merely sending on a few light ships to assist in the siege, and by using the main body of his fleet to keep open Wolfe's sea communications and to prevent a French counterstroke against Louisburg or Halifax, decided to accompany Wolfe with the whole of his fleet and to co-operate with him in the attack on Quebec. Never before had a battle fleet been taken up the St. Lawrence, but by splendid seamanship the ships arrived safely off the Isle aux Coudres. There yet remained the dreaded Traverse passage, thick with dangers to navigation, with currents up to seven knots on the flood and nearly nine on the ebb. But, thanks to the help of some charts seized from the French, to the work of Captain Cook in navigation, and to the assistance obtained from some French pilots impressed for the work, the task, which even the French pilots genuinely believed to be impossible, was accomplished with the utmost success. On the 26th the fleet anchored off St. Laurent, and the next day Wolfe landed on the Isle of Orleans with the bulk of his army.

So soon as the army was ashore, Wolfe, accompanied by his chief engineer and by an escort, proceeded to the western end of the Isle of Orleans to view the goal of his expedition. The western front of Quebec was, of course, hidden from him. All he could do was to gaze at the apex of the city—formed by the junction of the St. Charles with the St. Lawrence—and thus obtain a foreshortened view of the whole city-triangle save for the base. There is not a single line of authentic record extant as to the impression made upon Wolfe by his first sight of Quebec, but it is possible that his first feeling was one of surprise, for Quebec, looked at across the four-mile stretch of water from where Wolfe stood, could not have given the immediate impression of a powerful fortress. To the left of the rocky plateau on which stood the city there was, indeed, a bold elevation overlooking the river and crowned by a redoubt, which suggested military strength, but the first feature which must have riveted Wolfe's attention was the row of spires, roofs and pinnacles silhouetted against the western sky, and giving to Quebec the appearance less of a fortress than of a cathedral city. It must have appeared in striking contrast to Louisburg. Through his glasses Wolfe would have been able to pick out the works and gun positions, which would discount the impression, but these came as no surprise to him, seeing that he had long been in possession of a plan supplemented by a full description of the place. The appearance of strength must, however, have been diminished by the Lower Town, which lay naked and unprotected along the water at the base of the cliff upon which stood Quebec. On the whole it is possible—though the reader must remember that this is pure conjecture—that viewed from the Isle of Orleans, Quebec may have seemed to Wolfe an objective less formidable than he had previously imagined. One thing must certainly have seemed abundantly clear: provided that suitable gun positions could be obtained, the city would be extremely vulnerable to bombardment, especially the Lower Town, the complete destruction of which would be but a matter of time.

After his first rapid glance at the city Wolfe experienced a profound feeling of dismay. As his glass swept past the right of Quebec—as he looked at it—and across the River St. Charles, he must instantly have realized that his preconceived scheme for reducing the place would require a great modification. For eastward from the River St. Charles, for mile upon mile along the wooded bluffs which looked down upon the foreshore of the northern bank of the St. Lawrence, could be seen lines of entrenchments, supplemented here and there by redoubts, and apparently occupied everywhere by troops. The line did not cease until it disappeared in the River Montmorenci, some eight miles from the St. Charles. Here was a double disappointment. It was upon this strip of land that Wolfe had proposed to throw his army ashore, and he had not expected serious opposition until he should have to fight his way across the St. Charles on his way to the western flank of Quebec. But clearly now, should such a landing be attempted, very heavy fighting must be looked for long before the St. Charles could be reached, and there was even the question whether such a landing might be feasible at all. The second disappointment was in the length of the line held by the French, for if it was held in anything like strength, then the numbers of the enemy were clearly much greater than those at the disposal of Wolfe.

Nevertheless, although the appearance of lines of entrenchments along the Beauport shore must have seriously disconcerted Wolfe, the action of his enemy in occupying a position so close to Quebec was in the nature of a forced move. So far from being a source of strength to Canada, Quebec was, in 1759, in some respects a weakness. It attracted to itself the bulk of the French mobile forces in Canada, and the necessity of supplementing its inadequate defences by a field army compelled Montcalm to throw to the winds the plan of campaign he had conceived. The military possibilities of Quebec were very great—meaning by the term " Quebec " not the collection of civil, military and ecclesiastical buildings perched on Cape Diamond, but the land and water area of which that cape, the opposite shore, and the Isle of Orleans are all part. Clearly such an area was capable of being turned into a strong barrier, preventing ingress to the heart of Canada, in the event of the fall of Louisburg and the opening thereby of the Gulf and River St. Lawrence to a hostile amphibious expedition. A parallel from modern times is suggested by the Gallipoli campaign of the Great War, Montreal for the moment taking the place of Constantinople, and the Dardanelles being represented by the St. Lawrence from Montreal down to Quebec and for some distance beyond that city. Disregarding for a moment the question of mines and submarines, the land defence of the Dardanelles consisted chiefly of well-sited coast artillery in various works, with a mobile field army—not glued to entrenchments under the walls of the capital, as was the army of Montcalm—ready to act as circumstances might require. The Turkish works held their own against the tremendous fire brought against them by ships' guns, and, as a matter of fact, the naval attempt to force the maritime defile had to be abandoned. In this comparison between 1759 and 1915 the point to be borne in mind is that the Turks did not entrust the defence of the Dardanelles merely to an exposed city of mosques, palaces, minarets and government buildings to which the fortifications were but a secondary consideration. The comparison between the Gallipoli campaign and that of Quebec must, however, not be pressed too far. As Lord Bryce has well expressed it, "History *never* repeats itself," and we may legiti-

THE QUEBEC CAMPAIGN, 1759   337

mately add as the converse that "No military problem has ever had an exact precedent." Thus, although we may be tempted to discover analogies between the Quebec campaign and those of the Crimea, Vicksburg and Gallipoli, reflection will show us that many specious resemblances are often obliterated by innumerable differences. It is true that Clausewitz committed himself to the advice regarding military problems: "Examples from history make everything clear," but when put to the test this oft-quoted *cliché* will be found a very feeble guide indeed.

In any case, the consideration in the preceding paragraph as to the ideal use to which the land and water area about Quebec might have been put is entirely academic. We are concerned with the position as it existed in 1759. By that date Quebec had been a city for over a hundred years, and Montcalm and his subordinates could no more have willed away the non-military excrescences of it than they could have emulated Joshua and have bidden the sun to stand still. The fatal mistake made by the French was to expect a fortified city—and poorly fortified at that—to do work which required a fortified area in which there should be nothing but military works, stores, supplies, and personnel; in which civilians, except labourers and artificers, would be out of place; and in which the presence of women and children would be simply unthinkable. But if Quebec was not to be a fortified area, but a city—a governmental, residential and ecclesiastical capital like Constantinople—then the St. Lawrence below it should have been made its Dardanelles, and the intricacies of the navigation of that river, supplemented by coast artillery, might have afforded Quebec the security of a practically impassable maritime defile. Most unfortunately for themselves, the French greatly exaggerated the perils of the notorious Traverse, and this exaggeration gave rise to the wholly inaccurate opinion that Quebec could not be reached by a hostile fleet of war.

From this, again, there resulted a neglect even to make the best of Quebec as it then existed. The place, even as a fortified city, had distinct natural advantages, but they had received little assistance from the skill of engineers. Some writers are, indeed, dubious as to whether it is not a misuse of terms to call Quebec a fortress at all. Its condition in 1759 must have made Vauban turn in his grave. The land front, against which an attacking army was bound to operate, was protected merely by a wall some twenty-five to thirty feet high, of no great thickness, with " ditches of sorts," *des espèces de fossés*, but with no advanced works, and although mounting fifty-two guns, these were very badly sited. The home government was by no means entirely to blame for the condition of the capital of Canada. The great importance of making it impregnable had long been recognized, and money had been poured out like water to that end, but the dishonesty and corruption which, like a

THE QUEBEC CAMPAIGN, 1759   339

cancer, were eating away the efficiency of Canadian administration, prevented any real strengthening of the place. As late as 1752 a competent engineer, who had been sent out to report, found the works at Quebec in a most disgracefully unserviceable state.

In spite of this, Vaudreuil, the governor-general, had bombastically declared that Quebec was impregnable. But the news brought by Bougainville of Wolfe's expedition led to intense anxiety for the capital and to the diversion thither of the bulk of the force available for offensive operations. The troops told off to reinforce Quebec consisted of five regular battalions—weakened by detachments sent to Niagara and Ticonderoga; 1,200 colonial infantry; the sailors who were disembarked from the few French ships, which had been sent for safety far up the river beyond Quebec; some 6,000 militia and 700 to 800 Indians, as well as the militia garrison of Quebec, under 2,000 strong. Montcalm had hurried to Quebec to take command in person, and at once it was decided to send eight vessels down the river to be sunk in the Traverse so as to block the passage there. The scheme, however, was never put into execution, for a careful survey proved that the navigable channel was at least four times wider than had been believed. It is something of a reflection upon that "centralized command" which historians often assert gave Canada an advantage, that the government was totally ignorant of the navigation of the St.

Lawrence in the neighbourhood of Quebec, and that the government pilots had laboured for at least a century in deplorable error. The British fleet came through the dreaded Traverse without the slightest mishap, and from a contemporary account it seems that the sailing masters on board treated the so-called difficulties with amused contempt. Foiled in their attempt to block the navigation of the river, Vaudreuil and Montcalm had to decide upon the best position for the army covering Quebec, the decision reached being to occupy the northern bank of the St. Lawrence from the River St. Charles to the Montmorenci. At the date of Wolfe's arrival the number of troops under Montcalm was about 10,000 exclusive of the mixed garrison of Quebec—regulars, sailors and militia of some 1,500 effectives—and including a mounted force more than 200 strong. During the summer the Canadian army was reinforced by numerous volunteers, who could have claimed exemption as being above or below military age, but against this a large number of desertions took place on the part of militiamen wishing to return to their farms. It is, however, difficult to assess the exact numbers present under Montcalm along the Beauport shore at the time of Wolfe's first survey of it, for there is an astounding discrepancy between the various authorities consulted. The figure of 10,000 given above may be taken as the minimum, but some accounts give the number as twelve, fourteen, or even sixteen thousand of all ranks.

THE QUEBEC CAMPAIGN, 1759   341

For the moment Wolfe had other things to occupy his attention beside the question of how to deal with the new situation brought about by the discovery of French troops on the Beauport sector. While he was actually examining the Quebec position from the end of the Isle of Orleans, a sudden storm arose, blowing hard from the northeast, and the fleet, which was in a badly exposed anchorage on the south side of the island, was immediately in difficulties. The storm passed away as quickly as it had come, but not before considerable damage had been done. Next night the French sent down seven fire ships, but the attempt was almost a complete failure, for the captains of them lit the charges too soon, and picket boats from the English fleet pluckily tackled the blazing ships and towed them ashore. This danger having been dealt with, Wolfe determined to gain a footing on the south bank of the St. Lawrence, opposite Quebec —a step which he was led to take for three reasons. By occupying Point Lévis he could ensure a safe anchorage for the naval part of the expedition, for Saunders had wished to move his ships from their present awkward position and to the part of the river lying between Point Lévis and the Isle of Orleans. In the second place, by pushing along the south shore Wolfe would be able to view the western front of Quebec, and to get some idea of the ground upon which he wished to place his army. In the third place he could look out for possible gun positions whence he could bombard

Quebec—an operation which would facilitate the running of the gauntlet of Quebec by some of Saunders's ships. It will be remembered that before Wolfe had sailed from Louisburg he had put on record that " It is the business of our naval force to be masters of the river both above and below the town," and he had also mentioned the possibility of " stealing a detachment up the St. Lawrence and landing them three, four, or five miles above the town." It is reasonable to suppose that, as Wolfe had been cooped up with Saunders on board the *Neptune* for over ten weeks, he was referring to a plan which had been discussed with the admiral and had been approved by him.

The next few days were busy ones. On June 29th Monckton, with four battalions, occupied Point Lévis practically without opposition, and entrenched himself there, his force being augmented by some marines from the fleet. Next day Townshend's brigade moved up to the Point d'Orléans at the western extremity of the island, and Saunders brought his ships up to the new anchorage, which was now guarded on either side. On July 2nd Wolfe, with a strong escort, pushed on westwards along the southern shore, and examined the ground at Pointe des Pères, immediately opposite Quebec. The result was satisfactory, and in a few days mortars and siege guns were being landed at Point Lévis and were brought by road to Pointe des Pères. Two days later Murray moved still further up the south bank to view the west front of Quebec

THE QUEBEC CAMPAIGN, 1759   343

and to examine the shore above the city. All this time Wolfe was acting in close co-operation with Saunders, who accompanied him several times during his reconnaissances on shore.

Now that the preliminary measures had been successfully undertaken, Wolfe had time to consider his real problem—the taking of Quebec. The task with which he was confronted was indeed a formidable one. In order to place his army on the Heights of Abraham, facing the land-front of Quebec, it would be obviously necessary to deal first with Montcalm's army on the Beauport shore, unless Wolfe could move up the river past Quebec with his landing force, but at present this operation was not feasible. For the moment the immediate problem was to land on the north shore of the St. Lawrence, below Quebec, and to defeat the covering army there entrenched. The mere tactical defeat of that force would, however, be quite insufficient. Montcalm's army must be so overwhelmed as to be temporarily incapable of further effective action in the field. It must either be squeezed into Quebec—where the accession of strength to the garrison would be neutralized by the extra demand on the scanty rations in the city—or it must be so dispersed as to lose all coherence, or it must be forced to retreat so far westward towards Montreal, and in such a disorganized condition, as to be unlikely to interfere with Wolfe's investment of Quebec. For clearly Wolfe would find it difficult, if not impossible, to maintain a footing on the Heights of Abraham if an enemy field army still in being were to menace his flanks and rear. The task of putting Montcalm's army completely out of action—even for a time—was, however, one of immense difficulty, seeing that in numbers it was clearly superior to the force which Wolfe could throw against it, and even allowing for the fact that Wolfe's veteran regulars were probably superior as a fighting machine to the heterogeneous mixture which made up the French force.

By taking a broad and detached view of the situation Wolfe could realize that without committing himself too deeply, and by merely amusing Montcalm, his army would still be performing very valuable service, for it was obvious that the mass of French troops used to cover Quebec implied a diminution *pro tanto* in some other part of the theatre of war. There could be merely a delaying force in front of Amherst, and a reasonably rapid advance by the commander-in-chief must infallibly force Montcalm to take steps to deal with him even at the expense of weakening his hold upon Quebec. For it must have been diamond clear to Montcalm, and no less so to Wolfe, that, after all, the real deadly thrust at Canada was that being carried out by Amherst by the classic Lake Champlain-River Richelieu route. Success at Quebec would be important, but it would result merely in the slow strangulation of Canada; whereas the arrival of Amherst on the St. Lawrence would be to sever the artery through which pulsed the life-blood of the colony. But although Wolfe probably saw the strength of such argument, he was correct in disregarding it. He had been definitely ordered to take Quebec, and in this task time was an important factor, for before the beginning of October Saunders's vessels might have to leave if they were to escape being ice-bound. Wolfe's was not a nature that would be content merely with " holding " Montcalm while the decisive blow was being struck elsewhere and by another hand. And, as a matter of fact, any reliance upon even a reasonably rapid advance by Amherst would have been misplaced, for the commander-in-chief, although he acted surely, acted with extreme slowness.

To attack Montcalm with any prospect of success it would be necessary to force him to unglue himself from his defensive position, to change his front, and to fight a battle on ground of Wolfe's choice. To bring this about Wolfe proposed to land portion of his army east of the Montmorenci, to move up the left bank of that river till he could find a ford above the Falls of Montmorenci, and then, if possible, to act against Montcalm's left rear. Accordingly, on July 8th, leaving a detachment on the Isle of Orléans, Wolfe sent Murray's and Townshend's brigades across the river to the left bank of the Montmorenci. Wolfe's army was now split up into three parts—one on the south bank of the St. Lawrence, opposite Quebec, a detachment on the Isle of Orléans, and the bulk of the troops east of the Montmorenci—a dissemination of strength which had its obvious dangers. As for the proposed operations against Montcalm's left, these came to nothing. A large body of Indians, belonging to the French force, crossed the river and scalped thirty-six rangers who were looking for the ford, and it was soon clear that a turning movement by that route was not likely to be a success. Montcalm, on his part, refused to budge, and although his left was annoyed by some of the artillery of the British, who had entrenched themselves, he refused to make any attempt to dislodge them. Matters here came, therefore, to a deadlock, but the action of Wolfe had an important moral effect, for the Canadian militia became so uneasy that now, for the first time, they began to desert.

On July 12th the batteries upon Pointe des Pères were ready for action, and that night, at a given signal, the guns and mortars opened fire upon Quebec. The inhabitants of Quebec, alarmed at the prospect of bombardment, had already sent a force to reconnoitre the artillery position, with a view to attacking it. The attempt was made on the night of July 13th, when a mixed column, under the command of the town major, embarked above Quebec. The strength of the column is variously given at a figure ranging from 1,200 to 1,500, and it consisted of 100 volunteers from the regulars, some hundreds of militiamen, some citizens of Quebec, and a band of pupils from the Catholic Seminary. Scarcely had the expedition reached the southern bank when it gave, according to contemporary accounts, *signes d'une agitation nerveuse*. The young seminarists loosed off their muskets, although at least three miles from their enemy, doing some execution amongst the expedition. Three times did this happen during the march, and before the objective was reached the militiamen were seized with panic and a wild stampede was made for the boats, the unfortunate mob arriving at Quebec at dawn *accablés de désespoir et de honte*. Thereafter the garrison at Quebec contented itself with replying to the British fire, but doing very little execution.

A week later Quebec had another shock; even Montcalm, the imperturbable, was shaken out of his calm. Taking advantage of the darkness and a flood tide, and under cover of a storm of fire from the batteries on Pointe des Pères, Saunders sent a few of his ships, with three transports, carrying three companies of grenadiers and a battalion of Royal Americans up past Quebec. The French were completely taken by surprise, and even when the ships were discerned the fire opened was feeble. The venture was completely successful; only three shots took effect, and the damage was negligible. And although the *Diana*, of thirty-two guns, ran aground and was badly injured by the mishap, she was got off safely in daylight. The campaign had now entered upon a new phase; but although the running of the gauntlet of Quebec reflects the very highest credit on the navy, it is doubtful whether it quite deserves Sir Julian Corbett's description of it as a " desperate attempt." The river was about three-quarters of a mile wide, the garrison of Quebec was indifferent, and the venture was made under cover of a fierce and sustained fire and assisted by a racing tide. In a riverine campaign to run past a fortified position is nearly always part of the game. To gain command of the river above Quebec was part of the duty which all along Wolfe had considered would fall to the navy, and in this it is almost certain that he had the promise of Saunders. It is clear from entries made by Wolfe in his diary that he considered that the attempt might well have been carried out at least two nights before the venture was actually made. It is difficult to believe that the passage of the St. Lawrence at Quebec was as desperate as the passage of Farragut past the forts below New Orleans in 1862, or past Vicksburg or Port Hudson, or even Porter's running the gauntlet of the second of those places in 1863. Historical comparisons, of course, always require some qualification, and it must not be forgotten that Farragut had steam-power as against the wind and tide of the enterprise in 1759. But against this can be set the fact that the Confederate ordnance was heavier and more accurate than that at the disposal of the French in Quebec. It is also worth mentioning that in the other successful attempts to run past Quebec very little damage was received. One diminutive transport, ironically named *The Terror of France*, got by in broad daylight.

Although the successful passage of Quebec on the night of July 18th gave Wolfe the command of the St. Lawrence immediately above the city, he did not consider a landing there on the north side of the river a feasible project, although for a moment he thought that the attempt might be worth making. As he wrote, some weeks later, to Pitt : " What I feared most was that if we should have landed between the town and the river of Cap Rouge the body first landed could not be reinforced before they were attacked by the enemy's whole army." It seemed to Wolfe that another attempt against the Beauport lines was called for, especially as Montcalm might have weakened his force by detaching a force to meet a possible danger above Quebec ; and, in fact, Montcalm had sent Bougainville, with 600 men, to guard the few paths up the cliffs along the twelve miles between Quebec and Cap Rouge. In order still more to distract Montcalm, Wolfe ordered his quartermaster-general Carleton to make a raid at Pointe aux Trembles, a place further up the river. But although the raid was duly carried out, and a number of important prisoners were carried off, Montcalm refused to allow himself to be influenced by it. Accordingly, on July 23rd, a council of war was held on Saunders's flagship, at which it was decided that the attempt against the Beauport lines should be carried out. Another step of a drastic kind was resolved upon. On his first arrival Wolfe had issued a rather bombastic proclamation, offering the colonists immunity if they would keep aloof from his contest with the King of France's army. The proclamation had been without effect, and it was now decided that unless by August 10th the colonists should accept the offer of neutrality, the whole country would be laid waste and every inhabitant taken would be made a prisoner.

On the night of the 28th the French made another attempt to destroy the fleet of the invaders, sending down a hundred rafts tied together and laden with combustibles which were set on fire. But once again, with coolness and resource, the sailors grappled with the danger, and the imposing engine of destruction was towed ashore. Three days later, on July 31st, took place the attack on Montcalm's position. The task was one of immense difficulty, and it seems that Wolfe had never much confidence in its success. Briefly, Wolfe's plan was to ferry over all the available grenadier companies, and part of Monckton's brigade from Point Lévis and the Isle of Orléans, and to land the force opposite the left of Montcalm's position, where it would be joined by Murray's and Townshend's brigades, which were to cross the Montmorenci River where it was fordable near the mouth. The navy was to co-operate by sending some transports, fitted as floating batteries, which were to be run inshore till they took the ground, while Saunders himself, in the *Centurion*, was to take up a position in the North Channel, where his ship did excellent service with her guns. The initial objective was to be a redoubt which the French had erected to bar the passage of the tidal ford near the mouth of the Montmorenci.

After attempting a feint against Montcalm's right, the boats—so soon as the tidal ford of the Montmorenci was passable for Townshend and Murray—dashed for their real landing-place opposite the French left. Misfortune dogged the enterprise from the start. A long delay was caused by a reef, which had not been discovered before, and Montcalm had time to make his necessary movements while Wolfe was searching for a fresh landing-place. Thirteen companies of grenadiers were the first ashore, followed by 200 men of the Royal Americans, but, without waiting to form up, the various companies of the grenadiers—urged on doubtless by inter-regimental rivalry—rushed headlong for the redoubt, which the French hurriedly evacuated. The redoubt was, however, commanded by the French entrenchments above— a fact which Wolfe had not anticipated—and the grenadiers came under such a withering fire that they recoiled for a moment. Some, however, made a most gallant attempt to struggle up the steep slippery ascent on the summit of which the French were posted, but the attempt was hopeless, and the assailants were heavily punished by the French musketry. It was now growing dark, a storm of rain came on, and the tide had begun to make, threatening the retreat of Townshend's brigade, which had passed across the ford at the mouth of the Montmorenci. In these circumstances Wolfe realized that a continuance of the attempt would be highly imprudent, and he accordingly ordered a retirement. Thus the affair had been a complete failure, and it had cost Wolfe nearly 450 casualties, including thirty-three officers. He himself, while on board the cat-boat *Russell*, had been struck three times by splinters, and had his stick knocked from his grasp by a cannon ball. The affair was in every way unfortunate. It shook Wolfe's confidence in himself; a little later he talked of himself as " a man that must necessarily be ruined." Smollett relates how Wolfe was often seen to sigh, and was often heard to complain, and how he realized that to return unsuccessful would expose him to the censure and reproach of an ignorant populace. The confidence, too, of the soldiers in their leader was affected, and many of the officers talked freely of the disastrous July 31st. The abortive attack seems also to have led to a little friction between Wolfe and Saunders. And finally the *moral* of the French rose so high at their success that Vaudreuil declared triumphantly: " I have no more anxiety about Quebec."

It was clearly now advisable to exploit the passage of Quebec. Deserters had brought Wolfe the intelligence that supplies were running short in Quebec, and early in August he discovered by the same means that some fifty miles up the river the French had formed large depôts of food, clothing, and ammunition at Deschambault. In consultation with Saunders, Wolfe decided to make an attempt to destroy this depôt—a step which, in conjunction with the ravaging of the fields everywhere within reach of the troops, would, he hoped, materially assist in the reduction of Quebec. Accordingly, on the night of August 5th, Murray, with 1,260 men, marched some distance up the south bank to embark in flat-bottomed boats, which had run past Quebec during the same night.

For the next three weeks this further dissemination of Wolfe's force left him in a position in which he was unable to take any decisive step until the result of the up-river diversion had become known, and the troops making it had returned. Murray, however, instead of at once proceeding to act against the depôt at Deschambault with Holmes, who was the admiral in charge of the naval side of the upstream operations, decided to attack Pointe aux Trembles, many miles short of the objective against which he had been directed to operate. The reason for this divergence from his orders was a wish to assist the admiral in the capture of some floating batteries which had been observed off the place. Two attempts were made upon Pointe aux Trembles, both of which failed, and Murray was compelled to retire to the southern bank, having lost over a hundred in killed and wounded. Murray's action, when the news of it reached Wolfe on the 11th, seems to have been considered an uncalled-for operation, and was the subject of some comment in camp. Within a week, however, Murray and Holmes were able to bring off their great *coup*. On the night of August 18th, leaving tents standing and fires burning at the camp opposite Pointe aux Trembles, and under cover of a feint against that place, they slipped up-stream with a flowing tide and landed five miles below their objective at Deschambault. No opposition was encountered. The surprise was complete, and after setting fire to a storehouse containing stores and clothing, the troops re-embarked without the loss of a single man. Having accomplished his task, Murray set his force in movement along the south bank to rejoin headquarters.

Wolfe had expected Murray back by the middle of the month, and had been chafing at his delay—so much so that on August 19th he wrote to Monckton : " I wish we had Murray's Corps back so that we might decide it with 'em " ; and four days later : " Murray, by his long stay above, and by detaining all our boats, is actually master of the operations, or rather puts an entire stop to them." For Wolfe was still set upon the idea of a further attempt upon the Beauport position. His perseverance in that project, and his refusal to exploit the up-river situation, and thus to control the line of supply by which Quebec was fed, have been the subject of considerable criticism. Wolfe, however, considered the up-river movements purely as a means to an end, that end being to force

THE QUEBEC CAMPAIGN, 1759   355

Montcalm, if not to evacuate his trenches, at any rate so to weaken himself by sending detachments up the St. Lawrence as seriously to reduce the defensive strength of his position. Such expectation on the part of Wolfe was not without justification. Before even Murray had started up river, a deserter who surrendered to the frigates below Quebec reported that Amherst had been very successful at Ticonderoga. Montcalm would, of course, have heard this news, and would probably be forced to take action about it. Actually on August 9th he not only had confirmation of this report, but heard also of the loss of Fort Niagara—intelligence which compelled him to send off Lévis at once to Montreal with 800 men, of whom 100 were regulars.

Then, as Wolfe foresaw, the burning of the French magazines at Deschambault had a most disturbing effect on Montcalm, who was at last goaded into action. He rushed at once to the scene of action— where he arrived too late—and during his absence the Beauport position was without not only the French commander-in-chief, but his two chief subordinates, Lévis and Bougainville, as well. The absence of the three senior officers at the same time would certainly be disturbing to the French troops on the Beauport position. Again, Wolfe knew perfectly well that the French must rely upon getting in the harvest if they were to continue to exist, and the need for gathering it was accentuated by the fact that the summer had been abnormally wet and the harvest a poor one. During the month of August, indeed, Montcalm had to give leave to 2,000 Canadians for the purpose, and it seems that the bulk of these had taken the law into their own hands and that the grant of leave was simply a face-saving concession wrung *ex post facto* from Montcalm. The Indian allies, too, of the French were not likely to appreciate the Fabian tactics to which they found themselves committed, and indeed, when Montcalm endeavoured to assure them of speedy victory, the red men ironically pointed to the shells crashing in Quebec, and to the British ships and camps still undisturbed.

Wolfe had clearly some justification in looking for a certain disintegration of the French force on the Beauport position and a certain depression of their *moral*—a depression bound to be accentuated by the sight of Quebec crumbling under their eyes. The arrival of a convoy gave Wolfe almost unlimited ammunition, and even by August 4th 4,000 shells and nearly 10,000 round shot had been discharged against the city. The damage done had been very severe, and during the night of the 8th–9th the Lower Town—which was the richest and most thickly populated part of the city—was set on fire and almost totally destroyed. The Upper Town had also suffered severely, and early in the month the guns on Pointe des Pères were reaching even the northern suburbs of Quebec. These considerations do not pretend to be exhaustive, but reflection on them may perhaps help the reader to understand why Wolfe was reluctant to abandon the idea of an attack upon the Beauport position. He was clearly right in wishing to dispose of Montcalm's covering army before attempting the investment of Quebec, and that army was his initial objective. It is curious to reflect that his persistence has been criticized chiefly by writers who maintain that there are "rules" of strategy—and that amongst these so-called "rules" that of "maintenance of objective" takes a prominent place.

The intense strain which the responsibility of command had imposed upon Wolfe was, however, too much for his frail constitution. From the beginning of August he had been a sick man, and the failure of the attempt of July 31st told heavily on him. He struggled to attend to his duty, but about August 19th or 20th, to the dismay of the army, he was forced to take to his bed in the little house which he occupied at Montmorenci. Five days later he was reported to be on the road to recovery, and about this time he prepared a memorandum addressed to his three brigadiers, requesting them, in order that the public service might not suffer by the indisposition of the general officer commanding, to meet to consider the best method of attacking the enemy, submitting to them three variations of a general plan for dealing with Montcalm's army. The alternatives suggested were as follows :—1. To ford the Montmorenci, eight or nine miles above the falls, and then to penetrate the rear of Montcalm's line. 2. To ford the river below the falls and then scale the heights. 3. For all the troops to attack the Beauport shore at low water.

The brigadiers met at Lévis, and, after considering Wolfe's proposals, were unanimous in rejecting them. They then drew up a proposal of their own, and on August 29th went on board the flagship to communicate it to Saunders. In this document, after exposing what they considered the drawbacks of Wolfe's proposals, they went on to say :—

" We are therefore of opinion that the most probable method of striking an effectual blow is to bring the troops to the south shore, and to carry the operations above the town. If we can establish ourselves on the north shore, the Marquis of Montcalm must fight us on our own terms ; we are between him and his provisions, and between him and the army opposing General Amherst. If he gives us battle and we defeat him, Quebec, and probably all Canada, will be our own, which is beyond any advantage we can expect by the Beauport side ; and should the enemy pass over the River St. Charles with force sufficient to oppose this operation, we may still, with more ease and probability of success, execute the General's third proposition (which is, in our opinion, the most eligible) or undertake anything else on the Beauport shore, necessarily weakened by the detachments made to oppose us above the town."

When this proposal was submitted to Wolfe he acquiesced in it—a fact which, at first sight, might suggest irresolution on his part ; for to adopt the plan put forward by the brigadiers was to forgo the idea of attacking Montcalm in his Beauport position, to which Wolfe had long been wedded. On the other hand, it must be pointed out that the concluding lines of the proposal of the brigadiers distinctly foreshadowed a possible reversion to Wolfe's idea ; and, further, having directed the brigadiers to consider three alternative schemes, Wolfe would have been ill-advised, to say the least of it, to act contrary to their unanimous decision. To persist in attempting to carry out a scheme of his own, knowing that his subordinates disapproved of it, was not the best way to ensure victory. Wolfe, therefore, agreed to put the suggestion of the brigadiers to the test, but was unable, in his condition of health, to feel much enthusiasm for it. It is certainly remarkable that he sent, on August 31st, a force of some 1,600 down the St. Lawrence merely " to lay waste such parishes as shall presume to persist in their opposition." This detachment did not rejoin until a week after the battle for Quebec. In a despatch to Pitt, dated September 2nd, 1759, there is almost a touch of despair. Wolfe admits that " In this situation there is such a choice of difficulties, that I own myself at a loss how to determine. The affairs of Great Britain, I know, require the most vigorous measures ; but then, the courage of a handful of brave men should be exerted only when there is some hope of a favourable event." Two days earlier he had written a short note to his widowed mother, and in it the same dejection is revealed. " My writing to you will convince you that no personal evils, worse than defeats and disappointments, have fallen upon me. The enemy puts nothing to risk, and I can't, in conscience, put the whole army to risk. My antagonist has wisely shut himself up in inaccessible entrenchments, so that I can't get at him without spilling a torrent of blood, and that perhaps to little purpose. The Marquis of Montcalm is at the head of a great number of bad soldiers, and I am at the head of a small number of good ones that wish for nothing so much as to fight him; but the wary old fellow avoids an action, doubtful of the behaviour of his army. People must be of the profession to understand the disadvantages and difficulties we labour under, arising from the uncommon natural strength of the country."

On September 3rd the troops were skilfully withdrawn without loss from the camp on the Montmorenci, and on the following night a flotilla of flat-bottomed boats passed successfully above the town with the baggage and stores. On the 5th seven battalions marched westward along the south shore from Point Lévis, and embarked, together with Wolfe himself, on Admiral Holmes's ships. The movement at once upset Montcalm, who sent off large reinforcements to Bougainville, who had his headquarters at Cap Rouge, with detached fortified posts down the river, including one at Anse du Foulon, a cove set in the wooded and precipitous heights, from which a fair winding road, leading up from the beach, emerged on the

THE QUEBEC CAMPAIGN, 1759   361

Heights of Abraham, a mile and a half above Quebec.

Within the next few days there took place some movements up and down the river, the obviousness and simplicity of which are apt to be obscured by the technical terms sometimes used to describe them. The phrases "amphibious operations," "interior and exterior lines," "communications," and "strategic pressure" are often employed. The reader will be well advised to reject this pseudo-scientific jargon and to concentrate his mind on two simple facts and the corollaries of them. The first fact is that the St. Lawrence is tidal at and above Quebec, and the tide was so impetuous as to reach a velocity of four knots. It follows from this that troops moving with the tide—either up or down stream—either in boats aided by oars or in ships aided by the wind, could obviously move faster than an enemy flying column trying to move parallel with them on the bank. The second fact is that tides have ebb and flow, the beginning, termination and duration of which are exactly known. To every journey made with the stream a return journey with the same assistance—except in the case of certain conditions of wind, when ships with sails were in question—was guaranteed. The importance of these two facts when a landing on the northern bank was in question must be obvious. The British soldiers, resting in boats, could proceed rapidly, say, downstream, with the French flying column trying to keep pace with them ; and at the turn of the tide the soldiers could either attempt to force a landing where they were or, if the place looked " unhealthy," could then glide rapidly back again and search for another landing-place, leaving the enemy, already exhausted, to follow as best they could. This, in a few words, was the secret of the " tactics " or the " strategy " of those few days.

Wolfe, however, taking counsel with himself alone, decided to dot the i's and cross the t's of the scheme submitted by his brigadiers. They had contemplated, apparently, a landing by a *coup de main* a little above Cap Rouge, but Wolfe saw that by drawing Bougainville further up-stream, and by making a feint simultaneously against Montcalm on the Beauport lines as well, it might be possible, secretly, under cover of darkness, and using the flowing and ebb tide in succession, suddenly to emerge on the Heights of Abraham close to Quebec by means of the cove at Anse du Foulon. It was a daring plan, although the dangers inseparable from it have perhaps been somewhat exaggerated. It was on September 9th that Wolfe formed his decision, and that decision was entirely his own. On his return to Holmes's flagship he simply informed the brigadiers of his intention, and on the next day took two of them and some of the staff to view the selected landing-place from the south shore. The exact details were, however, kept secret almost to the last moment, and even a few hours before the venture was launched the brigadiers drew up a formal remonstrance, protesting that they were not sufficiently informed as to the exact landing-place, to which Wolfe replied, with a dignified firmness, not unmixed with tartness, giving exact details of the landing-place, and of how the operation was to be conducted, and definitely assuming for himself responsibility to King and country for the consequences.

It seems that during a reconnaissance—probably that made on September 10th, when the Anse du Foulon was pointed out to the two brigadiers—mention was made of Gray's " Elegy," and that someone in the boat quoted the line " The paths of glory lead but to the grave," whereupon Wolfe replied that he would rather be the author of that poem than take Quebec. The more popular legend is that Wolfe recited the stanza, and made the remark during the actual passage down the river on the night of the actual attempt. For this preposterous perversion there is not a particle, a scintilla, an iota of evidence. It may be mentioned that several leading modern historians omit this " Elegy " incident altogether.

The plan of Wolfe, although simple in general outline, required thorough co-ordination between the navy and army, as well as perfect staff work and professional skill on the part of the former service —qualities which were splendidly displayed. A good part of the plan was essentially naval. Below Quebec, Admiral Saunders was to move out of the South Channel with his main fleet and, with lowered boats, manned by sailors, marines and such soldiers as were available below Quebec, was to make a feint of landing on the Beauport shore—an operation which would certainly tend to pin Montcalm to his position. Above Quebec a feint was to be made up-stream by some ships from Cap Rouge, but it is not clear to what extent this ruse was actually carried out. As for the real attack, the arrangements were as follows:—From Cap Rouge, when the tide should begin to ebb, about 2 a.m. on the morning of September 13th, 400 light infantry, under Colonel Howe, as the advanced guard, followed by 1,300 men under Monckton and Murray, were to embark in flat-bottomed boats and drop down to the Anse du Foulon, where the boats were timed to arrive at 4 a.m. This force of 1,700 was all that the boats could carry in one trip. A further 1,900 were to be brought downstream in the ships, which were to anchor as near the landing-place as possible. Then were to come the vessels carrying artillery and entrenching tools. The remaining troops allotted to the attack were to be marched to Goreham's Post from Point Lévis, ready to embark as soon as the second landing had been made at Anse du Foulon. Finally, the batteries opposite Quebec were to fire with increased intensity upon the city.

According to a tradition which seems well founded, Wolfe spent some time on the eve of the battle with his old school-fellow Captain John Jervis—afterwards the Earl of St. Vincent—of

H.M.S. *Porcupine*, entrusting to him the miniature of Miss Lowther, which, by the terms of his will, was to be returned to her set in diamonds. At 1.30 a.m. on the morning of the 13th a lantern was shown in the rigging of the *Sutherland*—Holmes's signal for the boats to gather round—and at 2 a.m. they were cast off down the river, Wolfe himself being in one of the leading boats. In due course the other vessels followed with the second division of the troops and the artillery and stores. Everything was carried out in perfect order, and the boats, sloops and frigates moved in the darkness down the river in absolute silence. The procession consisted first of the boats under the direction of Captain Chads, R.N. Then followed the armed sloops, and behind them came those with stores and ammunition. These were followed by H.M.S. *Lowestoft*—on board of which was Admiral Holmes—accompanied by the *Sea Horse* and *Squirrel*, and two transports, all full of troops, the *Sutherland* having been left behind to " Keep an eye on the Enemy's Motions, their Floating Batteries and Small Craft." Then, for one breathless moment, it seemed as if disaster were imminent. Under the north shore was lying H.M.S. *Hunter*, waiting to intercept a French provision convoy which was expected to try to run down to Quebec that night. As the leading boats of the attacking force drew near, those on board them heard the crew of the *Hunter* rushing to quarters. Fortunately it was possible to explain matters before the *Hunter* opened fire, and the expedition slipped silently by. For two hours the boats moved on unchallenged until they were close to Anse du Foulon, where a French sentry called out *Qui vive?* Instantly Captain Fraser, of the Highlanders, replied *France. A quel regiment?* called out the voice from the shore. *De la Reine* was the reply, naming one of the regular regiments known to be with Bougainville. This satisfied the sentry, who, knowing that a convoy was expected, allowed the boats to pass without demanding the countersign. The racing ebb tide carried the leading boat a little beyond the intended landing-place, and the troops in them disembarked below the path on a narrow strand at the foot of the heights. A forlorn hope of an officer and twenty-four other ranks of the Light Infantry dragged themselves up the cliff side, and soon rifle-shots and loud hurrahs told Wolfe that the first step had been gained. The rest of the troops landed, and the boats went successively to bring the second division from the frigates and transports, and from the south bank of the river. Before the sun was well up, Wolfe's force, some 4,500 strong, had reached the plateau, and was moving across the plateau towards the Sainte Foy road. No opposition had been encountered after the surprise of the French post at the top of the path, except a rather galling fire from the left, and from the fire of batteries at Sillery and Samos on the rearmost boats. These guns were quickly taken in reverse by some of the Light Infantry and silenced.

Wolfe meanwhile had gone forward to reconnoitre, and drew up his force, facing generally east, on a tract of grass land known as the Plain of Abraham : fairly level ground for the most part, though broken by patches of corn and clumps of bushes. The right of the line rested near the brink of the heights, which here overlook the St. Lawrence ; the left flank was " in the air " and lay about one-third of the way between the Quebec-Sainte Foy and the Quebec-Sillery roads. On the extreme right was the 35th Regiment. Next in succession, working from right to left, came the Louisburg Grenadiers, the 28th, the 43rd, the 47th, Fraser's Highlanders, and the 58th, less two companies. On the Sillery road was posted a brass six-pounder which had been pulled up the steep path at Anse du Foulon. The left flank was refused with the 15th Regiment and the 2nd Battalion Royal Americans. The 48th Regiment was in reserve. Guarding the landing-place were two companies of the 58th, while the 3rd Battalion Royal Americans kept open the communication with it. The Light Infantry, under Colonel Howe, were posted about half a mile to the left rear, between the Sillery and Sainte Foy roads. Monckton commanded the right and Murray the left, Townshend being in charge of the troops available as a reserve. Wolfe himself remained with Monckton's brigade on the right. Quebec was not a mile distant, but was hidden from view by a low ridge some six hundred yards in front of the line.

Montcalm at his headquarters had passed an anxious night, for no sooner had his alarm at the false attack by Saunders begun to subside when the guns from the west of Quebec were clearly heard. No information having reached him by six o'clock, Montcalm, accompanied by Johnstone, one of his *aides-de-camp*, rode off to the bridge over the St. Charles, where he had his first sight of the British drawn up on the plateau west of the city. "There they are where they have no right to be," he exclaimed, adding: "This is a serious business." He at once sent off Johnstone at a gallop to bring up all the troops left at Beauport except a small guard of 200 men. Close by was the Guienne Regiment, which had been twice told off for duty on the Heights, but had been twice withdrawn by order of the governor-general. Montcalm at once sent it forward, and it moved up to the high ground to reconnoitre.

Meanwhile the centralization of command on the French side was beginning to work havoc with Montcalm's plans. Vaudreuil, from the bridge over the St. Charles, was issuing orders of his own, with the result that the troops on the left of the Beauport position were kept in their trenches; and when Montcalm applied to the governor of the fortress for twenty-five field guns, only three pieces were given him. As the troops crossed the bridge over the St. Charles, they moved upon Quebec, entering the city on the north side, and, passing through the narrow streets, emerged upon the plain by the gates on the western front. Montcalm was unable fully to deploy his troops owing to the clumps of bushes which dotted the ground, and the advance took place in an irregular line of quarter columns. A hurried council of war now took place on the French side, and it was unanimously decided to push forward at once in order to deny to the enemy the possibility of entrenching himself and receiving reinforcements. By nine o'clock the French line was formed. On the right was a battalion of Quebec colonials. Then came the white-coated regiments of La Sarre, Languedoc, Béarn and La Guienne, with the blue mass of the Royal Roussillon on their left, and next, on the extreme left of the line, the colonial infantry of Montreal and Three Rivers. The flanks were covered by Indian and Canadian sharpshooters, who made skilful use of the features of the ground. The Canadian militiamen—some of whom were apparently placed among the regulars—had no bayonets, and neither they nor the Indians were of much use on open ground. In numbers the French force was approximately equal to that of the enemy.

The battle began with a duel between the sharpshooters on the French side and the skirmishers whom Wolfe had thrown forward to meet them, followed by an artillery combat between Montcalm's three field guns and the solitary six-pounder on the Sillery Road. Then about ten o'clock the French line advanced with loud shouts to the real attack, firing so soon as they came within long range. The first shots were fired when the lines were apparently two hundred yards apart, and came apparently from the non-regular troops, who not only opened fire without orders, but, following their usual custom, threw themselves flat on the ground to reload. The French formation was thus spoilt and the flanks uncovered, for some of the Canadians began to steal off to join the skirmishers who were fighting from behind cover. The regulars, however, moved on, but began to lose direction, sheering off to right and left and fighting shy of the British centre, opening as they did an irregular and half-hearted fire.

Until the French advance began the British troops had been lying down. They then sprang to their feet and stood steady with recovered arms. Nearer and nearer drew the multi-coloured French line—but a line no longer—and it lurched forward unsteadily with a fire ragged and uncontrolled. Wolfe had been struck in the wrist, but had merely wrapped his handkerchief round the wound and called out to the men to be steady and reserve their fire. Then, when less than forty yards separated the two armies, there came from the British right a sharp word of command. A volley crashed out, followed almost instantaneously by other volleys right along the line, the detonations blending into one frightful crash as if from some monstrous cannon. The front line of the French went down like corn before a sickle, and from behind the curtain of smoke rose yells and oaths and the clatter of arms. In a moment the British had reloaded, and a second series of volleys crashed out. The French right reeled and broke, streaming in disorder from the field. Almost immediately the centre gave way in confusion, and the left, after a brief stand, in turn broke up and fled.

At this moment Wolfe rushed to the front of the Louisburg Grenadiers and gave the order to charge. Little resistance was encountered, except from the fire of the sharpshooters on the flanks, and the French army was but a panic-stricken mob flying in terror from the bayonets and claymores of the pursuers. Just as the charge began Wolfe was struck by a bullet in the groin, but he continued to advance until another bullet passed through his lungs. Two or three officers and a private soldier carried him to the rear and laid him down. He refused to see a surgeon, saying: " There is no need ; it is all over with me," and sank into a state of semi-consciousness. He was aroused by a cry of " See how they run ! " " Who run ? " asked Wolfe, like a man roused from sleep. " The enemy, sir. Egad ! They give way everywhere." " Go, one of you lads, to Colonel Burton," said Wolfe earnestly, " and tell him to march Webb's regiment with all speed down to Charles River to cut off the retreat of the fugitives from the bridge." Then, turning on his side, he added : " Now God be praised, I will die in peace," and sank back dead.

The body of Wolfe was borne to Anse du Foulon,

and at eleven o'clock was brought on board the *Lowestoft*. The next in order of seniority to the dead commander was Monckton, but he had been wounded, and command passed to Townshend. Almost at once he was called upon to deal with a danger which, had it occurred but a short time previously, might seriously have prejudiced the British chance of victory, for Bougainville's force now appeared and threatened the rear of the British. Townshend, however, had reformed his men as quickly as possible, and, with two regiments and two field guns (a second gun had been brought up), turned on Bougainville, who, realizing that Montcalm's army had been driven off the field, retired in good order on Ancienne Lorette, nine miles north-west of Quebec. Townshend now gave orders to the army to entrench, and parties of sailors continued their task of getting guns and stores up from Anse du Foulon.

On the French side all was confusion. Montcalm, on a big black horse, had been conspicuous in the fight, desperately endeavouring to rally his flying troops, but he had been borne along in the headlong rush to the city. On the way he was shot through the abdomen, but, supported in the saddle, he rode through the St. Louis Gate. Some terrified women, seeing his bloodstained uniform, shrieked out, " Oh God ! The marquis is killed ! " Montcalm endeavoured to reassure them, and was then borne to the house of a surgeon. Informed that he had but a day to live, Montcalm replied : " So much the better. I am happy not to live to see the surrender of Quebec." He was still, however, able to take some small part in affairs. A hurried council of war was assembled by Vaudreuil in a work by the bridge over the St. Charles, by which many of the fugitives had passed. A message was sent to the dying Montcalm for his advice. In reply he suggested three methods: a renewal of the battle; a retirement westwards to the Jacques Cartier; or surrender. The second course was adopted, and at nine o'clock that night the demoralized French army, abandoning all the stores and camp equipment of the Beauport position, streamed away in disorderly and panic-stricken flight, Vaudreuil, the braggart governor-general, accompanying them. Before leaving he had written to Ramezay, the governor of Quebec, authorizing him to surrender so soon as provisions should fail. Inside the city the dying Montcalm passed away just before dawn, and some hours before his death he had addressed a letter to Townshend, commending the French sick and wounded to his care.

The utter confusion prevailing in the French higher command outside the city was reflected within the fortress itself. The governor-general had directed Ramezay to hold out until compelled to give up the place through lack of provisions; but the dying Montcalm was under the impression that the fate of the city was in his hands, and in the letter, referred to above, to Wolfe's successor, he opened with the phrase *Obligé de ceder Quebec à vos armes*. The governor of the fortress continued, however, to resist for several days, during which time the guns of the fortress were particularly active, awaiting the provisions and reinforcements promised by Vaudreuil. The place was in a serious condition. One hundred and eighty houses had been destroyed by fire, and the total in ruins was over five hundred. Practically the whole of the Lower Town had ceased to exist. The cathedral was entirely consumed. Many of the citizens were without shelter for the coming winter. Nine hundred of the garrison had deserted, and the town was on the verge of starvation. The British on their side were anxious to enforce an early capitulation, for soon the larger ships would have to depart, and the others would shortly have to follow. There was the danger, too, that the broken remnants of Montcalm's army, uniting with Bougainville's force and with the detachment under Lévis, who had been summoned by Vaudreuil to come up from Montreal to take command, might attack the British from the rear.

This danger was not one, however, so serious as it might seem, certainly not after September 17th, by which date the British had got up from the river sixty guns and fifty-eight mortars. Two days earlier the mayor and citizens of Quebec had presented a memorial to the governor begging him to save the city from the horrors of starvation or assault. Ramezay temporized for a couple of days, but Townshend, with the threat of a combined naval and military attack on the 17th, induced the governor to hoist the white flag. Ramezay attempted to gain time by prolonging negotiations, but Townshend replied that unless the place was surrendered by 11 a.m. he would take it by storm. The tragic situation of Quebec was now being tinged with a blend of farce. Desertions, even in broad daylight, were taking place in considerable numbers. A sergeant who had charge of the defences in one of the weakest parts of the town not only deserted, but took with him the key of one of the city gates, which he handed over to the British commander. It was in circumstances such as these that Ramezay signed the capitulation. The terms were lenient, the garrison being allowed to march out with arms and baggage, drums beating, lighted matches, with two guns and twelve rounds—and this although the land defences of the fortress had not withstood even a single cannon shot. The garrison was, however, to be transported to France. For the British the capitulation was perhaps fortunate, for before the messenger with the signed articles reached Townshend, mounted men rode into the city with provisions and a cheering message that Lévis was on his way with a relieving force. Early in the afternoon of the 18th the British entered the city, the soldiers occupying the Upper and a naval brigade taking possession of the Lower Town. At four o'clock the Union flag of Great Britain was hoisted in three conspicuous places. The French troops marched out with the honours of war and, on the 22nd, were sent to France in British transports.

With the hoisting of the British flag over the fortress the task which had been set Wolfe to accomplish was achieved. He had been told to attack and take Quebec, and it was only his death in the hour of victory which robbed him of the glory of putting the seal of completion on his efforts. There cannot be the slightest doubt that the daring conception formed by him but a few days before the battle was entirely his own, and he is entitled to every credit for having refused to be shaken in his determination by the disquiet which the apparently desperate nature of his scheme aroused not only in his brigadiers but in the admiral co-operating in the attack as well. There has arisen a school of criticism within recent years whose members assert that the fall of Quebec by no means represented the complete success which Wolfe ought to have achieved. It is contended that if he had adopted the scheme submitted to him by his brigadiers, namely, to land at Pointe aux Trembles, twenty miles above Quebec—although it is worth while pointing out that the brigadiers, in their memorandum of August 29th, said nothing so definite as that—such operation, if successfully carried out, would have given him command of the whole road system leading to Quebec, and in this way he could have absolutely blocked all land and water communication between Quebec and Montreal. In these circumstances, so it is contended, Montcalm, from mere self-preservation, must have evacuated his position and moved westward to attack.

The weakness of this line of argument seems to lie in the fact that Wolfe had no transport and no horses for his guns. Montcalm, on the other hand, could have been accompanied by mobile artillery, and, picking up Bougainville's detachment *en route*, he would have had the further mobility and reconnoitring power afforded by over 200 cavalry —for the mounted troops had been given to Bougainville. In numbers Montcalm, thus reinforced, might have been at least fifty per cent. stronger than Wolfe, and even if he had preferred to avoid the gage of battle, his manœuvring ability would have enabled him to pass his army round Wolfe's outer flank, when he could have based himself on the French supply ships above the Richelieu rapids. This would have been to leave Wolfe between him and Quebec. But would this have been a disadvantage to Montcalm? Could Wolfe have moved to his long-wished-for position on the Heights of Abraham, where he would have the guns of Quebec in front and the unbeaten, mobile, numerically superior and well-supplied army of Montcalm to his rear? Further, it must be remembered that the removal of Montcalm's army from the neighbourhood of Quebec would have prolonged the resisting power of the fortress so far as the question of food supply was concerned. It would, of course, be absurd to dogmatize without accurate knowledge of the capacity of the up-river magazines and ships for the supply of food, stores and ammunition. But in war it is often wise to take *omne ignotum pro magnifico*, and the experience of the following year tends to show that the capacity of the supply depôts and of Montreal was adequate. But all that the present writer wishes to do here is to suggest a line of thought which quite probably may have occurred to Wolfe, but has certainly escaped the notice of some of his critics.

To turn now from a consideration of what might have happened to an examination of what actually took place, there is the question whether Montcalm's action in immediately attacking Wolfe was the best in the circumstances of the case. Here, again, there are two different schools of thought. The protagonists of one school assert that Montcalm was clearly in the right, maintaining that prompt action was necessary, seeing that every minute's delay would give the British the chance of strengthening their position and of getting up artillery from the river; while the other school holds that it was above all things imperative for Montcalm to unite with Bougainville so as to present an unquestioned numerical superiority to the enemy, a victory over whom, seeing the difficult position of the British, might well have been decisive. The author of this book is convinced that the members of the latter school of thought have reached the correct opinion. In the actual battle Montcalm began his attack about ten o'clock; Bougainville appeared on the field at eleven o'clock; but, for all the influence he was then able to exert upon the destiny of Canada on that fateful September 13th, 1759, he might just as well have been in Europe. It will be noted that between Montcalm's attack and the appearance of Bougainville about one hour elapsed, and it is difficult to see how within a period so brief the position of the British could have been materially strengthened, especially as Montcalm could have harried them all that time with his Canadian sharpshooters and his Indians. If Montcalm had manœuvred to his right until he joined hands with Bougainville, he might then have forced the British to accept battle against a superior force, with their backs to the precipitous banks of the St. Lawrence and their sole line of retreat down the steep Anse du Foulon road. And in the worst event for Montcalm he could himself have retreated with Bougainville to Cap Rouge, bringing about a situation analogous to that outlined a few pages back.

To carry out the plan above suggested as the most favourable for Montcalm would, however, have been rendered difficult by the fact that he had clung so long to the Beauport lines; for the left units on that position were nearly eight miles from Quebec, and his manœuvring power was hampered by the time required in collecting troops from a position extending so far to the east. The present writer cannot help feeling that, once it was clear to Montcalm that Wolfe had moved the bulk of his army up river, Montcalm was wrong in keeping his force on the Beauport position. There was henceforth always the possibility—if, indeed, not the probability—that the long-delayed battle would take place west of Quebec, and for such an event Montcalm's army was now unhandily placed. There seem good grounds for believing that a more central and concentrated position, say, astride the River St. Charles at the double bridge-head, where the bridge of boats crossed it, would have made Montcalm *in utrumque paratus*, able to deal, and deal swiftly, with any attempt on the part of Wolfe to strike a blow west of Quebec or—should the up-river movement turn out to be a mere ruse—able to revert once again, and in sufficient time, to his old position on the Beauport front.

What actually happened was that the French army was beaten in detail. Montcalm's force, hurriedly brought into action and incomplete, was routed, and Bougainville's detachment was driven off the field. Wolfe took great risks, but the situation was one which demanded such a course. Wolfe hoped that by accepting the risks he would out-manœuvre his opponent. He did so. The immediate fall of Quebec was the result. " It was a famous victory," and it is commemorated in the British Army not only by the battle honour

borne on the colours of the victorious infantry, but by the creation of a regiment—now the 17th Lancers—whose badge of the Death's Head, with the scroll bearing the terse alternative " Or Glory," was approved by George II as a commemoration for all time of the unflinching resolution and impetuous courage of the victor of Quebec.

CHAPTER SEVEN

THE SURRENDER OF CANADA TO THE BRITISH CROWN.

DURING the year 1759 people at home had been following the course of the war with some anxiety. Apart from the struggle at sea, England was fighting France on four fronts and in four continents, the bulk of the army abroad being engaged in Germany and North America. It was known that France was making great preparations to invade Great Britain, and it was realized that the force of regulars left in England was insufficient. The news of the great victory won in Germany at Minden on August 1st came, however, as a welcome relief, and, little over a fortnight later, Boscawen had overtaken the French Mediterranean fleet, which was endeavouring to unite with that of the Channel, and had overwhelmed it off Lagos. Even this did not exhaust the harvest of good tidings. The beginning of the month of September was distinguished " by a torrent of prosperous news." On September 8th news of American victories began to come in. Amherst had captured Ticonderoga and Johnson had taken Niagara—a combination of good fortune which augured well for the final settlement of the contest with France for America, and sent all England wild with delight. Horace Walpole wrote that we had taken more places and ships in a week than would have set up such pedant nations as Greece and Rome to all futurity, and playfully suggested Ticonderogus and Niagaricus as appellations for the victors. Then some five weeks later came the sobering anti-climax brought about by Wolfe's gloomy despatch written while he was smarting under the failure of his second attempt to dislodge Montcalm from the Beauport position. This reached Pitt on October 14th. Wisely he attempted no concealment. He at once sent the despatch to the *Gazette*. He himself was under no illusions; he gave up all hopes of success and said so publicly.

The mortification of the people at the failure was extreme, and not less so for the fact that Wolfe apparently despaired of being able to do anything further to accomplish what was eagerly looked for—the absolute conquest of Canada. But on October 16th, two days later, before the country had had time to realize the full extent of its disappointment, Colonel Hale arrived with news of the great victory. To the chagrin which had been felt there succeeded a frenzy of joy: " all was rapture and riot: all was triumph and exultation," wrote Smollett, who added also that the praise of the all-accomplished Wolfe " was exalted even to a ridiculous degree of hyperbole." All over Great Britain every town and village blazed with bonfires and illuminations. One spot alone was dark. At Blackheath, where Wolfe's mother mourned for her only son, her neighbours, in sympathy with her sorrow, refrained from the display of their participation in the national joy.

While the rejoicing in England was at its height, the body of James Wolfe had begun its last long journey home. After the corpse of the general had been brought from the field of battle on board the *Lowestoft*, it was embalmed, and on September 20th was transferred to another vessel for the voyage to England. The fleet was sent off in instalments, some to Halifax and the remainder to home waters, Saunders sailing with the last vessels to leave about the middle of October. The *Royal William* had the honour of bearing Wolfe's remains. She arrived at Spithead on Friday, November 16th, 1759, and at 7 a.m. on the following morning two guns fired from her announced the beginning of Wolfe's obsequies. Punctually at eight o'clock the body was lowered into a twelve-oared barge, which was towed by two others, and attended by twelve more similar craft. During the hour of the passage of the body from the *Royal William* to the Point of Portsmouth minute guns were fired from the ships at Spithead. The body was received by a regiment of Invalids and by a company of soldiers of the garrison. At nine o'clock the coffin was placed in a travelling hearse, followed by a mourning coach, and, passing through the garrison, moved out to the Landport Gate, preceded by the company of soldiers and followed by the Invalids, both with arms reversed. As the procession passed through the town the flag above the fort flew at half-mast, bells tolled in muffled peals, and minute guns were fired. When the Landport Gate was reached, the soldiers opened to the right and left, and the hearse and coach moved out by the road to London. On arrival at Blackheath the coffin was brought to the Wolfes' house, where it remained for a day, and on November 20th the body of James Wolfe was placed by that of his father in the family vault within the parish church of Greenwich.

On the day following the burial the House of Commons decided to erect a monument to Wolfe in Westminster Abbey. The motion was brought in by Pitt, who, in a low and plaintive voice, pronounced a kind of funeral oration. His speech on this occasion, unlike most of his speeches, was premeditated. It lacked animation and power, and, according to Horace Walpole, was perhaps the worst harangue he ever uttered. But the enthusiasm of his hearers supplied every deficiency. Pitt moved, too, in general terms, thanks to the generals and admirals, mentioning them all, and particularly Admiral Saunders, whose merit, he said, had equalled those who had beaten armadas. " May I anticipate ? " he cried, " those who *will* beat armadas." The monument to Wolfe was subsequently executed by Wilton, and represents the dying commander, whose right hand presses his mortal wound, sinking into the arms of a grenadier, who points to Fame hovering overhead. In the background is a mourning Highlander. During the Great War the colours of the Canadian regiments were grouped upon the monument, and the dying Wolfe was almost hidden by those emblems of loyalty of those Canadians of French and British stock who had come from overseas to fight for their common empire.

The words used by Pitt about future beating of armadas proved prophetic—more than prophetic even, for before they were spoken England had achieved a great victory over France at sea. During the summer the Brest fleet had been closely blockaded by Hawke, but when the autumn gales had driven the English admiral from the French coast, Conflans seized the opportunity to sail forth with his fleet of twenty-one ships of the line and five cruisers, with the object of defeating a small force under Captain Duff before Hawke could come to its assistance. Hawke, however, effected a junction with his subordinate off the point of Quiberon before Conflans could attack it. The French admiral drew his ships close inshore towards the mouth of the Vilaine—a coast guarded by granite rocks and islets above and by shoals and quicksands below. In spite of the protests of his pilot, Hawke led his fleet, in a gale of wind, into these perilous waters. Before night two French ships had struck; four others, amongst them the flagship of Conflans, had been sunk; the rest, more or less damaged, sought safety by running up the Vilaine. A finishing blow had been given to the naval power of France for the remainder of the war.

QUEBEC HOUSE, WESTERHAM, KENT. Known as Spiers during the period of occupation by the Wolfe family, 1726-1738.
(*By permission of " Country Life."*)

The victory of Quiberon Bay put an end to the fears of a French invasion; and although early in the following year the French made a raid on Carrickfergus and forced Belfast to supply victuals to the raiding ships, the effort was but a flash in the pan, and the raiding force was later captured off the Isle of Man by British cruisers. Towards the solving of the great question of the conquest of Canada the victory of Quiberon was obviously another step forward. The French navy was reduced to relative, if temporary, impotence; Louisburg was lost to it; the French troops in Canada—including regulars, colonials and militia —were outnumbered by the regulars and provincials opposed to them; and the victory of the English at Quiberon Bay enabled them to send overseas any military reinforcements they wished, while denying this power of reinforcement to the French. It was not unnatural, therefore, that opinion in England regarded the destiny of Canada as already settled, and that the belief should exist that the capture of Quebec, succeeding that of Louisburg, had now solved the question once for all. Actually this was not quite the case. In the early pages of this book the statement has been made that the destiny of Canada was decided amid the shoals of Quiberon Bay no less than upon the Heights of Abraham, and that this is true is simply a matter of history. But at the close of the year 1759 there was a danger that undue optimism might exist, and, as a matter of fact, such feeling did prevail. The fact was overlooked that in the American campaign of that year the French had succeeded in what they had set out to do, namely, to keep New France in being for another year.

The marooned British army in Quebec might be attacked and defeated by the French troops in Canada during the winter, before assistance could reach it, and Quebec might thus be retaken. Or, even supposing that Quebec should hold out all the winter, when the ice broke up in the spring French reinforcements and supplies might, notwithstanding that command of the sea was theoretically with the British, evade notice and slip up the St. Lawrence before the blockading fleets were in position, just as had happened in the spring of 1759; in which case English men-of-war might arrive to find that Quebec had just rehoisted the French flag. Or, finally, by the prolongation of the war, the French might by diplomacy recover what they had lost in battle. By the end of 1759 the war had been in progress over three years. Quite obviously it could not continue indefinitely, and when peace negotiations should begin, unless Canada had meanwhile been entirely and unmistakably conquered, France, by concessions elsewhere, might make out a good claim to be left with the bulk of her North American possessions. In the War of the Austrian Succession Louisburg had been wrested from France, but she had declined to make peace unless the lost fortress was restored to her. A similar obstinacy might be expressed over Quebec.

THE FALL OF CANADA 389

It was clearly, therefore, the object of England to push on with the entire conquest of Canada with the minimum of delay. But conditions of climate, topography, and the experience of Canadians in winter operations meant that it was possible for the French army in Canada to attack and retake Quebec before Amherst could begin to exert pressure against Montreal. Briefly stated, it might be assumed that Quebec was certain to be attacked before the ice broke up in the St. Lawrence, but this aspect of the case was generally overlooked in England, not only by the Horace Walpoles, but by the country at large.

The garrison left behind in Quebec amounted, in round numbers, to 7,300 of all ranks, Murray having been left in command. Before they sailed the English ships landed great quantities of stores, the task of unloading, which was one of heavy labour, increased by the fact that, as there were no horses in Quebec, the casks and bags had to be manhandled up a very steep hill from the Lower to the Upper Town. The first consideration, after the supplies had been landed, was to put Quebec into a satisfactory condition of defence. The wall on the west side of the city was not proof against gunfire, and, further, it was commanded by a ridge upon the Plain of Abraham. A great deal of damage, too, had been done to the city both by the guns of the fleet and by those of the battery on the opposite bank. Murray took immediate steps to repair the breaches, to open embrasures, and to mount some guns, but so far was Quebec from answering to the requirements of a fortress that at a very early stage Murray made up his mind, in case of attack, not to trust to the defences of Quebec, but to move out to meet his enemy, and, with this end in view, he established a couple of advanced posts a few miles west of Quebec at Sainte Foy and Old Lorette.

The long, cold Canadian winter was a severe trial to the garrison. By December the cold was intense, and all ranks suffered from want of fuel, from inadequate accommodation, and from a lack of fresh meat and vegetables. Sentries were relieved half-hourly, but, even with this precaution, frost-bite was of constant occurrence. The Highlanders suffered especially, until some of the nuns of the city, moved by compassion, knitted for them long woollen hose. During the winter five hundred houses, damaged during the bombardment, were repaired. The chief anxiety was about cordwood, so the regiments were instructed to obtain it themselves, the men being allowed extra pay when engaged in cutting it and bringing it to town. Owing to the scarcity of horses, the sleighs were drawn by soldiers, and many on this duty were frost-bitten. In the week before Christmas over 150 men were affected. On one occasion there were over 60 cases in one day, and of a party of 200 sent to the south bank of the river there were 198 cases. More serious than frost-bite was the scurvy which broke out. The garrison was victualled entirely with salt-pork provisions, and, owing to the laying waste of the country by Wolfe's orders during the summer, fresh meat was almost impossible to obtain. Fed upon salt pork and beef with insufficient vegetables, and insufficiently clothed, the men were unable to resist the disease. On December 24th, out of 6,400 of all ranks, 1,400 were unfit for duty, and as time wore on there was hardly a soldier in the ranks really free from the effects of scurvy.

An extraordinary feature of life in Quebec at the time was that there was scarcely any money to pay the troops. A sum of £20,000 had been despatched from Halifax, but the sloop of war conveying it reached the St. Lawrence too late in the season and was forced to return. From October 24th the pay of the troops was in arrear. Murray declined to issue paper money, and he forbade the circulation of the discredited paper money which had been used by the Canadians. Before the ships sailed away the officers of the navy had collected £4,000, which they lent to the army, and when a further supply was required Murray issued his own and Colonel Burton's notes at six months for £8,000, and asked the garrison to volunteer advances of cash on the security thus offered. The sum was promptly made up, one quarter of it being subscribed by Fraser's Highlanders.

In spite of the severe conditions and the monotony of the life, the *moral* of the garrison was high, and the soldiers cheerfully responded to all the calls made upon them. At first, however, discipline had begun to relax, and the supply of liquor found in the place brought about a considerable amount of drunkenness—so much so that Murray withdrew the licences which he had granted to some of the taverns, and any soldier found drunk was sentenced to receive twenty lashes every morning until he gave information as to where he had obtained the liquor. Murray was not the man to allow the safety of the garrison to be imperilled by the insubordination of a few. He ruled Quebec with a stern hand. The gallows and the triangles did their work. A soldier was hanged for theft, as was a Canadian for inciting soldiers to desert, a soldier who had taken off his uniform being discovered in his house. The sentences of a single court-martial show the severity of the discipline enforced. One soldier was sentenced to a thousand lashes for absence from duty and for using expressions tending to excite mutiny and desertion. A second, for being disguised with intention to desert, and being out of his quarters at an undue time of night, received three hundred. A third was awarded a thousand lashes for intention to desert, and a fourth for desertion and endeavouring to inveigle others to desert was condemned to death.

To turn now to the French, it will be remembered that the surrender of Quebec anticipated by but a short time the arrival of Lévis with a relieving force made up largely of the army which had streamed away from the city in panic-stricken flight on the night of September 13th, but the *moral* of which he had swiftly restored. By the death of Montcalm Lévis was now in chief command, and, after the failure to relieve Quebec, it was necessary to select a position for the French army. The main body of it was posted at Jacques Cartier, with detachments at Pointe aux Trembles and Saint Augustin, the last-named place being about two days' march from Quebec. The position at Jacques Cartier was a high bluff on the left bank of the river, and was so strengthened by the French engineers that in the end the fort there was the last point on the St. Lawrence where the French flag was lowered. When the winter definitely set in some of the regulars were kept in garrison at the outposts, the remainder being quartered among the inhabitants of Montreal and in the surrounding country; while the Canadians were dismissed to their homes subject to recall to service by the governor-general.

Both Vaudreuil and Lévis were determined to make an effort as early as possible to retake Quebec, although the latter sometimes cherished a wild scheme of leaving Canada to its fate and of leading his forces further into the interior, past Lake Ontario and Lake Erie, and thence down the Ohio and the Mississippi into Louisiana. This was, however, in his darker moments, and what he really hoped was to keep Canada "alive" until peace negotiations might be begun. There was in the colony a pathetic, but misplaced, confidence that so soon as conditions would admit of it in the following spring, France would make every effort to send assistance at the earliest possible moment to Canada. Lévis was for some time in favour of a winter attack on Quebec, and to take the place by escalade, but on the advice of his chief engineer he abandoned the idea. In the end it was resolved to defer the attack until the spring, but when the frost was still in the ground, and Murray could not throw up defences on the Plain of Abraham ; and, once in Quebec, the victors would there await that succour from France without which every plan must fail.

It was plain to Murray that he must expect an attempt to retake Quebec, and his surmise was confirmed by reports of deserters and spies. The situation was one of some gravity, for as the winter wore away, the strength of the garrison had been steadily diminishing from the ravages of scurvy, while the dwindling food supply threatened the defenders with actual starvation. By the middle of April those fit for duty in Quebec numbered barely 3,000, and there were no less than 700 corpses temporarily interred in the snow until the ground should thaw sufficiently to enable regular burial to be carried out. As for the strength that Lévis could bring against him, Murray could merely form a conjecture, but the enemy force would certainly outnumber the troops fit for duty in Quebec, and one report asserted that Lévis would appear at the head of 10,000 men. Actually the case was not quite as bad as that, for the force at the disposal of Lévis was not quite 7,000. These, however, had been carefully organized into a useful army by blending the militia with the regular regiments, except in the case of the Montreal militia, who were brigaded with the cavalry force—just over 200 strong—and a body of Indians, 270 in number, with eight officers. A disquieting feature, from the British point of view, was that immediately the navigation of the St. Lawrence should be open local command of the river would be with the French, for they had four frigates above the Richelieu rapids, whereas Saunders had left but two small vessels behind when the fleet had sailed away in the previous October.

Hearing that the French were about to attempt a landing at the mouth of the Cap Rouge River, Murray sent a detachment, on April 17th, to occupy a position there, and a minor action ensued. Realizing that the expected attack upon Quebec would be not much longer deferred, Murray ordered all Canadians to leave the city. This order was issued on the 21st, and on the same day Lévis had begun his voyage down the channel, now open in the river, with his frigates and transports under sail, and hundreds of small boats propelled by oars. Pausing for a day at Pointe aux Trembles, Lévis landed at St. Augustin during the forenoon of the 26th, and moved against the British advanced posts, which fell back upon Sainte Foy, followed up by the advanced guard of the French army. Lévis himself followed with the main body by a march through terrible weather conditions — a violent storm with cold rain lasting throughout the night.

About three o'clock in the morning of April 27th a French artilleryman was brought before Murray in Quebec. The man had been found unconscious on an ice-floe about midnight, and he told how in the landing at St. Augustin his boat had been crushed by ice, and that a large force under Lévis was marching upon Quebec. Murray immediately moved out upon Ste Foy with a detachment of about 500 men, with two field guns, supported by three battalions—so weak that they totalled little more than 700 between them. Murray at first proposed to take up a position and await attack, but, finding that the French in increasing numbers were working round his left flank, he thought it prudent to order a retirement upon the city. Before the retreat began the church at Ste Foy was blown up by Murray's orders, as there was no means of removing the ammunition stored inside it.

Murray was now in a difficult position, but, as he wrote afterwards to Pitt: "When I considered that our little army was in the habit of beating the enemy, and had a very fine train of artillery," then it seemed better to go out boldly and attack the French than to await attack behind the wretched fortifications of Quebec. Accordingly, at half-past six on the morning of the 28th he led out his little army from the city. It mustered scarcely more than 3,000 men—and of these many were really unfit to take part in a battle—with three howitzers and twenty field guns. The force moved out in two columns until it reached the ridge where Montcalm had deployed seven months before. Here the British force now formed into line. The field guns were distributed in pairs to each battalion, and were drawn by soldiers owing to the lack of horses. The ground was soft and slushy, but with a hard bone of frost beneath, and in the hollows the half-melted snow lay deep.

What followed was in the nature of an encounter battle, and the engagement, highly honourable but disastrous for British arms, may be briefly summarized. When Murray went forward to reconnoitre he saw that only the French advanced troops were in position and that the French main body was still debouching in columns from Sillery Wood, and he hoped by a rapid advance to destroy the French force before it could fully deploy. The numerical odds against him were at least two to one, and indeed Murray believed that Lévis had at least 10,000 men with him. The British advance resulted in some initial success on both flanks, but when the French brought into play their great superiority of numbers, the tide of battle turned. The whole British left was crumpled up after a gallant resistance, and although Murray put in two more battalions, they arrived too late, and the left wing was ordered to fall back. The men were furious at the order, some saying " Damn it !

What is falling back but retreating?" There was, however, no help for it. On the right, too, a similar outflanking movement by superior forces took place, and a general retreat, in which all the guns, except two, had to be abandoned, was necessary if the British army was to be saved from destruction. Murray arrived in Quebec during the afternoon, having lost, in addition to his artillery, one-third of his force in killed and wounded. The French had followed pursuit, but the British retirement was conducted in tolerable order, and Lévis thought it more prudent to recall his troops.

Once in Quebec the *moral* of the army gave way for a moment, and for a day or two the bonds of discipline were broken. But Murray, partly by a manly appeal to the troops and partly by sterner measures—a man was hanged without trial on the 30th " as an example to the rest," and all liquor belonging to the sutlers was spilled—restored the spirit of the garrison. Strenuous efforts were made to strengthen the defences and to mount more guns, while the French, on their part, were disembarking artillery and stores at the cove at Anse du Foulon, where Wolfe had landed on that memorable September night of the previous year. It was an anxious time for Murray, for the hungry and debilitated garrison was in no condition to withstand a siege, and it could be but a matter of days before the French would have their guns in position. Then, on May 8th, a French sloop which, four days earlier, had run the gauntlet of Quebec, on her way down the river, was seen flying up the river before an east-south-easterly gale. Her return indicated that her departure had been hindered by a British ship or ships. Sure enough, upon the 9th a frigate sailed into the Basin which saluted the garrison with twenty-one guns, and from which the captain put off in his barge to come ashore. The vessel was the *Lowestoft*. All Quebec went wild with delight. Officers and men mounted the parapets in full view of the enemy, waved their hats, and cheered for almost an hour. The garrison, the enemy's camp, and the country round resounded to the roar of artillery, "for the gunners were so elated that they did nothing but fire and load for a considerable time."

The arrival of the *Lowestoft* meant, however, no military reinforcement to the beleaguered garrison, and there was yet the chance that the French army, whose batteries were being got ready under a fierce fire from the fortress, might yet assault and capture the place even at the eleventh hour. Nevertheless, the sight of the British flag flying from a man-of-war in Quebec Basin exhilarated the defenders of the fortress and steeled them to vigorous efforts, while it profoundly depressed the French, who now realized that the French reinforcing fleet of transports could not arrive, for it was obvious that the *Lowestoft* was but the first of a relieving squadron. Lévis, however, made his effort, and, on May 11th, four French batteries opened upon Quebec. The execution done was considerable and justified the distrust Murray had always felt in the western fortifications of Quebec. It seemed as if the French were now at last in a position where a vigorous assault might give them back their lost fortress, but the French guns and ammunition were indifferent, and when more British men-of-war arrived, and when these dashed at the French frigates and drove them up river with heavy loss, Lévis saw that the game was lost. He decided to raise the siege, and on the evening of the 16th, abandoning forty guns, he began a retirement on Montreal, dropping garrisons as he retreated at Pointe aux Trembles, Jacques Cartier and Deschambault.

The Marquis de Vaudreuil now decided to concentrate the bulk of the forces at Montreal, and to remain on the defensive. In order to revive the spirits of his troops, and especially of the Canadians, he issued a letter to the officers of militia thanking them for their services in the recent victory at Ste Foy, and announcing great news from Europe: "The truth is His Majesty is in person in Holland with an army of 200,000, and the Prince de Conti in Germany with 100,000." Inaccurate and bombastic reports of the war in Europe could not, however, do much to assist the French in their now desperate situation in North America. Three armies were now combining against them, for Amherst, the British commander-in-chief, had decided to attack the heart of Canada from east, west, and south, all three expeditions being water-borne. Murray was to ascend the St. Lawrence from Quebec ; a central column, under Brigadier-General Haviland, was to enter Canada by Lake Champlain, while Amherst himself would lead the main body down the St. Lawrence from Lake Ontario. Before the campaigning season opened Amherst had to detach a force of some 1,300 to South Carolina to suppress a rising of Cherokee Indians. On May 19th it seemed as if the whole plan would have to be readjusted, for on that day an express arrived from Quebec giving the news of the French victory at Ste Foy, and it was not until June 11th that Indians reported that the French had raised the siege owing to the arrival of British men-of-war—intelligence which was confirmed ten days later by the arrival of two officers who had been prisoners in Montreal.

The short campaign which ensued is of interest rather as a triumph of organization than as a collection of tactical incidents. Of pitched battles, of serious engagements even, there was none, although some small forts were taken, not without fighting. Amherst had the largest force, consisting of British regulars, provincial troops, and some hundreds of Indians, amounting to 11,000 all told ; but he had likewise the longest and most difficult navigation to achieve. There was a minor naval action on Lake Ontario on August 17th, when a French 10-gun brig was attacked by row-galleys, but so soon as the brig saw the boats threatening to board, she struck her colours at once. The most difficult portion of Amherst's advance was the passage of the rapids in the St. Lawrence, in which operation more than eighty were drowned, which Amherst attributed to excessive rashness amongst the regulars and excessive caution amongst the provincials. Early in September the three columns gained touch near Montreal. The combined total of the British now united under Amherst amounted to 17,000 men. Against this disciplined force, flushed with victory, Vaudreuil could oppose but a mere handful. The militia had all returned to their homes. The Indians, quick to desert a lost cause, had vanished into the woods. Even in the regular regiments desertions had been numerous. With less than 2,500 men all told, Vaudreuil realized that resistance would be useless. Articles of capitulation were accordingly drawn up and carried by Bougainville to Amherst on September 7th. Vaudreuil claimed that the French should march out with the honours of war, to be met, however, with a stern refusal from Amherst, who decided in this way to punish the French for their "series of bad behaviour during the present war in the country, in setting on the Indians to commit the most shocking cruelties." Vaudreuil had no choice but to submit, and on the following morning, in the words of William Amherst, "surrendered to the British Crown more than was ever given to any Crown before." The whole of Canada formed the trophy of conquest of British arms. The Treaty of Paris in 1763 left the arrangement undisturbed when France formally ceded to England the provinces of Canada, Nova Scotia, and Cap Breton, and yielded also that part of the vast territory of Louisiana east of the River Mississippi.

Thus fell New France. The dissolution of an immense empire was unprovided with a dramatic setting. It came not as the result of a fiercely contested and decisive world battle, but after a parley and with scarce an exchange of shots between the opposing outposts. The contrast between the tameness of the ultimate and bloodless surrender enforced by Amherst at Montreal and the dramatic victory gained by Wolfe at Quebec just twelve months earlier inevitably threw the latter into bold relief and produced a distorted perspective which is only to-day in process of readjustment. The news of the triumph at Quebec had been accentuated by its receipt at a moment when the national mind had been depressed by Wolfe's own confession of failure; the consciousness of the country was starving for happy tidings when the manna of the victory on the Heights of Abraham fell as from the heavens. In the sharp and vivid reaction from despair to joy the pathos of Wolfe's death in the moment of victory, the cutting short in early manhood of a life so full of promise, and the dying words, so eloquent of soldierly self-sacrifice, of the hero of Quebec, invested the battle in which he fell with a glamour of its own. His end struck his contemporaries less as death than as an apotheosis. The very darkness which had prevailed when the brilliance of his victory flashed forth but showed up with greater vividness the radiancy of the meteor which burnt for the moment and then vanished in the blaze of its glory and of its fame.

To the lay mind the taking of an enemy's capital is apt to be considered synonymous with victory over the entire country in which that capital exists. This was certainly the case in 1759 in England, when the exaggerated estimate of the strength of Quebec as a fortress fostered, and indeed augmented, the belief that by its fall the fate of Canada had been for ever sealed. The preceding pages of this chapter will show how far was this from being the case. Quebec, for nearly eight months after it had received the British army within its walls, had as much as it could do to hold its own, and a little more promptness on the part of France in endeavouring to send reinforcements into Canada, a little more tenacity and dash on the part of Lévis, must infallibly have brought about its recapture. As it was, Murray retained his hold upon the fortress merely by the skin of his teeth. This unexpected development came as a shock to the people in England, who had been lulled into the belief that the struggle was over, and that Canada had fallen. In June, 1760, everyone was startled at being forced to realize that the French were still fighting hard to hold their empire in North America, and that in their effort to regain Quebec they had won an unquestioned tactical victory, and had even come within an ace of entire strategic success.

"Who the deuce"—wrote Walpole angrily—"was thinking of Quebec? America was like a book one has read and done with, but here we are on a sudden reading our book backwards."

The shock was, fortunately, but temporary, and as the memory of it faded after the capitulation of Montreal, there arose from the confused record of a struggle of a century and a half, terminating with a six-year spell of intensive warfare, a miasma of inaccurate thought from which emanated the Wolfe legend. The capture of Quebec was an incident complete in itself; *totus, teres atque rotundus;* definite, understandable and clear-cut. Everyone knew where Quebec was, and many confused it and some identified it with Canada. The Lake Champlain-River Richelieu corridor was, in comparison with the St. Lawrence, probably as little known in England as was some obscure Welsh tarn or Highland burn in comparison with the Severn or the Thames. Goldsmith remembered enough of his narrative of the war, in his "History of England," to treasure up the names Oswego and Niagara for inclusion in "The Traveller" as sonorous synonyms for North America, and it is doubtful if to his readers they conveyed much more. It is hardly possible that the average Englishman, to whom the word "lake" connoted some acres of water in Westmorland or Wales, could visualize the 100,000 square miles that made up the inland seas known as the Great Lakes of North America, or could realize without a mental effort that Lake Ontario—the smallest among them—was nearly 500 miles in circumference, that great billows could be raised by storms upon its surface, and that ships of war could ride and fight upon its waters.

As a result of a combination of ignorance of actual facts and of a kind of mental slovenliness in which narratives of campaigns are often read, there arose a tendency to exalt the work achieved by Wolfe at the expense of a corresponding depression of the work of others who were engaged with him in the great task of winning a dominion for the British Crown. In spite of the efforts of some of the ablest historians of the day—notably Sir John Fortescue and Professor George Wrong—to straighten the distorted perspective in which the last scene of the fall of Canada is viewed, there are undoubtedly even to-day many spectators upon whom the readjustment of the picture is thrown away. To John Richard Green we owe the description of Wolfe as "The Grandsire of the United States"—a phrase which has seduced many lesser writers into the paths of plagiarism. It is difficult adequately to criticise an epithet so vague ; but if implicit in the words there is supposed to lie the idea of nation-forming which exists in describing Washington as "the father of his country," then no refutation is required other than that which will be gained from a perusal of "The Fall of Canada" or of "The History of the British Army." Wolfe has also been hailed as "The Conqueror of Canada"—a description so unwarranted by fact as to call for no serious discussion. If to but one aspect of the struggle—the military, or land, one—our attention is to be turned, and if to one man alone the palm is to be awarded, then that man is Jeffery Amherst. As Sir John Fortescue says, and says truly : "The fame of the man is lost in that of Wolfe, and yet it was he, not Wolfe, that was the conqueror of Canada." It should never be forgotten—although, as a matter of fact, no military item is more persistently overlooked—that Wolfe, although acting in temporary independence upon orders received direct from the King, was still a subordinate. In 1759 and 1760 Amherst was commander-in-chief in North America. The expedition to Quebec was rendered possible only by the striking success achieved in the previous year. It has always been a mystery to the writer of this book that although every schoolboy knows of the taking of Quebec in 1759, yet many people are apparently in complete ignorance of the fall of Louisburg in the year before. This success was gained by Amherst, and although there the gallantry of Wolfe gained for him the reputation of the " hero of Louisburg," this no more entitles him to the credit of that successful siege than the gallantry of any particular general on June 18th, 1815, should be allowed to rob the Duke of Wellington of the credit of Waterloo. When Amherst was made commander-in-chief the difficulties which confronted him were appalling, and although the plan of campaign for 1759 was laid down for him at home, it was to his remarkable powers of organization, to his correct if cautious tactics, to his capacity for leadership, to his imperturbability and coolness, and to the tact and skill with which he welded the elements of his force into a disciplined whole, that the ultimate triumph is almost entirely due.

In this selection of a recipient for the palm a reservation was made in the preceding paragraph, due to the fact that the present writer prefers to consider the conquest of Canada as accomplished, not by one man, nor by one service, but by a co-operation and co-ordination between statesmen, sailors and soldiers of a kind until then unique and unparalleled in the history of England. At the head of this happy organization was Pitt, who was responsible for the policy of the nation and technically also for the plan of campaign, which, although not without its serious dangers, led to the greatest results. But a study of the work done by Pitt in administration, as revealed in Professor Basil Williams's " Life of William Pitt," will show that, except on the supposition that the great minister was a monster of erudition for whom time stood still, it was a sheer physical impossibility that the plans of campaign and the detailed instructions required by them could possibly have been entirely the work of his hand and brain. The outside professional assistance on which he undoubtedly relied came from Anson, the First Lord, and from Ligonier, the Commander-in-Chief. These orders were carried out with zeal, faithfulness and resolution by the admirals and generals to whom they were entrusted. The conquest of Canada was achieved by the harmonious co-operation of the two services officered by men like Boscawen, Hawke, Saunders, and Holmes, and by soldiers of the calibre of Amherst, Forbes, Rogers, Johnson, Wolfe, Murray, Monckton and Townshend. To attempt to assign to any member of this band his exact share in the conquest of Canada is a task as futile as it is invidious. The words used by an American admiral concerning an operation within our own days may well be applied to the winning of New France : " There was enough glory to go round."

Nothing, however, not even the infatuated adoration of his worshippers, can ever diminish or obscure Wolfe's title to fame. He carried out the difficult task assigned him. What he was called upon to do he did ; he did it within the time limit imposed, in circumstances of unexpected difficulty, with a force which in numbers fell far short of the figure upon which he had counted ; and in doing it he gave his life. In the long annals of the British Army, for devotion to duty, for untiring resolution, for dauntless courage, for the sure grasp of a chance fleetingly offered, for the gifts of personality and leadership, no name stands higher than that of James Wolfe :—

> Wolfe, where'er he fought,
> Put so much of his heart into his act
> That his example had a magnet's force,
> And all were swift to follow whom all loved.

INDEX

Abenakis, 43, 69, 148, 150
Abercromby, 243, 276, 277, 279, 280, 281, 282, 290, 291, 292, 293, 300, 301, 304
Abraham, Heights of, 10, 329, 343, 361
Abraham, Plain of, 367
Acadia (see also Nova Scotia), 25, 26, 31, 35, 53, 58, 59, 60, 68, 146, 153, 168 et sqq., 217, 220
Ahrenberg, 88, 89
Aix, Island of, 270, 272
Albany, 23, 52, 59, 70, 128, 129, 130, 140, 164, 171, 214, 225, 226, 248, 258
Albemarle, Earl of, 198, 199, 200
Alexander VI, Pope, 12
Alexander, Sir Wm., 27, 35
Alexandria, 217
Allanton, Sir H. S., 115
Alleghanies, 71, 133, 221
Alleghany, River, 71, 208
Amherst, Jeffery, 282, 295, 296, 300, 301, 302, 303, 304, 305, 306, 307, 320, 322, 344, 355, 358, 382, 389, 400, 401, 402, 403, 407, 409
Amherst, William, 298, 312
Annapolis, 151, 152
Anne, Queen, 58, 59, 61, 68, 122, 179
Anse du Foulon, 360, 362, 363, 364, 367, 371, 372
Anson, 76, 167, 178, 408
Antwerp, 117, 172
Arcot, 216
Argall, Samuel, 26
Arkansas, 49
Austria, 236, 238, 241

Banff, 192, 194
Barbados, 300
Battle of Blenheim, 122
Battle of Culloden, 114, 115, 194
Battle of Dettingen, 97 et sqq.
Battle of Falkirk, 112 113
Battle of Fontenoy, 102–103, 225
Battle of Lagos, 178
Battle of Lauffeld, 118
Battle of Malplaquet, 122
Battle of Minden, 178, 225
Battle of Monongahela, 222 et sqq., 232
Battle of Oudenarde, 122
Battle of Quebec, 178, 225
Battle of Quiberon Bay, 11, 178
Battle of Ramillies, 122
Beauport (lines, or position), 335, 349, 354, 358
Beauséjour, 217, 220
Bedford, Duke of, 269, 316
Bic, Isle de, 302, 311, 327, 331
Bienville, Céloron de, 208
Bigot, 243
Black Hole, 252, 298
Blake, 121
Blandford, Lord, 316
Boscawen, 178, 219, 233, 235, 282, 283, 284, 295, 382, 409
Boston, 38, 42, 43, 58, 146, 299
Bougainville, 244, 323, 324, 326, 331, 339, 355, 360, 372
Bourlamaque, 244
Boyne, 198
Braddock, 217, 218, 221, 222, 223, 224, 226, 231, 232, 243, 249, 296, 298, 322
Bradstreet, 296, 307, 308
Brattleborough, 69
Brebeuf, 42
Brittany, 14
Brown's " Estimate," 253
Brulé, Etienne, 28
Bryce, Lord, 126, 336
Burton, Colonel, 314, 371, 391
Bury, Lord, 190, 198
Byng, 236, 252, 276, 318

INDEX

Cabot, Sebastian, 13, 14, 19
Calcutta, 252
Caldwell, 310, 312
California, 142
Canada, Chap. I, *passim*, 69, 70, 124 *et sqq.*, 207, 243 *et sqq.*, 277 *et sqq.*, 300 *et sqq.*, 324 *et sqq.*, 383 *et sqq.*, Chap. VII, *passim*.
Canseau, 146, 152, 156
Cap Breton Island, 14, 25, 31, 35, 123, 146
Cap Rouge, 349, 360, 362, 395
Cape Cod, 23
Carignan Regiment, 46, 47
Carillon, Fort, 291
Carleton, 349
Carlisle, 109
Carlyle, 75
Carnatic, 216
Carolinas, 74, 208, 211
Caroline, Queen, 179
Carrickfergus, 387
Cartagena, 76, 87
Cartier, Jacques, 15, 17
Casco, 55
Cataraqui, Fort, 49
Cathcart, 78
Cayahoga, 303
Centurion, H.M.S., 350
Chads, Captain, R.N., 365
Chambly, 143
Champlain, 15, 17, 23, 24, 28, 31
Chancellor, 19
Charlevoix, 132, 136, 148
Charles I, King, 34, 36, 37
Charles VI, Emperor, 79
Chartres, 144
Chebucto (see Halifax)
Cherbourg, 299
Chesterfield, Lord, 180, 198, 200
Chignecto, 168
Chouaguen, River, 138
Clark, Mary 44
Clive, 178, 216, 237
Colbert, 38, 40, 45, 46, 47, 50, 51
Colorado, 71
Company (London), 26, 29
Company of New France, 27, 31, 32
Company (Plymouth), 26
Company of the West, 40, 45
Connecticut, 55, 155, 277
Constantinople, 336

Conway, 265
Cook, Captain, 332
Coote, Eyre, 178, 238
Cope, Sir John, 106, 107, 108
Corbett, Sir Julian, 78, 313, 348
Cornwallis, 184, 265
Corry Arack, 107
Coudres, Isle aux, 319, 332
Coureurs de bois, 40, 62, 135, 136, 145
Crevelt, 299
Crimea, 337
Cromwell, 38
Crown Point, 70, 143, 166, 218, 225, 226, 229, 248, 281, 301
Cumberland, Duke of, 83, 89, 94, 95, 101, 102, 103, 109, 111, 113, 114, 115, 117, 118, 174, 182, 262, 298, 314
Cumberland, Fort, 223

Dale, Sir Thomas, 25, 26
d'Anville, Duc, 163
Dardanelles, 336
Dearfield, 57
De Lancey, 280
Delaware, 47
Denonville, 52
Deschambault, 354, 355
Detroit, 59, 147
Diana, H.M.S., 347
D'Iberville, 56
Dieskau, 218, 226, 233
Dinwiddie, 211
Dongan, 52
Doreil, 323
Dover, 203, 204
Drake, 21
Drucour, 290
Druilletes, 43
Duchambon, 161
Dundee, 192
Dupleix, 216
Duquesne, Fort, 129, 213, 218, 221, 229, 230, 231, 294, 302
Duquesne de Merreval, 209, 210
Duquesnel, 151, 153
Durell, 312, 327, 331, 332
Dutch, 40, 41, 46, 51, 121

Edward, Fort, 226, 248, 262, 280
Eliot, 42
Elizabeth, H.M.S., 104

INDEX   413

Elizabeth, Czarina, 239, 240, 241
Elizabeth, Queen, 16, 18, 19, 21, 22, 36
Eltham, H.M.S., 157
England, in North America, Chap. I, Chap. III, 237, Chap. VII
Exeter, 204, 265

Farragut, 348
Fielding, 182
Fitzmaurice, Wm., (later Earl of Shelburne), 267
Fleury, 68, 81
Florida, 57
Foch, 197
Forbes, 278, 294, 296, 302, 409
Fortescue, Hon. Sir John, 98, 406, 407
Fouras, Fort, 271
Fox, Indians, 59
France, in North America, Chap. I, Chap. III, 237, Chap. VII
Franklin, 215, 221
Fraser, Captain, 366
Frederick II, King of Prussia, 78, 80, 96, 239, 240, 241, 242, 299
Fronde, 37
Frontenac, 49, 61, 136
Frontenac, Fort, 49, 126, 130, 138, 141, 225, 226, 248, 249, 250, 293, 308

Gabarus, Bay, 158, 285
Galissonnière, de la, 145–147
Gallipoli, 337
Gasperau, Fort, 220
George I, King, 68
George II, King, 80, 83, 89, 91, 92, 93, 96, 110, 117, 178, 238, 241, 254, 301, 381
Ghent, 65, 101
Gibraltar, 122
Gilbert, Sir H., 22
Glasgow, 184, 188, 201, 202
Glenfinnan, 105, 107
Goldsmith, Edward, 86, 331
Goldsmith family, 65, 86
Goreham's Post, 364
Grammont, 90, 91, 92
Grant, 313
Gray and "Elegy," 178, 182, 316, 363
Great Meadows, 213, 214

Green Bay, 144
Green, John Richard, 406
Greenwich, 76
Guadaloupe, 306
Guy, Captain, 85

Hale, 383
Halifax, 60, 126, 146, 151, 163, 167, 206 *et sqq.*, 229, 257, 258, 284, 299, 306, 311, 327
Hampton, 217
Hanover, 68, 96, 235, 238, 241, 254
Hawke, Admiral, 11, 178, 235, 237, 270, 299, 314, 386, 409
Hawkins, 20, 21
Hawley, 111, 113
Haverhill, 58
Haviland, 401
Henrietta Maria, 34
Henry VII, King, 17, 18
Henry VIII, King, 18
Highlanders, 193
Holbourne, 256, 257, 264
Holmes, 353, 354, 360, 365, 409
Holy Roman Empire, 79
Hoosac, River, 172
Hopson, 256, 300
Horton, 170
Hoskins, Miss, 186, 188
Houtan, la, 136
Howe (George), Lord, 282, 288, 291
Howe (Richard), Lord, 219, 275
Howe (Hon. W.), 364
Hudson's Bay, 53, 56, 59, 60, 145
Hudson River, 46, 48, 70, 124, 128, 129
Huguenots, 32, 33, 35, 63
Hunter, H.M.S., 365
Hurons, 40, 41, 43
Hutchinson, Mrs., 45

Ile Royale, 123
Illinois, 49, 50, 147
India, 217, 234, 237
Indians (*see also* Iroquois, Hurons, etc.), 41, 42, 43, 48, 49, 50, 51, 52, 53, 54, 55, 57, 58, 59, 120, 133, 136, 137, 139, 144, 168, 207, 215, 221, 223, 232, 251, 253, 295, 329, 339, 346, 356, 395, 401

414 INDEX

Inverness, 107, 116, 194
Inversnaid, 116
Inwood, Mrs., 196
Iowa, 49
Iroquois, 40, 41, 43, 44, 46, 47, 48, 54, 57, 59, 69, 70, 124, 140, 150, 215

Jacobite rebellion, 1745, 105 *et sqq.*
Jacques Cartier, 393
James I, King, 25, 27, 29, 30, 34
James River, 23
James Town (later Jamestown), 16, 23, 25
Jenkins, 72, 73, 74, 75
Jervis (later Earl St. Vincent), 364
Jesuits, 33, 34, 40, 41, 42, 43, 44, 48, 61, 62, 136, 148
Johnson, Samuel, 178
Johnson, William, 217, 226, 229, 382, 409
Joliet, 49, 50

Kalm, 216
Kennebec, 41
Keppel, 221
Kingston, 49, 130
Kirke, Gervase, 35
Knowles, 271
Kolin, 264
Königseck, Count of, 102

Labourdonnais, 216
Lake Champlain, 47, 70, 128, 171, 248, 280
Lake Erie, 42, 48, 50, 125, 308
Lake George, 129, 229, 281, 291
Lake Huron, 12, 28, 41, 43, 50, 125, 138
Lake Michigan, 42, 50
Lake Ontario, 28, 41, 49, 125, 126, 129, 226, 248, 249, 253, 293, 401
Lake Superior, 41, 42
La Salle, 50, 51, 71
Launceston, H.M.S., 157
Lawrence, 67, 68
Lawson, Elizabeth, 185 *et sqq.*
Le Bœuf, Fort, 210, 212
Le Caron, 28
Le Loutre, 170, 220
Lee, 197

Leeward Islands, 300
Lévis, 244, 249, 260, 355, 374, 394, 395, 399, 400
Ligonier, 408
Lion, H.M.S., 104
Logstown, 208
Loudon, Earl of, 242, 248, 255, 256, 276, 279
Louis XIV, 68, 121
Louis XV, 117, 121, 241
Louisburg, 60, 106, 123, 124, 130, siege of (1745), 156 *et sqq.*, 162, French attempt to recover, 162 *et sqq.*, 166, 167, 172, 173, 184, 230, 256, 257, 258, 264, 282 *et sqq.*, 297, 298, 301, 306, 311, 321, 326, 328, 330, 387, 388
Louisiana, 40, 50, 51, 57, 60, 71, 207, 325, 393, 403
Lowestoft, H.M.S., 365, 372, 384, 399
Lowther, Katherine, 183, 317, 330

Macaulay, 252, 253
Mackellar, 320
Mackinaw, 54
Magellan, 19
Mahan, Captain, 306
Mahon, Lord, 180, 315, 316
Maine, 43, 53, 56, 69
Maria Theresa, 80, 81, 83, 96, 239
Marlborough, Duke of, 65
Marlborough, Sarah, Duchess of, 180
Marquette, 49, 50
Mary, Queen, 18
Maryland, 14, 211, 214, 227, 251
Mascarene, Major, 153
Massachusetts, 43, 45, 55, 56, 58, 69, 143, 154, 168
Mayflower, 13, 27
Medina, 231
Membertou, 15
Mercer, Colonel, 251
Mermaid, H.M.S., 157
Merrydan, Captain, 85
Meserve, 280
Miami, 144
Michigan, 59
Minorca, 235, 236, 252
Mississippi, 40, 48, 49, 50, 51 53, 56, 57, 58, 60, 71, 144, 150, 208, 303, 308

INDEX 415

Mobile River, 303
Mohawk River, 129, 225
Moltke, 82, 90, 197
Monckton, 217, 220, 314, 331, 342, 364, 372, 409
Monongahela, 71, 205
Montana, 71
Montcalm, 137, 244, 245, 248, 249, 259 et sqq., 291, 315, 322 et sqq., 339, 340, 346 et sqq., 356 et sqq., 372 et sqq.
Montmorenci River and Falls, 334, 345, 350
Montreal, 10, 15, 28, 41, 54, 55, 59, 62, 70, 126, 135, 142, 143, 164, 165, 277, 301, 336, 402
Monts, Sieur de, 25
Mordaunt, Sir John, 185, 265, 270, 274
Moscow, 19
Murray, James, 314, 331, 353 et sqq., 364, 389 et sqq., 409

Napoleon, 196
Necessity, Fort, 214
Nelson, 317
Neptune, H.M.S., 318, 326
Newcastle, Duke of, 165, 234, 254, 298, 300
New England, 14, 27, 39, 47, 51, 69, 155, 166, 172, 214, 217
Newfoundland, 13, 22, 59, 60, 123
New France, Chap. I, *passim*, 133
New Hampshire, 143, 277
Newhaven, 39, 43
New Jersey, 47, 52, 211, 217, 251, 277
New Netherlands, 46, 47
New Orleans, 60
Newport, I. of W., 77
New Sweden, 46, 47
New York (harbour, town, or state), 14, 46, 47, 51, 53, 55, 57, 59, 124, 128, 129, 143, 146, 155, 214, 217, 251, 261, 276, 277, 280, 299
Niagara, 42, 70, 125, 126, 130, 138, 140, 141, 143, 146, 150, 218, 225, 231, 302, 304, 307, 308, 339, 355, 382
Noailles, 89, 90, 91
Normandy, 14
North Carolina, 14, 278

North-East Passage, 19
North-West Bay, 260
North-West Passage, 20
Northumberland, H.M.S., 163
Nova Scotia (see also Acadia), 14, 27, 68, 123, 151, 205, 220, 229, 230, 233, 403

Ohio, 49, 50, 71, 144, 147, 208, 209, 210, 215, 231, 249, 294, 303, 322, 326
Onondaga, 138, 293
Orleans, Isle of, 311, 341
Osborne, 299
Ostend, 83, 97
Oswego, 70, 126, 129, 141, 145, 171, 225, 250, 253, 258, 262, 284, 293, 302, 308
Ottawa, 28
Oudenarde, 65

Panama, 73
Parkman, 22, 36, 140, 170, 230
Penn, 52
Pennsylvania, 52, 59, 211, 212, 214, 227, 251, 278
Penobscot, 23
Pepperell, Colonel, 155, 156
Perth, 190, 191
Peterhead. 193
Pilgrim Fathers, 11, 13, 14, 15, 29
Pitt, William (later Earl of Chatham), 74, 178, 182, 183, 233, 234, 235, 252 et sqq., 263, 274 et sqq., 281, 283, 290, 298 et sqq., 315, 319, 322, 328, 349, 359, 383, 385, 386, 396, 408
Pittsburgh, 71, 129, 208, 213
Placentia, 151
Plymouth (U.S.A.), 11, 15, 27, 30
Pocahontas, 23
Point Lévis, 341, 342
Pointe aux Trembles, 349, 393
Pointe de Pères, 342, 346, 347, 356
Pompadour, 199, 239, 240, 241, 324
Pope, Alexander, 178
Porcupine, H.M.S., 365
Portland, 55, 129
Porto Bello, 72
Port Royal, 15, 16, 25, 26, 36
Portsmouth, 37, 283
Portugal, 12, 20

INDEX

Potomac, 217
Poulett, Lord Harry, 318
Poutrincourt, 15
Pragmatic Sanction, 80, 97, 150
Presqu'ile, 210
Preston Pans, 108
Prevost, 242
Prussia, 79, 96, 238
Putnam, 296

Quakers, 40, 44, 45, 52, 212, 228
Quebec, 9, 10, 11, 13, 16, 23, 32, 35, 36, 41, 42, 43, 44, 51, 54, 55, 56, 59, 62, 63, 121, 122, 126, 127, 128, 129, 130, 135, 139, 142, 146, 162, 164, 230, 238, 256, 277, 292, 300, 301 *et sqq.*, 311, 325, 326, 329, 333 *et sqq.*, 352 *et sqq.*, 365 *et sqq.*, 376 *et sqq.*, 387 *et sqq.*, 394 *et sqq.*, 404, 407
Quiberon Bay, Battle of, 11, 386, 387

Rainy Lake, 142
Raleigh, Sir W., 22, 34
Ramezay, 373, 375
Rasles, 149
Reading, 203
Rebecca, 72, 74
Red River, 48
Reformation, 12
Rémusat, Madame de, 197

Regiments (French)—
  Artois, 218
  Béarn, 218, 249, 369
  Bourgogne, 218
  Carignan, 46, 47
  Guienne, 218, 249, 368, 369
  Languedoc, 218, 219, 369
  La Reine, 218, 219
  La Sarre, 244, 249, 369
  Royal Rousillon, 244, 369
Regiments—
  Barrell's (4th), 103
  Duroure's (12th), 82
  15th, 367
  Lord George Sackville's (20th), 176, 190
  Shirley's, 218, 250
  28th, 367
  35th, 243, 246, 367

Philipp's (40th), 151
42nd Highlanders, 243, 247, 255, 292
43rd, 367
44th, 217, 221, 246
47th, 367
48th, 217, 221, 246
58th, 367
Royal Americans (60th), 242, 243, 261, 346, 350
Fraser's Highlanders, 285, 367, 391
Pepperell's, 218, 250
Temple's, 65
Renaissance, 12
Rhode Island, 14, 155, 277
Richardson, 178, 182
Richelieu, 31, 37, 121
Richelieu, River, 46, 47, 70, 128, 129, 130
Richmond, Admiral Sir H., 163
Rickson, 185, 193, 273
Rio Bravo del Norte, 53
Rochefort, 264, 269 *et sqq.*, 298, 321
Rocky Mountains, 71, 141
" Roderick Random," 305
Rogers, Robert, 253, 296, 409
Roland, 118
Rolfe, 135
Rosebery, Lord, 196
Royal William, H.M.S., 384
Russia, 238, 241

Sackett's Harbour, 250
Sackville, Lord George, 176, 189, 283, 284, 295, 316
St. Augustin, 393
St. Charles River, 329, 335, 340
St. Contest, 199
St. Joseph, 144
St. Laurent, 333
St. Lawrence, River, and Gulf of, 10, 14, 22, 24, 42, 48, 71, 123, 124, 125, 128, 131, 139, 142, 146, 150, 243, 256, 297, 302, 303, 307, 309, 322, 361
St. Louis, 144
St. Malo, 299
St. Sauveur, 25, 26
Ste. Foy, 395
Salem, 43
Salmon Falls, 55
Saratoga, 171

INDEX

Saskatchewan, River, 142
Sault Ste Marie, 41, 48
Saunders, 282, 306, 307, 312, 318 *et sqq.*, 327, 330, 341 *et sqq.*, 350 *et sqq.*, 358, 363, 385, 409
Saxe, 98, 100, 102, 116, 118, 127, 196
Saxony, 241
Schenectady, 55
Sea Horse, H.M.S., 365
Seignelay, 50
Shirley, William, 154, 157, 164, 166, 218, 225, 226, 228, 243, 248
Silesia, 80, 239
Smith, Captain John, 23
Smollett, 178, 182, 304, 305, 352, 383
South Carolina, 57, 278
South Sea Company, 72, 73
Spain, 12, 20, 21, 64, 71, 72, 73, 75, 76, 275
Spiers, 66
Squerryes, 67, 81, 82
Squirrel, H.M.S., 365
Stair, Earl of, 83, 88
Stanhope, Philip, 198, 200
Sterne, 178
Stirling, 114, 184
Stuart, Charles Edward, 100, 104, 105, 107, 108, 109, 110, 111, 114, 161
Sulpicians, 48
Surinam, 47
Sutherland, H.M.S., 365
Susquehanna, 28
Sweden, 241
Swift, 178, 182
Swinden, Rev. S., 77

Talon, 47, 124
Temple, Lord, 315, 316
Temple, Sir R., 65
Terror of France, 349
Texas, 51, 53, 71
Thackeray, 180
Three Rivers, 54, 129, 259
Ticonderoga, 143, 226, 249, 251, 252, 257, 260, 291, 293, 301, 322, 355, 382
Townshend, 314, 331, 342, 345, 350, 351, 352, 372, 375, 409
Traverse, 332, 339, 340

Treaty of Aix-la-Chapelle, 131, 172, 174, 181, 205
Treaty of Ryswick, 56
Treaty of Utrecht, 53, 59, 63, 64, 68, 69, 121, 123, 131, 147, 148, 149, 237
Turtle Creek, 222

United States, 12, 406

Vauban, 60, 123, 338
Vaudreuil, 148, 245, 323, 326, 339, 368, 373, 374, 393, 400, 402
Vaudreuil, Rigaud de, 259
Venango, 211
Vendôme, 65
Vera Cruz, 72
Vergot, 220
Vermont, 53, 69
Vernon, 76, 77, 110
Verrazano, 14, 17, 23
Vicksburg, 337
Vigilant, 160, 161
Vincennes, 144
Virginia, 24, 29, 30, 38, 51, 59, 208, 212, 214, 227, 278

Wade, General, 65, 98, 101, 108, 109, 110, 111
Walker, Sir Hovenden, 58, 59
Walpole, Horace, 274, 382, 385
Walpole, Robert, 68, 73, 74, 80, 81, 178
War, The, of the Austrian Succession, 38, 79, 87, 161, 241
War, The Seven Years', 38, 142, 181, 233, 263 *et sqq.*
War, The, of the Spanish Succession, 38, 57, 64
War, The Thirty Years', 37
War, The, of Jenkins's Ear, 75 *et sqq.*
Warde, George, 67
Warde, John, 188
Warren, Admiral, 156, 157, 160, 165
Washington, George, 205, 210, 211 *et sqq.*, 222, 223
Webb, Colonel, 243
Wellington, Duke of, 197, 317, 407
Westerham, 66, 81
Wheelwright, John, 45
Whitmore, 282

418 INDEX

William III, King, 57, 253
William Henry, Fort, 262
Williams, Professor Basil, 408
Williams, Roger, 45
Wolfe, Edward (father of James Wolfe), 64, 65, 77, 78, 86, 108
Wolfe, Edward (brother of James Wolfe), 66, 86, 87, 91, 97, 98, 99
Wolfe family, 65
Wolfe, Henrietta (mother of James Wolfe), 65, 66, 186
Wolfe, James, Summary of Quebec campaign of, 9–11, 63 ; birth of, 1727, 66 ; friendship with Wardes, 67 ; schooling, *ib.*, 68, 71, 72 ; schooling at Greenwich, 76 ; proceeds to camp at Newport, I. of W., 77 ; sent home owing to ill-health, *ib.*, 79 ; begins career of active service, 81 ; receives his commission, *ib.* ; monument to commemorate, 82 ; transferred to 12th Foot, *ib.* ; embarks for Ostend, 83 ; progress in his profession, 84 ; letter to his mother, 12th Sept., 1742, 85 ; hardships of campaign, 87 ; at Battle of Dettingen, 1743, as acting adjutant, 91 *et sqq.* ; noticed by Duke of Cumberland, 95 ; appointed adjutant of 12th Foot, *ib.* ; at Ostend winter of 1743–4, 97 ; promoted captain in Barrell's Regiment, 98 ; letter to his mother on his brother's death, 99 ; misses Fontenoy, 103 ; first experience as staff officer in the '45, 105 ; do. 109, 111 ; letter *re* Battle of Falkirk, 113 ; aide-de-camp to Hawley, *ib.* ; at Culloden, 115 ; at Inverness, 116 ; at Inversnaid, *ib.* ; returns to London, *ib.* ; embarks with his regiment for Holland, January, 1747, *ib.* ; recommended for lieutenant-colonelcy of 8th Foot, 117 ; wounded at Battle of Lauffeld, 118 ; incident at, *ib.* ; comes of age in London, 119 ; summary of his military career to that time, *ib.* ; marked by his superiors as a coming man, 174 ; wishes to travel abroad, 175 ; practises chess, 176 ; major in 20th Foot, 1749, *ib.* ; personal characteristics, 176–7 ; review of conditions of English society during his early manhood, 177 *et sqq.* ; false impressions *re* Wolfe, 183–4 ; joins 20th at Stirling, 184 ; acting in command, *ib.* ; to Glasgow, *ib.* ; takes lessons in Latin and mathematics, 184–5 ; love affair with Miss Lawson, 185 *et sqq.* ; bows to his parents' wishes, 186–8 ; comments on his conduct, 188 ; dislike of Presbyterian divines, 189 ; inspection of 20th by Lord George Sackville, *ib.* ; roadmaking in Highlands, *ib* ; " quite out of conceit with Scotland," *ib.* ; his opinion of the officers of 20th, 190 ; is regarded as a paragon, *ib.* ; at Perth, 191 ; ill-health, *ib.* ; promoted lieut.-colonel of 20th, 191 ; to London, on leave, November, 1750, 192 ; alleged dissolute conduct, *ib.* ; remarks *re* Nova Scotia in letter to Captain Rickson, 193 ; suggestion *re* Scottish Highlanders, *ib.* ; ill-health at Peterhead, 193 ; troubled with stone, *ib.* ; at Banff, 194 ; his opinion of inhabitants of Inverness, *ib.* ; revisits Culloden, *ib.* ; his studies, 195–6 ; " shamefully beat at chess," 196 ; visits Ireland, 198 ; obtains leave to visit France, *ib.* ; reaches Paris, October, 1752, *ib.* ; how he spent his days there, 199 ; wishes to undertake a further tour, 201 ; but is recalled, *ib.* ; rejoins 20th at Glasgow, *ib.* ; more roadmaking in Highlands, 203 ; 20th ordered to England, *ib.* ; his poor opinion of Scotch people, *ib.* ; 20th proceeds to Dover, *ib.* ; his poor opinion of his officers, *ib.* ; dislike of Dover, 204 ; regiment moves to Exeter, *ib.* ; his views on Braddock's defeat in letter to his father, 4th Sept.,

Wolfe, James, Summary of Quebec campaign of—*continued*.
1755, 224; comment on this letter, 225; appointed quartermaster-general to Rochefort expedition, 265; his passion for soldiering, *ib.*; reputation as a regimental commander, 266; description of Wolfe by Wm. Fitzmaurice, 267; Wolfe's reading, 268; applied for by Duke of Bedford to go to Ireland, 269; the Rochefort expedition, 269 *et sqq.*; Wolfe's share in it, 270-1; his views on the failure, 272-3; at the commission of inquiry and court-martial on Sir John Mordaunt, 274; Pitt attracted by Wolfe, *ib.*; remarks on Wolfe by Horace Walpole, 274-5; appointed brigadier to Louisburg expedition, 282; his opinion of Portsmouth, 283; voyage to America, *ib.*; reaches Halifax, 284; his views on the military situation, *ib.*; indignant over service of supply, *ib.*; arrival of expedition off Louisburg, 285; landing of Wolfe's party, *ib.*; his share in the siege, 288 *et sqq.*; copies tactics of *carduchoi*, 289; Wolfe's criticisms on the siege, 295; and on the operations generally, 296; his opinion of American soldiers, 296; prophecy as to future of North America, 297; employed in minor operations in Gulf of St. Lawrence, *ib.*; returns to England, *ib.*; appointed to command Quebec expedition, 301; Wolfe not particularly attracted by American service, 309; his letter to Pitt, 24th Dec., 1758, upon the situation in North America, 310-12; his appreciation of naval side of the problem, 312; repartee of George II to detractors of Wolfe, 313; his appointment popular in England, 313-14; tribute to his ability by army in North America, 314; choice of subordinates, 314; is confident of success, 315; curious conduct of Wolfe at Pitt's house, 315-6; remarks on, 316; comparison of Wolfe and Nelson, 317; engagement to Miss Katherine Lowther, *ib.*; departure of Wolfe for North America, 14th Feb., 1759, 318; considerations on the task of Wolfe, 321-2; arrival at Halifax, 327; unforeseen circumstances hamper Wolfe, 326-8; his comments thereon, 328; death of his father, *ib.*; his views on drill, 329; letter to his uncle dealing with prospects of campaign, 329-330; writes his will, 330; " state " of the expeditionary force, 331; arrival off Quebec, 333; he views the city and its vicinity, 333-4; his plan requires alteration, 335; some comments on the situation, 335 *et sqq.*; a storm, 341; French send down fire-ships, *ib.*; Point Lévis occupied, 342; Wolfe reconnoitres westward along southern bank, *ib.*; further considerations upon Wolfe's task, 343 *et sqq.*; 8th July, unsuccessful attempt to dislodge Montcalm from Beauport position, 345-6; batteries erected opposite Quebec and fire opened, 346; French attempt to capture these batteries fails, 346-7; some of the British ships run past Quebec, 347; Wolfe's opinion of the attempt, 348; operations west of Quebec not yet considered feasible, 349; another attack upon Beauport position decided upon, *ib.*; proclamations to inhabitants, 350; French send down fire-rafts, *ib.*; the attack upon the Beauport position, 350-2; consequences of the failure, 352; subsidiary up-river operations, 352 *et sqq.*; Wolfe falls ill 20th Aug., 357; submits proposals to brigadiers for another attempt upon Beauport position, *ib.*; they are unani-

Wolfe, James, Summary of Quebec campaign of—*continued*
mously rejected, 358; decided to operate above Quebec, 359; Wolfe's despondency, 359; troops successfully withdrawn from Montmorenci and passed up-river, 360; his project to land at Anse du Foulon, 362; the incident of Gray's "Elegy," 363; the popular legend a preposterous perversion, *ib.*; the passage down the St. Lawrence in the early hours of the morning of 13th Sept., 1759, 365-6; landing at Anse du Foulon, 366; Battle of Quebec, 367 *et sqq.*; death of Wolfe, 371; comments on the campaign, 376 *et sqq.*; Wolfe's body brought home, 384; funeral, *ib.*; monument decreed in Westminster Abbey, 385; his share in the conquest of Canada examined, 403 *et sqq.*

Wolfe, Major Walter (uncle of James Wolfe), 272, 295, 329, 331
Wolsey, Cardinal, 18
Wrong, Professor Geo., 406
Wyoming, 71

Xenophon, 289

Young, 182
Ypres, 98

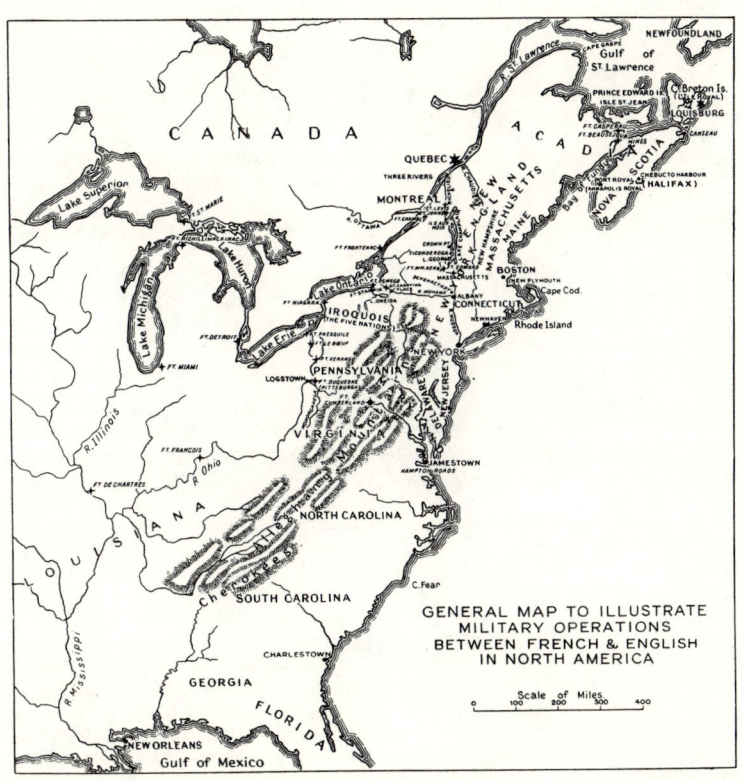